MR CHARLES BOOTH'S INQUIRY

MR CHARLES BOOTH'S INQUIRY

LIFE AND LABOUR OF THE PEOPLE
IN LONDON RECONSIDERED

ROSEMARY O'DAY
AND DAVID ENGLANDER

THE HAMBLEDON PRESS

LONDON AND RIO GRANDE

Published by The Hambledon Press, 1993
102 Gloucester Avenue, London NW1 8HX (U.K.)
P.O. Box 162, Rio Grande, Ohio 45674 (U.S.A.)

ISBN 1 85285 079 5

A description of this book is available from
the British Library and from the Library of Congress

Typeset by York House Typographic Ltd, London
Printed on acid-free paper and bound in
Great Britain by Cambridge University Press
Digitally Reprinted 2004

Contents

Preface

In writing a book of this kind there are always more debts of gratitude than one can possibly acknowledge. Some we must mention. We owe a great debt of gratitude to the Open University. Specifically we would like to thank the Faculty of Arts Research Committee for its continuing financial and moral support. We mention especially the support and encouragement of Joan Bellamy, formerly Dean of Arts. Also, we acknowledge with great pleasure the help accorded us by Dr Angela Raspin and Ms Sue Donnolly of the British Library of Political and Economic Science. Dr Raspin, an external member of the Charles Booth Research Group at the Open University, has not only produced documents tirelessly and cheerfully but has also given us the benefit of her considerable knowledge of the archival possibilities of the project. We are also pleased to acknowledge the helpful service provided by the Archivists of the University of London Library at Senate House, the University of Liverpool Library, the Modern Records Centre, University of Warwick and by the librarians of the Open University Library.

The Charles Booth Research Group has provided a forum for the writing of this book. Professor Royden Harrison, an external member of the group, has generously commented on parts of this work. Dr Judith Ford, sometime research assistant on the Charles Booth Database project, assisted us considerably in the attribution of handwriting and in analysis of the street notebooks of the Poverty series. Dr Mark Clapson's work in designing the Charles Booth Database under our direction is gratefully acknowledged. Dr Hugh McLeod and Dr William Marsden alike deserve special mention for their significant contributions to the Charles Booth Conference that we organised in 1989. We are most grateful to Mrs Belinda Norman-Butler, Charles Booth's granddaughter, for her continued and valuable support.

We went into this work wondering what it would be like to work together on a book-length project. It has proved a rewarding experience. Dr O'Day was responsible for Chapters 1 and 3 and Dr Englander for Chapter 2. The Introduction was written jointly. There was continuous and close collaboration both during the research and writing of the book. This said, the authors are respectively responsible for their own individual work. The children, Andrew (now an adult), Daniel and Matthew, have helped us on the way, for which we are grateful.

Martin Sheppard of The Hambledon Press has been an understanding publisher and we thank him for his care with this book. Last but not least we thank Wendy Clarke of the Faculty of Arts for her sterling contribution in typing and co-ordinating the many versions of the text and producing final copy.

Rosemary O'Day   David Englander

March 1992

This book is dedicated to the loving memory of our mothers

Beryl Brookes (*née* Robinson) b. 1903 d. 1989

Eva Englander (*née* Amdur) b. 1909 d. 1989

Introduction

Introduction

Booth was a queer fellow. Contemporaries could not make head nor tail of him. Some claimed that he had done for social science what Copernicus did for natural science; others noted his slipshod methods and inability to generalise and formulate sociological principles. His politics seemed equally baffling. At one and the same time he was praised for his individualism and condemned for his socialism.[1] Historians have fared no better. He is sometimes confused with William Booth, often made a Conservative M.P., frequently described as a 'sociologist' and generally assumed to have acquired most of his information second-hand.[2] None of these statements is correct. Assessments of his work and influence are no less varied and just as questionable. Judgements range from the delirious – his poverty-line constitutes 'one of the greatest contributions of social science to social progress' – to the observation that Booth's principal defect as a social theorist was that he was not Marx:[3] *Charles Booth – Social Scientist*, the authorised biography by T.S. and M. Simey, though easily the best informed study, also lacked

---

[1] On Booth as a social scientist, see the varying estimates in BLPES Booth Collection, A58, fo.79 [press-cuttings], *Pall Mall Gazette*, 31 July 1891; M.McG.Dana, 'Charles Booth and his Work', *Gunton's Magazine*, x (1896), pp. 189-97; Helen Bosanquet, *The Strength of the People: A Study in Social Economics* 2nd edn (London, 1903), p. 102. On contemporary criticism of his politics, see A.M. McBriar, *An Edwardian Mixed Doubles: The Bosanquets versus the Webbs: A Study in British Social Policy, 1890-1929* (Oxford, 1987), pp. 65-66.

[2] For 'General Charles Booth', see John Maloney, *Marshall, Orthodoxy and the Professionalisation of Economics* (Cambridge, 1985), p. 271; for Booth as Conservative MP, see Gertrude Williams, *The State and the Standard of Living* (London, 1936), p. 19 and T.W. Hutchinson, *A Review of Economic Doctrines, 1870-1929* (Oxford, 1960), p. 412; for Booth as 'sociologist', A.D. Gilbert, *Religion and Society in Industrial England: Church, Chapel and Social Change, 1740-1914* (London, 1976), p. 65 and Owen Chadwick, *The Victorian Church*, 2 vols (London, 1970), pp. 234, 312. On second-hand methods, see Raymond A. Kent, *A History of British Empirical Sociology* (Aldershot, 1981), p. 75 and G.E. Mingay, *The Transformation of Britain, 1830-1939* (London, 1986), p. 15.

[3] H. & M. Wickwar, *The Social Services* (London, 1949, revised edn), p. 287; John Madge, *The Origins of Scientific Sociology* (London, 1963), p. 537.

balance. A dual image emerged. Booth, presented as the 'Founding Father of British Sociology', was also seen as a batty businessman with a bee in his bonnet, or, more accurately, as an awkward amalgam of both. Neither portrait squares with the archival record.

Thirty years have elapsed since the Simeys published their biography of Booth. Interest in his work and ideas, though, has not diminished. Two selections from *Life and Labour of the People in London* have been published and there has been a lively discussion about the nature and significance of Booth's ideas.[4] Recent studies of the assumptions and procedures of the Life and Labour Inquiry have exposed Booth's methods to careful scrutiny and added a fresh dimension to our understanding of the balance between continuity and innovation in the social thought of the period.[5] Booth's texts have also been used to debate certain epistemological problems involved in the historian's craft.[6] These studies, taken together, point to the need for a wider revision of the framework erected by the Simeys.

The Simeys wrote as social scientists, and came to Charles Booth in an attempt to locate a respectable pedigree for the empirical school of British sociology, which was then a despised relation to the great American tradition suffering a crisis of confidence. They saw a straight line of progression between Booth and academic social science in Britain.[7] It was a mantle which some members of the Booth family were only too pleased to accept on his behalf, without perhaps realising the unpleasant implications of pigeon-holing their great ancestor in this way. Historians have different preoccupations and different skills. It is no longer sufficient or satisfactory to discuss Booth as a precursor of modern social science — we assume too much if we begin with this premiss and we miss out a great deal that is important by so doing. It is a bit like discussing the chicken only in terms of the egg that appears in the nesting box. The chicken may or may not have laid it but the chicken is interesting in and for itself. There are also dangers in treating Booth as the Father of British Social Science: these are those of comparing

---

[4] Anthologies include Harold W. Pfautz, ed. *Charles Booth on the City* (Chicago & London, 1967) and A. Fried and R. Eldman eds. *Charles Booth's London* (1971). Debate on Booth's ideas can be followed in John Brown, 'Charles Booth and Labour Colonies', *Economic History Review*, 2nd ser. xxi (1968), pp. 349-60 and in Trevor Lummis, 'Charles Booth: Moralist or Social Scientist', *Economic History Review* 2nd Ser. xxiv (1971), pp. 100-5; also see the exchanges between E.P. Hennock, 'Poverty and Social Theory in England: The Experience of the Eighteen-Eighties', *Social History*, i (1976), pp. 67-91 and Gareth Stedman Jones, *Outcast London*, paperback edn (1976).

[5] See Rosemary O'Day, 'Interviews and Investigations: Charles Booth and the Making of the Religious Influences Survey', *History* (1989), pp. 361-77; David Englander, 'Booth's Jews: The Presentation of Jews and Judaism in *Life and Labour of the People in London*', *Victorian Studies*, xxxii (1989), pp. 551-71.

[6] K. Williams, *From Pauperism to Poverty* (London, 1981), pp. 309-44.

[7] In part this was a defence against W.J. Sprott's portrait of Booth as a fact-finder for fact-finding's sake, see W.J. Sprott, 'Sociology in Britain: Preoccupations' in Howard Becker and Alvin Boskoff, *Modern Sociological Theory in Continuity and Change* (New York, 1957), pp. 607-9.

his theory, and methodology, with those of later exponents of the academic discipline and finding him necessarily 'deficient'. He should not be held responsible for the intellectual and institutional weaknesses of British sociology.[8] As the work of Collini, Goldmann and others has shown, Booth and his contemporaries need to be located within the history of their own time and not in advance of it. Anything less confuses us and belittles them.[9]

Previous studies have failed to explain why Booth undertook his survey. They have repeatedly referred to the idea that Booth was simply reacting to Hyndman's work.[10] His own insistence upon the prime importance of 'collecting facts', upon the need to guard against bias, and upon the relationship between inductive reasoning and deductive reasoning have all been seized upon to convey the impression of a rather mindless individual, who almost accidentally stumbled upon the empirical method and piloted an enormous survey. By describing him simply as a man determined to show things as they were and obsessed by the desire to enumerate those living in differing degree of poverty, scholars have unintentionally marginalised him as an eccentric businessman for whom social investigation was a leisure activity – all absorbing but nonetheless a leisure activity. The Simeys tied themselves up in knots trying to spring from this picture to their conclusion that he was indeed the Father of British Sociology. But they and others have told only part of the story. In the first part of this book we have set it as a goal to explain what motivated him to engage in this form of social investigation. The form of the inquiry itself as well as his reflections upon it hold the key. There may remain questions for debate but it must become clear that the established view of Booth is far from proven.

When the Simeys produced their book current scholarly standards did not apply. Not only are the referencing procedures unsatisfactory, the Simeys' text is often distressingly inaccurate. For example, George Duckworth is credited with writing the abstract in the Star Volume whereas the work was Arthur Baxter's;[11] Esmé Howard is falsely said to have worked on the third series and Baxter, an important figure, is omitted.[12] The committee of five friends who assisted Booth in the study of Central London are in fact well-known, contrary to the Simeys' assertion.[13] These are small but

[8] Cf.P. Abrams, *The Origins of British Sociology, 1834-1914* (Chicago, 1968).

[9] See Stefan Collini, *Liberalism and Sociology: L.T. Hobhouse and Political Argument in England, 1880-1914* (Cambridge, 1979); Lawrence Goldmann, 'The Social Science Association and the Absence of Sociology in Nineteenth-Century Britain', *Past & Present*, cxiv (1987), pp. 133-71. See too the instructive remarks of Christian Topalov 'La Ville "Terre Inconnue": L'enquête de Charles Booth et le peuple de Londres, 1886-1891' *Geneses*, v (1991), pp. 5-34.

[10] See, for example, below pp. 30-1.

[11] See T.S. and M.B. Simey, *Charles Booth, Social Scientist* (Oxford, 1960), p. 158; BLPES, Booth Collection, A31, fos. 70 and 72. Duckworth produced an earlier abstract for the first two series.

[12] Simey, *Charles Booth*, p. 141.

[13] Simey, *Charles Booth*, p. 111, see below p. 185.

significant slips. As so very little in the Simeys' text is footnoted, the reader can have little confidence in their account.

Belinda Norman-Butler, Booth's granddaughter, described the printed survey as 'like the British Museum, much valued but seldom sampled'. This statement is yet more applicable to the papers of the survey itself. Past studies of Booth's work have not involved a detailed use of the immense archive. The Simeys dismissed the possibility of examining the archive in depth. They read parts of it, found it puzzling and incomprehensible, and gave it up as a bad job. In June 1956 Margaret Simey wrote to George Booth that 'we are at the moment deep in a slough of despond over the survey',[14] and in a letter to Lady Gore Browne, one of Booth's daughters, in the following November she confessed that 'to tell the truth, we are making heavy weather of the Inquiry [which] . . . is proving extraordinarily indigestible'.[15] Their dismissal of it as a valuable and usable source appears to have convinced historians. Gareth Stedman Jones did not use the archive for his important *Outcast London*. Belinda Norman-Butler's invaluable work, *Victorian Aspirations*, did not involve a study of the inquiry itself, although she played an important part in ensuring that future scholars had free access to the Booth Correspondence and showed an admirable awareness of its importance. The family also deposited the working papers of the survey at the London School of Economics and large numbers of draft materials at the University of Liverpool Library. Some scholars have as a result been able to dip into the archive of the inquiry to support or illustrate their arguments. Brian Harrison, Raphael Samuel, William Marsden and Hugh Macleod have all in different ways shown its possibilities for the student who has the imagination and stamina to profit by their example.[16] The correspondence has not been used even in this way.

An archaeology of the inquiry itself is, however, essential for any valid assessment of Booth's thought on social problems and the place of the great inquiry within it. The Booth archive is immensely rich. The Booth archive is difficult to work. It is unindexed; enormous; amorphous; daunting. Until someone lays out the chronology and methodology underpinning it, scholars will never be able to say much more about Booth as a social investigator

[14] Booth Correspondence, University of London Library MS 797 I/5990 (i), Margaret Simey to George Booth, 10 June 1956.

[15] Booth Correspondence, MS 797 I/5991 (ii), Margaret Simey to Lady Gore Browne, 18 November 1956.

[16] See Raphael Samuel, 'Comers and Goers' and Brian Harrison, 'The Pub and the People', both in H.J. Dyos and M. Wolff, eds., *The Victorian City: Images and Realities*, 2 vols (London, 1973); W.E. Marsden 'Residential Segregation and the Hierarchy of Elementary Schooling from Charles Booth's London Surveys', *The London Journal*, xi (1985), pp. 131-34; see also Hugh McLeod 'Working Class Religion in Late Victorian London: Booth's "Religious Influences" Revisited' and William Marsden, 'Charles Booth and the Social Geography of Education in Late Nineteenth-Century London', in David Englander and Rosemary O'Day eds., *Retrieved Riches*, forthcoming.

or to use the materials further with any degree of confidence. Scholars are to be forgiven for shying away from this intimidating task. However, our goal should be to compare the printed text with the archive to reveal Booth's skill in writing up the survey and what he chose to present. Also the archive presents a unique resource for the study of many aspects of life and work in late Victorian and Edwardian London. Moreover, there are now noises being made about the reworking of the Booth data for the study of long-term economic and social change. The difficulties here are formidable and insoluble without a clear understanding of the origins and meaning of the data. It is intriguing to note that Llewellyn Smith's New Survey foundered when neither he nor G.H. Duckworth could satisfactorily reconstruct Booth's earlier methodology.[17] Our work on the formation and character of the Booth archive will make for a satisfactory outcome.

The Simeys' biography focused attention on the measurement of poverty and this remains a major preoccupation of historians and social scientists. Booth's measure is said to have been ill-defined, impressionistic and applied inconsistently.[18] So it was in his own day. The sense of relief which greeted the publication of the first volume gave way to a more critical response as class fears subsided and the implications of the Life and Labour survey sank in. The Poverty Line became a contested concept once it was realised that it might provide the basis for an interventionist social policy designed to raise incomes. Such a policy, it was feared, would destroy self-reliance, subvert the family and undermine national character. These fears, sustained by Booth's own advocacy of universal non-contributory old age pensions and the misuse of his data by Radicals and Socialists, were heightened by the imprimatur which he bestowed upon Rowntree's study of poverty in York.[19] Booth's declaration in favour of Rowntree's methods, and above all his insistence on the comparability of their findings, initiated a heated controversy on the meaning, causes and effects of poverty. Critics in the Charity Organisation Society claimed that their data was unreliable, their assumptions unsound, their procedures dubious and their results worthless.[20] Critics from the universities, though more measured in tone, questioned the representativeness of their findings, noted discrepancies in timing and

---

[17] See BLPES, New Survey of London Life, 7/4 and 9/1.

[18] T.H. Marshall, *The Right to Welfare and Other Essays* (London, 1981), p. 37.

[19] See Charles Booth to B.S. Rowntree, 25 July 1901, in B.S. Rowntree, *Poverty: A Study of Town Life* (London, 1901), p. 300.

[20] Helen Bosanquet, 'Physical Degeneration and the Poverty Line', *Contemporary Review*, lxxxv (1904), pp. 65-75; Memorandum of C.S. Loch, *Inter-Departmental Committee on Physical Deterioration* [Cd. 2175] PP. 1904 (xxxvi), pp. 104-11; E.P. Hennock, 'The Measurement of Urban Poverty: From the Metropolis to the Nation, 1880-1920', *Economic History Review*, 2nd ser. xi (1987), pp. 208-27.

method, drew attention to Rowntree's sloppy arithmetic and expressed reservations about the comparability of the results.[21]

Rowntree spoke up for himself and enhanced his reputation.[22] Booth, alas, maintained a dignified silence. Booth's understanding of poverty, however, was wider than is sometimes suggested. The expert accounts of the School Board Visitors, about whom so much has been written, supplied but one dimension.[23] Working people themselves supplied another. The archive, as distinct from the printed text, not only shows the variety of his sources, but also suggests that his relativistic concept of poverty was grounded in the testimony of working people as well as in the statements of teachers, philanthropists, clergy and the other authorities whom he consulted.[24] While this book is largely concerned with the archive of the investigation, one of its major aims is to set the record straight and explain just what Booth was investigating. This involves setting the Poverty survey within the context of the entire work and, moreover, looking carefully at the Poverty survey itself to determine what it contained.

A proper appreciation of Booth himself must also be taken in the intellectual context of the period 1870-1916. Scholars have too easily accepted the idea that Booth rejected contemporary social theories and opted for a 'mindless' form of investigation. Such a contention is ripe for reexamination. Booth's reticence about method and his infuriating diffidence in respect of specific outcomes have to some extent wrong-footed scholars.[25] Selvin, for example, in seeking to account for the non-diffusion of techniques of statistical correlation explains Booth's indifference to Yule in terms of his 'limited intellectual powers'. Others have concluded, quite

---

[21] See David L. Green, 'The Poverty of an English Town', *Yale Review* (February 1903), pp. 347-60; D.H. Macgregor, 'The Poverty Figures', *Economic Journal*, xx (1910), pp. 567-72.

[22] See B.S. Rowntree, *The Poverty Line: A Reply* (London, 1904); J.H. Veit-Wilson, 'Paradigms of Poverty: A Rehabilitation of B.S. Rowntree', *Journal of Social Policy* xv (1986), pp. 69-99.

[23] Contrary to received opinion, he did not rely exclusively upon the School Board Visitors for information even in connection with the first streets survey of the Poverty series. For example, one of the notebooks contains information supplied largely by rent collectors and building managers – Ella Pycroft (Beatrice Potter's friend and colleague at Katharine Buildings) and Miss Coe among them. Booth Collection, B19 (notebook no. 12), gives the sources of information for three blocks of Peabody Buildings, for Katharine Buildings, Wentworth Buildings, George's Yard and St George's House. See Passfield, II (i) II, Ella Pycroft to Beatrice Potter, 3 October 1886 for Miss Coe, rent collector.

[24] Booth's well-documented lack of sympathy for those for whom supply and demand made no provision is sometimes dismissed as middle- class moralising. The existence of comparable negative valuations within the working class has not received sufficient attention. Middle-aged readers from respectable working-class backgrounds will know from personal experience that middle-class social investigators had no monopoly of censorious judgements on the disadvantaged.

[25] See Booth's evidence to *Select Committee of the House of Lords on the Sweating System*, [361] PP. 1888 (xx), qq. 304, 306, 313, 389, 391-93, 397-99; Almeric Fitzroy, *Memoirs*, 2 vols (London, 1926), i. p. 170.

erroneously, that Booth had never encountered Le Play, and read neither Mayhew nor Marx.[26] As will be shown below, Booth knew of the work of the Frenchman, had read the Englishman – and most probably the German too. A closer acquaintance with the archive will enable us to clarify Booth's procedures and place his thought within its proper context.

The object here is not to assess the worth of the printed survey (seventeen volumes in all) but to discuss the making of this survey in the light of the archive. There are three main parts to this archive: an extensive collection of notebooks, reports, miscellanea and correspondence held at the British Library of Political and Economic Science; a large collection of draft chapters at the Liverpool University Library; and a huge collection of private correspondence deposited at the University of London Library, Senate House. But there are also subsidiary archives – Collet, Passfield, Schloss, Llewellyn Smith – which have been little explored in this context. These archives are frequently not self-evidently concerned with the Booth Inquiry but we ignore them at our peril. For example, Maurice Paul's letters to Beatrice Potter and Ella Pycroft's correspondence with Beatrice are frequently ignored in this context and have led to a misreading of parts of the Booth archive.[27] It is true, as the Simeys bemoaned, that Charles Booth never sat down and wrote a concentrated essay on the methodology he adopted in pursuing his inquiry.[28] While often fragmentary, the documentation needed to reconstruct his methodology does exist scattered throughout these collections. As is demonstrated, the very information which the Simeys thought lacking about the Industry inquiry, on the basis of the printed text alone, occurs in daunting abundance in the archive at the London School of Economics.[29] They were led to make startlingly inaccurate statements as a result of their ignorance of the archive: 'In particular, very little of the evidence of individual workmen on which he had relied "to make the book readable" had been collected . . .'[30] It is hoped that this discussion – which has involved painstaking piecing together of chronology, collabo-

[26] H.C. Selvin, 'Durkheim, Booth and Yule: The Non-Diffusion of an Intellectual Innovation', *European Journal of Sociology* xvii (1976), pp. 39-51; Paul F. Lazarsfeld, 'Notes on the History of Quantification in Sociology – Trends, Sources and Problems', *Isis*, lii (1961), p. 322; Raymond A. Kent, *A History of British Empirical Sociology* (Aldershot, 1981), pp. 61, 198.

[27] BLPES, Passfield, II i (II), 7 & 8; see for example, M. Bulmer *et al*, *The Social Survey in Historical Perspective* (Cambridge, 1992), pp. 49-110, which is apparently unaware of this material in the Passfield Collection, and, in consequence, makes a number of errors and omissions ranging from the trivial but irritating to the serious. Bulmer and his associates also made no use of the abundant and enlightening Booth Correspondence at University of London Library, Senate House.

[28] Simey, *Charles Booth*, pp. 8, 71: 'the sources consist of no more than incidental references to the subject. Other sources are no less unhelpful'.

[29] Simey, *Charles Booth*, p. 126; see below pp. 103ff.

[30] Simey, *Charles Booth*, p. 129.

ration and content – will help reveal more accurately the motivation, meaning and method behind the Booth Inquiry.

One caveat seems appropriate. It is unwise to make any categorical statements about Booth's method of working. The documentation is apparently inexhaustible and the scholar employing it will always be in the position of producing 'working papers'. For example, statements by scholars that Booth's 'Team' was restricted to the named authors of essays in the series is shown by even limited use of the archive to be incorrect. One never ceases to be amazed at the number of fresh collaborators in the 'work' which each of the archives reveals – Green, Vaughan, Brooks, Scott, Allen, Hey, Lewis, Nevinson, to name but a few.[31] No fewer than thirty-four people were employed at one time or another on the inquiry. Moreover, people known to have contributed to one part of the inquiry are often found collaborating in another.[32] The nature and extent of the participation of, for example, Charles H. Skinner and Jesse Argyle can now be documented.[33]

This reconsideration aims to restore balance to the scholarly appreciation of Booth's work. The Poverty Series is seen to be much more than a set of statistics of dubious validity about London in the late 1880s. There is no attempt to recover ground already well trodden by scholars. The Poverty Series offers vivid and valuable detail about the occupants of London streets and a Booth who is reflective, humble and humane. It presents special studies produced by able associates, few of whom, apart from Beatrice Potter, have ever been acknowledged by historians and social scientists as in any sense important. Booth's survey was from the start a collaborative affair. Booth was certainly the 'Chief' – the moneybag, the manager – but the men and women who worked with him made important and individual contributions. Here we attempt to reconstruct the manner in which these special studies were conducted and written up, focusing on the work of a very few secretaries and associates. The recent discovery at the library of the London School of Economics of Schloss papers pertaining to the survey of the boot and shoe industry – used for the first time here – and the Booth archive at the London School of Economics have proved invaluable. The three surveys conducted by Beatrice Potter have been carefully documented. The Industry Inquiry, described by Mary Booth as 'dull', emerges from the archive as 'my beloved trades of London', explored through the workplace by Booth and his associates. The vibrant interview materials belie the dry-as-dust details of the printed work, making an unfavourable comparison with

[31] Passfield, II i (II), 6, 7, 8, 9; Booth Collection, A6, A7, 'Cabinet-Making', p. 350. See pp. 000 below.

[32] See, for example, Booth Collection, B58, B60, B64 for Clara Collet's work on Battersea for Graham Balfour.

[33] See, for example, Skinner's and Argyle's role in the special streets interviews of 1890. Booth Collection, B66-B74.

Mayhew's *London Labour and the London Poor* much less persuasive. Once again the 'Team' are extremely evident — Ernest Aves, George Duckworth, Arthur Baxter, Hubert Llewellyn Smith, Esmé Howard, Jesse Argyle and George Arkell. Then there is the Religious Influences Series, largely ignored by historians and social scientists, yet absorbing in the extreme to Charles and Mary Booth. The archive for this series is very full but incomplete. It contains material relevant to a study of the ministry in turn-of-the-century London, its morale, perceived problems and attitudes. It also provides many clues about the motivation and method behind the survey itself. Without this the import of the printed survey is difficult to ascertain. The Religious Influences Series was unique in that it was the only one of which Booth was sole 'author'. However, it too was at the investigative and literary level a collaborative project, drawing upon the skills and judgement of Duckworth, Baxter, Aves, Arkell and Argyle, as well as of Mary Booth, Charles' hidden collaborator.

It is difficult to establish the precise nature and extent of Mary Booth's contribution to the inquiry but it appears to have been considerable. The family later asserted that the two styles detected 'in the book' by the Simeys, 'one more direct and one more literary' were 'Father's and Mother's of course'.[34] George Booth told the Simeys, 'With regard to written contributions by my Mother and others, we are all conscious of many contributions from my Mother. . .'[35] The evidence is fragmentary but suggestive. Mary read widely both with and for Booth — Marx and Webb, James and Rowntree, Barnett and Price. She, and sometimes her eldest daughter 'Dodo', attended meetings with him. In 1887, for example, the two heard his address at the Royal Statistical Society and in 1893 Mary accompanied Charles to a discussion between the Webbs and the Co-operative Men at the Economic Club. Her letters to Beatrice Potter in the 1880s suggest that Mary was at least fully aware of the state of the inquiry;[36] in March 1892 it was she and Jesse Argyle who saw 'the Pauper' through proof and press;[37] she interviewed people on occasion for Booth and held a press reception on the publication of at least one of his works.[38] But her role in relation to the third series is by far the best documented — she played a major critical role during

---

[34] Booth Correspondence, MS 797 I/3030, Meg Booth Ritchie, daughter of Charles Booth, to George Booth, son of Charles Booth, 22 January 1956.

[35] Booth Correspondence, MS 797 I/2402 (ii), George Booth to Margaret Simey, 23 January 1956.

[36] Passfield, II(i)(II), 6, Mary Booth to Beatrice Potter, 1887; Mary Booth to Beatrice Potter, 11 August 1889.

[37] Belinda Norman-Butler, *Victorian Aspirations: The Life and Labour of Charles and Mary Booth*, (London, 1972), p. 121.

[38] Norman-Butler, *Victorian Aspirations*, p. 110. In January 1892, Mary interviewed J.A. Spender, author of *The State v Pensions in Old Age*; Mary Booth entertained the press to lunch in May 1890 to launch second volume of the Poverty Series, Norman-Butler, *Victorian Aspirations*, p. 120.

the authorship of the Religious Influence books and was left holding the Star Volume baby when Booth absented himself in 1903.[39]

One effect of this reassessment is to reveal a world, little known to historians, of professional or semi-professional researchers. There were immense opportunities for the newly educated woman – such as Clara Collet – or the young ambitious graduate – Maurice Eden Paul, Hubert Llewellyn Smith, Ernest Aves. The work had its pressures – part-time, poorly remunerated, insecure. Also there were opportunities for intelligent clerks – Argyle, Arkell – trained up to the work and themselves participating actively in some cases in analytical work of assessment and data handling and, as with Argyle, in social work of a kind. It was George Arkell who developed in Booth's employ new techniques and new expertise in the science of social geography. In so far as Booth's 'secretaries' have attracted attention, it has mainly gone to Beatrice Potter, one of the 'working rich', who, while fascinating, was not typical of Booth's collaborators.[40]

Noteworthy is the new light which such a reconsideration throws upon the role which the Toynbee Hall Settlement played in the inquiry. While historians have long recognised that certain of Booth's 'secretaries' were Toynbee men – Aves, Llewellyn Smith – and that Canon Barnett, after initial reservations about the work, ultimately gave his support, the extent to which Toynbee Hall was in fact a work station for Mr Booth's Inquiry has not before been evident. Barnett was responsible for introducing Booth and his 'secretaries' to East End officials, businessmen, clergy and tradesmen who could provide him with information.[41] It was from Toynbee that Booth drew many of his collaborators – not only known secretaries such as Aves but also men such as Henry Nevinson, Clem Edwards, E.W. Brooks, Percival Burt Allen, who now emerge as actively involved in collecting material for Booth.[42] Booth's 'secretaries' seem to have used the Toynbee Hall case books as a first port for data.[43] The Toynbee Economic Club was the forum

[39] See below for a detailed treatment of this pp. 180-87.
[40] Booth called all his assistants 'secretaries'; some, like Aves and Potter, were in reality 'associates', whereas Argyle and Arkell were not. In this book Argyle and Arkell are always termed as 'secretaries' but the others are variously described as assistants, associates, collaborators, colleagues and secretaries.
[41] See pp. 66, 68-9 below. Such introductions were not always effective. See page 120 for George Duckworth's unproductive interview with Mr Koenigsberg, of Commercial Road notwithstanding a Barnett letter of introduction.
[42] See pp. 109 below.
[43] See pp. 55, 68 below.

for a trial run of the Industry Series.[44] The collaborators attended (and perhaps inspired) conferences on subjects highly relevant to the interests of the inquiry.[45] Some held classes at Toynbee – Henry Higgs (on working men's budgets); Clara Collet; E.W. Brooks; George Arkell.[46] A few were residents of the Hall, more were not. (Ernest Aves, for example, was sub-warden and Llewellyn Smith was briefly resident, whereas most of the secretaries and helpers who had a Toynbee connection lived 'out'.)[47]

The Royal Statistical Society connection was also of vital importance. Sometime in 1884 Charles Booth became a Fellow of the Royal Statistical Society. The connections which he made through the society prove to have been very important. The Royal Statistical Society had its home in Adelphi Terrace, the Strand, close to the premises of the Registrar General. It rented part of its premises to Charles Booth in 1892, whence he removed from 2 Talbot Court as the headquarters of his inquiry. Several pieces of his work were in the first instance presented as papers for the society and he received criticism from its members.[48] He drew upon the expertise of Alfred Marshall of Cambridge, Leone Levi, Arthur Acland and Graham Balfour directly or indirectly through the Royal Statistical Society. Balfour, sometime President of the Royal Statistical Society, actively participated as an associate in the inquiry. It has emerged during the course of writing this book that Balfour followed Booth's methodology in his study of Battersea – recording information supplied by the School Board Visitors in notebooks which were available to Booth in 1890.[49] From 1892 to 1894 Booth was president of the society. In this capacity he led a delegation to the President of the Board of Trade asking for the creation of a permanent statistical organisation. The establishment in 1893 of the Labour Department as an outgrowth of the Labour Statistical Bureau (founded in 1886) owed much to the Royal Statistical Society's long campaign and Booth's support, together with the presence of A.J. Mundella, a fellow of the Royal Statistical Society, as President of the Board of Trade.[50] Immediately Booth's associates were

[44] *Toynbee Record*, viii (June 1896), p. 110, reports that at the last three meetings of the Toynbee Economic Club the speakers were Jesse Argyle, G.H. Duckworth and the President (Ernest Aves). *Toynbee Record*, x (December 1897), p. 104 reports that Aves addressed the club again on 23 November 1897; *Toynbee Record*, x (April 1898), p. 104 reports that Jesse Argyle delivered a paper on 'The Limits of Municipal Enterprise'.

[45] E.g. Women's Work and Wages, 1887, Working Men's Budgets, 1891, University of Warwick, MRC, Collet MS 29/3/13/5/16-17.

[46] Collet MS 29/3/13/5/16-17; Collet MS 29/8/1/55-110; see Calendar, *Toynbee Record*, viii (April 1896).

[47] Simey, *Charles Booth*, p. 101 states that Stephen Fox was a resident but his name does not appear in J.A.R. Pimlott, *Toynbee Hall* (London, 1935), pp. 283-99.

[48] See *Journal of the Royal Statistical Society*, 1886-94.

[49] E.g. Booth Collection, B72, fo. 199.

[50] See Simey, *Charles Booth*, p. 117; Roger Davidson, *Whitehall and the Labour Problem in Late Victorian and Edwardian Britain* (London, 1985), pp. 79-85, 95-98.

employed. Booth had also attempted a pilot study to demonstrate how important statistics could and should be collected by the Board of Trade. As a member of a committee set up to advise the Registrar General he had urged the inclusion in the census of 'some simple facts by which the position and manner of life of each family could be measured'.[51] Accordingly in the census of 1891 the Registrar General ordered his officers to record the number of rooms occupied by each householder living in four rooms or less and the number of servants employed in houses of five rooms or more. Booth met each of the registrars of the metropolitan sub-districts more than once to discuss the practicalities of this decision and was convinced that the enumerators (some 3,000 plus) did their work conscientiously and well.[52] These statistics were used by Booth.[53] He used the remainder of the series to demonstrate, among other things, what other information could usefully be collected for the Board of Trade at 'the epoch of any numerical census' – material on apprenticeships, trade organisation, family constitution and so on. 'With a little preconcerted arrangement, so that the information gathered by the Registrar General might lend itself easily to much further investigation, the work I have attempted might, I venture to suggest, be taken up by the Board of Trade with the certainty of a far larger measure of success.'[54] Such a social-industrial census, coupled with the numerical, should be quinquennial. The close relations between the Registrar General's office and the Board of Trade and the Royal Statistical Society ensured Booth a forum and partial success.

The place of other clubs and societies, notably the Charity Organisation Society, the Junior Economic Club and the British or Royal Economic Society, in the order of things is more shadowy. It has been possible, however, to build up a partial picture of Booth's activities in this regard. Clearly, Booth and his associates had connections with the Charity Organisation Society. Octavia Hill contributed to the inquiry and, despite her opposition to Booth's Old Age Pensions schemes, remained his friend to the last. C.S. Loch and Booth also disagreed fundamentally over the issues of Old Age Pensions and Pauperism but the lines of communication were open and frequently busy, especially in the 1880s. Beatrice Potter had been a member of the Charity Organisation Society; Clara Collet stayed a member from 1888-1906. Booth's daughter Imogen became secretary of the Hoxton Charity Organisation Society.[55] The Junior Economic Club was altogether a more academic affair and provided another important forum for discussion of and work on economic issues. It was founded on the initiative of one of

[51] *Industry*, 1, p. 16.
[52] *Industry*, 1, p. 12.
[53] *Industry*, 1, passim and especially p. 13ff.
[54] *Industry*, 5, p. 65.
[55] See Frederic Spotts, ed., *Letters of Leonard Woolf* (London, 1989), p. 179, Leonard Woolf to M. MacCarthy, 28 September 1912.

Booth's associates, Clara Collet. In mid June 1890 she suggested to Henry Higgs the formation of a club of young economists who had trained under Professor Foxwell at London and on 27 June, at a meeting of the Denison Club at University College, she founded the Junior Economic Club. It had a committee of nine (which included other of Booth's associates who were not products of London University − Ernest Aves, Llewellyn Smith − as well as Clara Collet and Higgs who were) and a score of members altogether. By the time of its first meeting on the second Tuesday of October 1890 it may have had fifty members, all carefully vetted by the committee and approved as 'trained economists'. Its meetings took several forms: discussions of major works (for example, in November 1890 Alfred Marshall came to the club to discuss his work;[56] later in 1899 Sidney Webb informed Beatrice that 'the Economic Club had had an evening over Industrial Democracy', with short papers on it. This was at Miss Collet's suggestion, 'in order to make the members read it');[57] considerations of chosen themes and questions in some detail (the first chosen was 'The Consumption of Wealth' which was to be examined under several heads including 'Curves of Demand', 'Theory of Utility', 'Standard of Comfort' and 'Luxury'); original investigation leading to publication (it was probably the Junior Economic Club that published a work on family budgets edited by Booth, Aves and Higgs in 1896). On 9 December 1890 Charles Booth, John Burnett and Alfred Marshall were invited to a meeting of the club to discuss family statistics. Charles and Mary Booth went 'To Economic Club in the evening' of 23 June 1893 to hear 'keen discussion between the Webbs and the Co-op men' on Co-operation, Production and Distribution.[58] It was clearly in the Economic Club that Booth's ideas and work were discussed and to some extent developed. (The Junior Economic Club should not be confused either with the British or Royal Economic Society, founded on 20 November 1890 at University College, or with the Toynbee Economic Club formed in November 1890 with Clara Collet as one of its vice presidents and with monthly meetings on the second Tuesday of the month. Sometimes such confusion will inevitably occur, The membership of the Royal Economic Society and the Junior Economic Club to some extent overlapped − Collet, Higgs, Foxwell, Edgeworth. The Toynbee Economic Club undertook parallel work on working men's family budgets which fed into the work of the Junior Economic Club).

Charles Booth belonged to the intellectual aristocracy that Noel Annan has described. Annan's concept of such an intellectual cousinhood is interesting but has its limitations. It has been possible here to move beyond a family tree to delineate the relationships which Booth had both with

---

[56] Document printed in 'Obituary of Henry Higgs', *Economic Journal* (1940), p. 561.

[57] Norman Mackenzie (ed.), *The Letters of Sidney and Beatrice Webb*, ii (Cambridge, 1978), p. 363, Sidney Webb to Beatrice Webb, 16 June 1899.

[58] Mary Booth's Diary, 23 June 1893, cited in Norman-Butler, *Victorian Aspirations*, p. 144.

members of that aristocracy, particularly Potter, Courtney, Grosvenor, Cripps, Duckworth, Harrison and Edgeworth, but also with what one might wish to call the '1st and 2nd XIs' of the intellectual world – Alfred Marshall, Llewellyn Smith, Sidney Webb, Ernest Aves, David Schloss, Clara Collet, Henry Higgs. These were people who themselves did not come from a background of wealth or high society, although they in some cases were connected by marriage to such backgrounds – for instance Marshall's wife was Mary Paley and Aves was to marry Ermengard (Eva) Maitland, daughter of Frederic. They were civil servants, university teachers with lively, sometimes original, minds, scholarly interests and great public spiritedness. They were drawn into the milieu of the intellectual aristocracy for these very attributes. This milieu included the great societies of the day, of course – the Economic Club, The British or Royal Economic Society, the Royal Statistical Society but it also took in the British Museum Reading Room, the University Settlements, the dinner table, the house party, and even the Booths' breakfast table. Booth's was an intellectually busy world. His life was lived at the very hub of the intellectual wheel.[59]

It was an environment that gave him enormous influence with professional, administrative and academic elites, but also served to isolate him from the political mainstream. Booth, though advanced in his social politics, preferred to address a professional audience and eschewed the journalism of the New Liberalism and the party platform made available by those who confused his Protectionism with Conservatism.[60] Booth was always his own man.

Booth had, as we have indicated above, an influence upon the Board of Trade which has been relatively overlooked. Clara Collet thanked Booth for his help when in 1903 she received promotion:

> As you were mainly responsible for my appointment, I think you will be glad to hear that I am promoted to be one of the two Senior Investigators; one of the vacancies being due to the promotion of Mr Schloss. Of course you already know that Mr Ll Smith will be the new Controller-General. So you must feel almost Permanent President of the Board of Trade.[61]

By 1907 David Schloss definitely had been promoted to the senior

---

[59] Booth also had contacts with the literary and artistic words – through, for example, close association with the Holman Hunts.

[60] On the importance of journalism in relation to advanced thought, see M. Freeden, *The New Liberalism, An Ideology of Social Reform* (Oxford, 1978). On the comparative unimportance of party political commitment in Booth's make-up, see Mary Booth, *Charles Booth: A Memoir* (London, 1918), p. 36.

[61] Booth Correspondence, MS 797 I/4803, Clara Collet to Charles Booth, 23 October 1903; this suggests that Schloss was a Senior Investigator before 1903, see Roger Davidson, *Whitehall and the Labour Problem*, p. 126.

secretariat of the Board as Director of the Census of Production. The list of Booth associates employed by the Board of Trade swelled when Ernest Aves, already an expert on the casual labour market and Home Office adviser on the Australian and New Zealand Wage Boards, joined their ranks as a Statistical Investigator.

Booth's influence stretched beyond obtaining jobs for his protegés. 'Mr Booth's influence at the Board of Trade has been abiding and unceasing', declared Collet in 1916. 'Both his scientific methods and personal character, working through Llewellyn Smith, raised the standard & purified the aims of the Labour Department.' 'Also,' she added, 'all the economic thinkers started from a new standpoint.'[62] Even when we allow for the eulogistic character of this letter to the recently widowed Mary Booth, the evidence certainly points to the truth of Collet's claim. In the words of Roger Davidson, their statistical philosophy 'had been largely moulded by their participation in the Booth Inquiry, and their primary concern was to provide a scientific exposé of the 'Labour Problem'; a careful, minute, systematic observation of working-class life as affected by environment, heredity and habit. This, they argued, would provide an impartial database for debate on labour issues, or on legislative proposals of a socialistic or autocratic kind that ignored the realities of the labour market and the complexities of social administration.[63] Schloss predicted that the database for legislators provided by the Labour Department would 'guide by the light of indisputable facts and figures the demands of the working classes' and show legislators what it was desirable and possible to do to meet these demands. Collet's own report on women's work acknowledged a debt to Booth, used his studies and statistics as a point of departure and comparison and followed closely his methodology.[64] Llewellyn Smith, of course, remained committed to Booth's empirical studies and it was he who directed the 'New Survey' which compared London forty years on with Booth's London. But it was not only Booth's methodology and Booth's vision which this group of social investigators took into the Board of Trade, it was an acute awareness through their experience as researchers of the lack of properly collected statistical data and the problems involved in amassing such data. It is by examining the work that Schloss, Collet and Smith did for the inquiry that we can gain insights into their future work in the civil service.

By concentrating on the archival material still extant it has been possible to study Booth's methods in some detail. The consequent findings are

[62] Booth Correspondence, MS 797 I/4804, Clara Collet to Mary Booth, 25 November 1916; for the institutional expression of Booth's influence see Roger Davidson's excellent *Whitehall and the Labour Problem* (London, 1985).

[63] Davidson, *Whitehall and the Labour Problem*, p. 119.

[64] See MRC Collet MSS.

important not only for an assessment of Booth's importance but also for any subsequent work on the development of research and survey techniques in the period of 1886 to the present. Far from relying exclusively on School Board Visitor material, Booth directly employed questionnaires, interviews, personal observation; collection of statistical data; collation of data; sampling; and statistical tabulation of data in his work. He adapted the scientists' method of observing and classifying data. He made use of other people's house-to-house and street-to-street surveys. He used the census. He invited a deluge of photographs and miscellanea. He was aware of the importance of social geography and his maps of contemporary London are a valuable resource today. Here we offer new insights into the manner in which he used these varied methodologies. While he was not always successful in his employment of them, his working experiments revealed their pitfalls to future generations of inquirers and encouraged them to discover ingenious avoidance strategies.[65]

In one sense Booth's methodology belonged to the long-standing tradition of data collection by central and local government departments, royal commissions and the ecclesiastical authorities. When Joseph Chamberlain wrote to Beatrice Potter in February 1886 about the existence of distress above the 'pauper line', he took it as axiomatic that empirically derived evidence of such distress was necessary before policy decisions could be taken by government: 'I am trying to collect facts from different sources but it is difficult to make them complete'.[66] Fact-finding was already an essential part of preparation for social action in Britain, even if it was often unsophisticated and ill-organised. Mary Booth was right in more ways than one when she likened Booth's enterprise and organisation to that of a government department. Booth's own family and that of his Macaulay wife knew this tradition well. Its premises – that empirical evidence, properly analysed, was essential before one could draw generalisations or, more importantly, move on to considered policy – set Booth against the approach of the Political Economists before he even started to read their works. The credo was one of optimism – one set out with the premiss that action was not only possible but necessary and desirable if only and when only one had collected the informative data.

It follows that one of Booth's major contributions to social investigation lay in the area of organisation. It has become clear from the archive that the inquiry did not consist of one man working with a group of docile research assistants, nor yet of one man, two secretaries and a group of independent scholars. The Chief directed the project but he did so in such a way that a nucleus of able young investigators felt committed to and deeply involved in

---

[65] See also Rosemary O'Day, 'Interviews and Investigations: The Making of the Religious Influences Survey', *History*, lxxiv (1989), pp. 361-77.

[66] Passfield, II i (II), 4, Joseph Chamberlain to Beatrice Potter, 28 February 1886.

the work that was being done, being able to use their own initiative in undertaking it whilst also engaging in constant debate both with the Chief and with each other. Of course there were varying degrees of commitment and enchantment. Collet found investigation a depressing business and Potter was clearly not cut out for Booth's special variety of social inquiry. Nevertheless, Booth experimented with ways of training his associates as interviewers and observers so that comparisons could be made between their findings while allowing these able individuals sufficient rein to use their particular talents. In the archive we see several examples of the attempt to impose uniformity of methodology – in the notebooks associated with the Poverty Series, for example, and in the interview books of the Religious Influences Series. The unifying role of the two secretaries, Argyle and Arkell, in the work on trades and industries for both the first and second series is strikingly apparent. Yet we see also the disparate essays contributed by Potter, Llewellyn Smith, Collet and Schloss in the first series and the highly individual reports drawn up by Duckworth and Aves for the third series. Lasting personal and working relationships developed between members of the 'team' – Llewellyn Smith, Collet and Schloss; Llewellyn Smith and Beatrice Potter; Collet and Potter; Schloss and Potter; Aves and Duckworth – which ensured that the concerns of Booth's Inquiry and the debates which it inspired lived on to inform other work of social investigation and deliberation. Smith, Collet and Schloss, for example, were founder members of the London Economic Club.

Booth emerges from the study as a man with a peculiar passion – to establish the truth about the condition of the people in London as a necessary prelude to the discovery of appropriate remedies. Here was no social scientist working in the abstract, in the ivory tower of one of the universities but a social reformer. He used and developed techniques which social scientists made their own or rejected and as such is an important figure in the development of social science. We must not, however, confuse his motivation and his meaning with his methodology. The Simeys, themselves sociologists, drew Booth in their own image. According to them he set out, as does the modern academic sociologist, with a set of hypotheses to prove or disprove:

> new hypotheses quickly emerged to take the place of the first and most naive of them, namely that Hyndman was wrong. The second series of hypotheses embodied the more complicated generalization that poverty could be regarded as a facet of the structure of society, as well as be attributed to the moral failings of individuals. This contention was validated by brilliantly successful statistical work, which provides a classic example of how sociological research should be be conducted.[67]

[67] Simey, *Charles Booth*, p. 190.

This was a dangerous description of Booth's work – dangerous not only because it propagated the myth that Booth's work was in its origins a reaction to Hyndman (for which see below, p. 31) and led scholars to neglect a study of other influences on Booth (such as the Political Economists and 'modern' thinkers such as Jevons, Walker and Marshall) but also because it read back modern sociological methods into Booth. When Booth described his work he mentioned no hypotheses or guiding ideas. 'The principles on which the inquiry was conducted' were 'dividing the people by districts and again by trades, *so as to show at once the manner of their life and work*'. No more, no less. There was no hypothesis carefully constructed and laid out and hence no work of validation or disproof. Later he commented that he 'undoubtedly expected that this investigation would expose exaggerations, and it did so' but this he did not formulate as a hypothesis.[68] Not an inkling of a hypothesis is to be found in the printed work, the archive or the correspondence.[69]

He was a great man, great because he was both humble and ambitious, not for himself but for his work. He saw the need for an enormous work and he had both sufficient drive and sufficient flair to see it through. While not himself a university product or a great reader, he was a clever man who thought a good deal, drew upon conversation with others, his own reading, the reading of others and the papers presented by others in order to develop his own project and his own approaches. Booth was not an original thinker and he was not a systematic thinker. But, as we seek to demonstrate below, he was influenced by the main intellectual currents of the period and did work on the basis of a theory which was derivative. A student of Comte, he remained convinced that empirically derived evidence of life as it was experienced, properly analysed, must form the basis of social action. When he said he had no bias, he seems to have meant that he sought to be open in his assessments and that he tried not to work on the basis of preconceived abstract theories such as those for long preached by the Political Economists. Booth was always willing, however, to modify his conclusions or those of other scholars such as Walker when the evidence he had collected seemed to dictate it. Far from being unreflective and unaware of the problems of his sources, he demonstrated considerable caution. He would seize upon a suggestion – such as that the School Board Visitors might be a source of much information – and involve himself in careful pilot studies to see whether that was the case or not. He was eclectic but intelligent in the choices he made. While he drew upon the expertise of others there is never a sense

[68] *Poverty*, 1, p. 5.
[69] See also Simey, *Charles Booth*, p. 254: 'It is this endeavour to develop working hypotheses, and apply them to the conditions of living society, that gives Booth his true significance as a sociologist'.

in which the inquiry was less than Booth's own. He was the Chief, the director.

One of the explanations for neglect of the Booth archive lies in its inaccessibility. It is largely unindexed and the index which does exist is often extremely misleading. It has proved difficult to establish how and on what principles this index was drawn up. Notes are in most cases grouped according to the appropriate chapters of the printed work but there is no attempt to discriminate between materials on trades and industries collected for the first and second series, for example. An important feature of the present volume is that it does discuss for the first time the nature of the archive in relation to the inquiry and its printed results and enables scholars to approach the sources with more confidence that they know what they are reading.

It has also been our aim to draw attention to important categories of material which have hitherto been lost to the eye. For example, the caches of material pertaining the lives of ordinary families, to social customs of the workshop; workplace design; the role of women in organised religion; the parochial ministry; working class religion; social geography of education.[70]

Life and Labour of the People in London is widely considered to constitute a landmark in the development of the sociological survey.[71] Contemporaries, too, considered it a significant innovation. What kind of innovation, though, was not entirely clear. All agreed that it was different in character from the fictional accounts of Walter Besant or other forms of writing. Mayhew's *London Labour and the London Poor* supplied the obvious referent. 'One naturally compares such a book with Henry Mayhew's widely known work', wrote one reviewer. The comparison, it was noted, was not always to Booth's advantage. The strength of *London Labour and the London Poor*, the reviewer remarked, lay in the testimonies 'taken direct from the lips of costers and street-merchants of every kind, whose friendship Mr Mayhew cultivated so assiduously'. Its weaknesses, though, were no less striking. 'It is really a mass of incidents of low life, told with dramatic intensity and simplicity by the actors themselves; but it fails to gather up its facts into any connected statement, or to point the way towards any solution of one of the greatest

[70] There is no sense in which this book aims to be an index to the collections. The authors, as Directors of the Charles Booth Group of the Open University, have, with the assistance of Dr Mark Clapson and Dr Judith Ford, prepared for publication a computerised calendar to the Poverty notebooks. There are plans to produce further computerised calendars relating to other aspects of the survey.

[71] A.F. Wells, *The Local Social Survey in Great Britain* (London, 1935); N. Carpenter, 'Social Surveys', in E.R.A. Seligman ed., *Encyclopaedia of the Social Sciences*, 15 vols (New York), 1930-35, xiv, pp. 162-65; C.A. Moser, *Survey Methods in Social Investigation* (London, 1958), pp. 18-20.

problems of modern civilization.' In all these respects, he or she concluded, Booth was Mayhew's superior.[72]

Even so, the comparison should not be pressed. The Booth Inquiry, like its predecessor, resisted easy classification. It is well to remember that, while Booth had no claim to priority in the application of survey methods in social investigation, the sociological survey had no established format when he began his inquiries. Booth himself had no idea that he stood at the head of a burgeoning 'social survey movement', and neither did his audience, who in general viewed his inquiry less as a blueprint for social action and more as a permanent work of reference, 'a statistical cycplopedia of life and labour in the greatest city of the world'.[73] Its compendious nature, gazeteer properties, impersonality and sheer scale impressed contemporaries almost as much as its optimistic interpretation of the social crisis. Critics invariably conceded the comprehensive scope and scientific character of the Booth Inquiry even if its specific remedies were politely denied or quietly ignored.[74]

For all that, *Life and Labour of the People in London* was a rather odd kind of standard reference. The uniform edition, bound in white vellum with gold decorations and green ribbon, was indeed almost as controversial as the content. The want of solemnity was confusing. 'The volumes savour too much of the *Englishwoman's Love Letters* in appearance', wrote Richard Mudie-Smith who also considered the binding 'quite unsuitable' and 'better fitted for a collection of poems than a work of reference'.[75] Yet this was no publisher's whimsy. The Booths, who bore the full cost of publication, had definite expectations about their readers' requirements and decided views about the design and presentation of their findings. Macmillan, who merely acted as the Booths' agent, were happy to comply.[76]

The format of the Booth Inquiry was equally striking. Although Booth knew what he was about, there was a discrepancy between his presentational skills and his technical accomplishments. The colossal scale of the publication, the want of integration and sheer weight of detail – testified to the experimental nature of the inquiry and the almost impossible task that Booth had set himself. The everyday experience of the urban masses eluded him as still it eludes us. The interviews and investigations that filled his notebooks were simply too rich, too vibrant, too variable and too many to

[72] Anon, 'Life and Labour in East London', *London Quarterly Review*, xxiv (1890), p. 316.

[73] Anon., 'East London', *Literary World*, xx (1889), pp. 251-53. Booth himself, it might be noted, concluded by the end of his investigation that his style of inquiry was not suitable as a policy- forming instrument: see his statement before *Inter-Departmental Committee on Physical Deterioration: Minutes of Evidence*, [CD 2210] PP. 1904 (xxxii), q 1,118.

[74] See, for example, W.J. Ashley, 'Booth's East London', *Political Science Quarterly*, v (1891), pp. 507-19.

[75] 'London's Religious Influences', *The Bookman* (June 1903), pp. 97-100.

[76] Booth Collection, A31, fos 81-82, 91-94, Jesse Argyle to Mary Booth, May-June 1903.

capture in cold print. Slippage was unavoidable, the prose uncontrollable. Time and again the project ran away from him. *Life and Labour of the People in London* expanded through three editions with differing methods, changing objects and much rearrangement of contents and chapters in what was ultimately a futile attempt to devise a satisfactory means of reporting his results. 'It is no depreciation of Mr Booth's effort to state that the problem was too great for it', wrote C.F.G. Masterman.

> We perused nine bulky volumes, mazes of statistics, ordered and classified, maps of picturesque bewilderment of colour, infinite detail of streets and houses and family lives. And at the end of it all the general impression left was of something monstrous, grotesque, inane; something beyond the power of individual synthesis; a chaos resisting all attempts to reduce it to orderly law. We are little nearer at the end than at the beginning to the apprehension of the conditions of Abysmal London.[77]

Masterman thought the poverty survey of York better connected and more helpful. His verdict, still current among many scholars, requires revision. The comparison is narrowing; it distorts our understanding and diminishes Booth's achievement. The York inquiry was essentially a poverty survey. It lacks the majesty and sweep of *Life and Labour of the People in London*, as well as its preoccupation with the civilisation of the workers. The Booth Inquiry, we shall show, was as much concerned with the values, beliefs and interests of the proletariat as with the enumeration of its deprivations and disadvantages. Our Booth, conscious of the influences on which poverty depends and on those which depend upon it, was equally interested in the institutions which might have had a direct or indirect bearing upon the life and labour of the London working class. Rowntree tells us how workers lived on tick; Booth tries to explain what made them tick.

The dismemberment of the Booth Inquiry obscures significant differences between the two studies. The severance of the Poverty Series reduces Booth's organising insights, leads to the erroneous assumption that he relied exclusively upon indirect inquiry and creates a questionable basis for comparison.[78] *Life and Labour of the People in London* should be seen less as

---

[77] C.F.G. Masterman, 'The Social Abyss', *Contemporary Review*, lxxxi (1902), p. 25.
[78] On comparative survey analysis and its limitations, see M. Bulmer, et al., *The Social Survey in Historical Perspective, 1880-1940* (Cambridge, 1991), pp. 189-216; also E.H. Hunt, *British Labour History, 1815-1914* (London, 1985), pp. 6, 103, 211.

the starting point of contemporary sociological inquiry, more as a unique
form of investigative reporting which was altogether more ambitious in
scope and grander in spirit than the modern social survey. No one was more
aware of its provisional nature then Booth himself. There could be no
finality when the printed text reported but a fraction of the information
recorded in the notebooks. Booth described them as 'mines of information'.[79] The challenge presented by these notebooks constitutes the unfi-
nished business of the Booth Inquiry. No longer need we see through a glass
darkly. Reading the published with the unpublished texts we can now see
face to face.

[79] *Poverty*, 1, p. 25.

I

The Poverty Series

Streets and Special Studies

The Poverty Series

Charles James Booth was born in Liverpool on 30 March 1840, the fourth of the five children of Charles Booth, a prosperous corn merchant. He had a happy childhood and an undistinguished career at the Royal Institution School, Liverpool, from the age of ten to sixteen, in the company of his more academic brother, Tom. After school Charles spent a year in London, Heidelberg and Appenzell and then began work in the offices of his father's second cousin, Mr Lamport, at the Lamport and Holt Shipping Company. He was four years there in training. In February 1862 Charles left their employ and went on a grand tour of the Holy Land, Greece, Italy, Switzerland and Germany before joining his brother Alfred in a new enterprise, a shipping company of their own. His great business experience was of enormous importance in his later investigative work. When he returned to Liverpool in 1864 it was to a life of public involvement. In the pages of Booth's family magazine, *The Colony*, his cousin Tom Fletcher described their motivation in the local campaign in Toxteth to give working men the vote. It arose not from a belief in the ideal working man but from disbelief in the assumed superior intelligence of the upper classes and 'the feeling that as self-interest governs the state, it is but fair that all people should have a chance of taking care of their own'.

Booth already distrusted philanthropy – later to be described as 'spoiling' by his co-workers – and looked about him for ways to encourage the working classes to stand on their own two feet and assume responsibility for the management of their own affairs. He abhorred the idea of organising men against their masters but saw collaboration between men and employers through trades unions as a potentially fruitful route. His relations with his cousin, the positivist Henry Crompton, seem to have encouraged such ideas. He was attracted to the positivist belief in the importance of service. He showed an early practical interest in trade union affairs, becoming a director of the Trades Hall project, enjoying the contacts with working men which ensued. The project failed. Booth had to be content with the foundation of a newsroom and reading room. His attempt to introduce settlement of disputes by arbitration also failed and at least one public

27

meeting set up to discuss it was broken up forcibly. Booth began a risk scheme for his own employees – this was part sickness insurance and part bonus provision. Booth's identification with positivism, through his attachment to the Crompton brothers and Emily and Dr Beesly, belonged to the 1870s. Nevertheless, ideas which he developed through this connection were to inform his later work in a way which historians have not hitherto acknowledged.[1]

In these years also Booth become involved in working for improved education of the masses. He joined Chamberlain's Education League and in 1869 launched a pilot scheme for universal education in Liverpool which met with a troubled reception. In this capacity he came across the enquiry made by A.J. Mundella, M.P. for Sheffield into the educational attainments of the children engaged in Mundella's own stocking factory, when Mundella spoke in Liverpool in defence of the Birmingham Education League.

Early in 1868 Booth, through his sister Emily, met Mary Macaulay. She was twenty, daughter of a senior civil servant at Somerset House, niece of Lord Macaulay and cousin of Beatrice Potter. By 1871 Charles and Mary were married.

1. The Youthful Pretender

Already in the 1870s Charles Booth was making connections in the East End of London. In the later years of the decade he was well known to Canon Barnett. Mary Booth reported a long conversation with Barnett in 1878 'about work and waiting and enthusiasm', which focused on the respective merits of immediate social action based on little or no information or 'holding your hand till you were quite sure'. By 1879 Booth was spending time getting to know the 'real' East End: 'I have been studying the ways of the people this evening having supped at a coffee palace and then gone to the nearest music hall to hear the Jolly Nash, etc . . .' This early acquaintance with the life of working people in the East End did more than convince Booth that their life 'was by no means all wretched and unhappy and in need of succour', as the Simeys believed.[1] It nurtured his growing conviction that the collection of statistics had to be accompanied by personal observation.

In the 1880s Booth determined to look more closely at the nature of the social problems facing British society. In the next chapter it is argued that

---

[1] See below pp. 144-48.
[1] T.S. and M.B. Simey, *Charles Booth: Social Scientist* (Oxford, 1960), p. 66.

this decision was Booth's response to the work of the Political Economists, which he found distressingly abstract, rather than a reaction to practical philanthropy or mere sensationalism or the work of Hyndman.[2] Unlike the Political Economists Booth had to describe things as they were. We know that he was actively involved in 'social diagnosis' during 1884 to 1885. Booth's attention had been drawn to the published reports of the census of 1881 (they appeared in 1883) and by 1884 had already become a member of the Royal Statistical Society. In that year the Lord Mayor of London, Sir R.N. Fowler, had opened the customary relief fund for the poor and had also initiated a more unusual step. He asked the Royal Statistical Society to give advice on how best to spend the fund. An inquiry based on the 1881 census tables was organised and housed in the Mansion House. Booth proffered his services in this context and seconded one of his clerks, Jesse Argyle, to the work.[3] Argyle, a cockney, had a good local knowledge of the East End.[4] When Beatrice visited Booth for two days in mid August 1885 she found the two men 'working away . . . on the Mansion House Enquiry into unemployment'.[5] The importance of this Mansion House inquiry in determining Booth's future approach has been very underestimated. Possibly Booth was responsible for designing the questionnaires which were sent to a variety of agencies in the City of London. Booth certainly had access to the completed questionnaires. An interesting example exists for Katharine Buildings.[6] Booth wrote to Marshall that he had just received 'the scheduled results of the Mansion House relief given' in the neighbourhood of St Paul's sub-registration district.[7] The Mansion House inquiry demonstrated what type of information could be extracted and some of the problems involved in extracting it. Above all the Mansion House inquiry combined the use of existing official statistics (the census) with newly and specially gathered information (in this case responses to a series of questionnaires) – the combination that was to be characteristic of Booth's great survey of the *Life and Labour of the People in London*. (Possibly he had been led in this direction

[2] See below pp. 145-52.

[3] Belinda Norman-Butler, *Victorian Aspirations: The Life and Labour of Charles and Mary Booth* (London, 1972) p. 71.

[4] Ibid, p. 117.

[5] BLPES, Passfield, MS Diary, 22 August 1885. This inquiry was published in 1887 as *Report of the Mansion House Conference on the Condition of the Unemployed*.

[6] BLPES, Coll. Misc.43, Katharine Buildings. Record of the inhabitants during the years 1885-1890.

[7] Booth Correspondence, University of London Library, MS 797 I/1311, Charles Booth to Alfred Marshall, 20 October 1886.

by his close association with Mary's father, Zachary Macaulay, a prominent senior civil servant at Somerset House. His own uncle, James Booth, an eminent legal draughtsman and a Secretary of the Board of Trade, had written a pamphlet called *Important Questions Affecting the Social Conditions of the Industrial Classes*. There seems to be little doubt that he consciously compared the task which he saw before him with that of a department of state collecting the information it required before evolving appropriate policies.)

Involvement with the Mansion House inquiry bore other fruits as well. The work for his paper on the Occupations of the People of Tower Hamlets was based upon the census papers made available to him in the context of the Mansion House inquiry and was completed in autumn/winter 1885-86. Under its auspices he was given privileged access not only to the published documents but also to the information recorded in the household schedules. Booth was led to criticise the manner in which the census department had done their work. His criticisms notwithstanding, the potential of the census was not lost upon Booth.

Yet he was a man open to new ideas – he looked to see what sources of information were available and where they did not exist he was willing and able to try to create them. By mid 1885 at the latest he seems to have become aware of the deficiencies of simply reworking other people's statistics. A proposal was shaping itself in his mind. In the late summer of 1885 he was talking to Beatrice Potter about the possibilities of social diagnosis and becoming acquainted with the readily available source materials for such – her personal experience of the management of Katharine Buildings; the work of the Mansion House inquiries into Permanent Distress and Unemployment; the minutes of evidence of the various Royal Commissions; recent private inquiries – such as W.T. Stead's *Pall Mall Gazette* investigation into the traffic in women, published as 'The Maiden Tribute of Modern Babylon'. He was already convinced, in the words of Beatrice Potter, of the need for something more than was currently being pursued: 'Plenty of workers engaged in examination of facts collected by others – personal investigation required. *Pall Mall* have started this – but in the worst possible way – shallow and sensational'.[8]

Booth's conviction that a new sort of inquiry was needed to ascertain the facts about the conditions of life in the metropolis empirically was emerging in mid 1885. It pre-dated the publication of the results of Hyndman's

---

[8] Passfield, MS Diary, 22 August 1885.

alleged inquiry in the autumn of 1885, which is said to have shown 25 per cent of the population to be living in conditions of extreme poverty. The two men did not meet until February 1886. Unfortunately the idea that Booth's great survey was the direct result of his reaction to Hyndman's conclusions was put forward strongly by the Simeys (p. 69) on the basis of their reading of Hyndman's comments in his autobiography[9] and is still given credence in influential modern works.[10] Hyndman's conclusions may well have disturbed Booth, as they did Beatrice Potter, but they certainly did not provide the main impetus for Booth's survey of the *Life and Labour of the People in London*. There is a great difference between alleging that Hyndman's findings met with Booth's disapproval and disbelief and concluding that Booth's proposal for an ambitious survey originated in this reaction to Hyndman. Rather it probably served to confirm him in his detestation of the habit of fixing on a theory or law and then finding the facts to fit it – a practice which he attributed to the socialist movement, specifically to the Social Democratic Federation and to the *Pall Mall Gazette's* so-called house-to-house survey of certain typical streets. According to Hyndman it was the validity of the evidence which Booth contested: 'He told me plainly that in his opinion we had grossly overstated the case'; while Hyndman defended his methodological rigour – 'I knew how thoroughly we had done our work . . . and I at once said I was quite sure that the more thorough any examination might be the more completely would our figures and statements generally be verified'. We know that at some time between 1879 and 1885 Booth invited two working men of socialist opinions (J.E. Williams and J. Macdonald) to spend three evenings at his house discussing socialism with himself and Alfred Cripps, husband of Teresa Cripps, Beatrice Potter's sister, but Booth was unconvinced that they had analysed the problem correctly or proposed the right remedies.[11]

---

[9] H.M. Hyndman, *Record of an Adventurous Life* (London, 1911), p. 331.

[10] Edward Royle, *Modern Britain: A Social History, 1750-1985* (London 1986), p. 199 restates Booth's indebtedness to Hyndman. For further refutation of the link see Daid Rubinstein, 'Booth and Hyndman', *Bulletin of the Society for the Study of Labour History*, xvi (1968), pp. 22-24 and E.P. Hennock, 'Poverty and Social Theory in England: The Experience of the Eighteen Eighties', *Social History*, i (1976), pp. 70-72. Hennock, however, confuses the issues of Booth's *Life and Labour* originating in an S[ocial] D[emocratic] F[ederation] survey and the verifiable existence of an SDF inquiry. These are distinct issues. Any suggestion that Hyndman's memory simply failed him or that he confused the issue with another survey done by the *Pall Mall Gazette* is *not* supported by Hyndman's assertions, which are assured and quite detailed in their claims. Either Hyndman lied or he was involved in a detailed SDF survey.

[11] Booth Correspondence, MS 797. 11/27/7, 'A Discussion on Socialism', C. Booth, A. Cripps, J.E. Williams and J. Macdonald, [?1879].

2. The Board of Statistical Inquiry

Charles Booth acted on his new conviction that personal investigation was necessary. Although April 1886 is often cited as the first meeting of the so-called Board of Statistical Inquiry, this had clearly taken place on a Friday in early March.[1] Booth had already signified that at this meeting he would present his 'proposals and general scheme of work and aims' to be commented upon. He found that the interest of others in his project was less than his own: he 'was yesterday rather depressed because nobody except himself turned up at the Friday afternoon meeting'. The situation improved a bit in April when Maurice Eden Paul, a young and clever medical student, son of the publisher Kegan Paul, engaged with Beatrice Potter in the management of Katharine Buildings, joined the Board. Benjamin Jones, Secretary of the Working Men's Cooperative Society; Radley, secretary of a trade society and Beatrice Potter were also in attendance. From that time until Potter returned to London in 1887, Booth, Paul and Argyle were the chief workers on the project.

In her diary Beatrice Potter commented on 17 April, 'Object of the Committee to get a fair picture of the whole of London society – the 4,000,000! by district and employment, the two methods to be based on census returns. We passed C. Booth's elaborated and detailed plan for the work; and a short abstract of it for general purposes . . .'[2] She added, ignoring lesser mortals such as Booth's hard-working, intelligent and knowledgeable clerks, 'At present Charles Booth is the sole worker in this gigantic undertaking. If I were more advanced in knowledge of previous conditions it is just the sort of work I should like to undertake. If I were free . . .'[3]

During the spring of 1886 Booth's work was still in the planning stage. No doubt Beatrice Potter relayed to him the profound scepticism which Canon Barnett expressed about his project.[4] She was out of London for much of the time but met C.S. Loch at Booth's office on 4 May. Loch expressed enthusiasm for 'accurate knowledge of the conditions of the poor'. 'Evidently, from his account, there are many who would like to devote themselves to investigation'. It was at this time that Beatrice contemplated writing an article in the autumn 'to explain what I mean by social diagnosis . . . If it

[1] Passfield, IIi(II), 6, see Mary Booth to Beatrice Potter, 13 March 1886.
[2] Passfield, MS Diary, 17 April 1886.
[3] Passfield, MS Diary, 17 April 1886.
[4] Passfield, MS Diary; 18 April 1886, see also Beatrice Webb, *My Apprenticeship* (Harmondsworth, 1971 edn.), p. 292.

were well written it would help Charles Booth's organization'.[5] And in the event it was in large part in conversations with her and letters exchanged with her that Booth refined his approach to the project and its organisation. This is not to say that Potter produced the ideas – she did not – but she did make Booth think and she drew his attention, according to Mary Booth, to one of the most important sources of evidence for his first foray into personal investigation – the School Board Visitors.

The way matters unfolded will always be, to a great extent, surmise on our part. But can it be sheer coincidence that, in a letter to Beatrice, Chamberlain put his finger on one of the main problems which would exercise Booth and his co-workers? 'My department knows all about Paupers and Pauperism but has no official cognizance of distress above the pauper line', he wrote.[6] 'Yet this is surely the serious part of the problem. I am trying to collect facts from different sources but it is difficult to make them complete.' He went on to say that 'the suffering of the industrious non-pauper class is very great and is increasing'. The remainder of the letter is a one-sided discussion of possible remedies – for example, labour exchanges. It seems highly probable that Beatrice Potter communicated these ideas to Booth when they met – for example on 17 April 1886, or 4 May or early June.

There has, however, been some misunderstanding concerning Chamberlain's early involvement with Booth's work. Looking back through the various accounts is reminiscent of Chinese Whispers, where a whisper is transformed as it passes around the group of party-goers. The Simeys report that, 'Ultimately a suggestion from Joseph Chamberlain, conveyed to Booth by Beatrice, gave him the idea of utilising the records kept by the School Board Visitors'.[7] In 1972 Belinda Norman-Butler elaborated on the myth that Chamberlain had communicated directly with Beatrice about Booth's search for a productive source of information; the project 'was now based on the suggestion which Chamberlain made to Beatrice about using School Board Visitors as the main source of information'. Both versions appear to owe their origin to a passage in Mary Booth's *Memoir* where she writes, somewhat ambiguously, 'It was some time before proceedings could begin, and Charles Booth was himself still doubtful as to the best way of setting to work. A suggestion of Mr Chamberlain, which reached him through his wife's cousin, Miss Beatrice Potter (now Mrs. S. Webb), was most helpful and was immediately acted on'.[8] Beatrice herself stated unequivocally in *My Apprenticeship*, 'In giving evidence before the Royal Commission on the Housing of the Poor, Joseph Chamberlain had incidentally mentioned that the Birmingham Town council, in preparing its schemes for the

[5] Passfield, MS Diary; 4 May 1886 see also *My Apprenticeship*, p. 292.
[6] Passfield, IIi(II), 4, Joseph Chamberlain, to Beatrice Potter, 28 February 1886.
[7] Simey, *Charles Booth*, pp. 80-81.
[8] Mary Booth, *Charles Booth: A Memoir* (London, 1918), p. 17.

clearance of slum areas, had found useful the very complete knowledge of each family possessed by the school attendance officers. Following this suggestion . . .'[9] No personal communication. No Beatrice as intermediary. One can be sure that she would have laid claim to such a role had the claim been valid. What Beatrice was doing was reading widely and alerting Booth to what she considered important or relevant.

In June 1886 Beatrice Potter was away from London and the inquiry. Apparently she wrote to her cousin Mary Booth expressing her worry on the one hand that the project would fold and on the other that she would be excluded from the work – that it would all be done by the time she returned. Mary comforted her on both counts: 'He says that though little is done everytime – the thing is alive and that he thinks the men he has got hold of by no means lose their interest in the idea', while 'I think you a little under rate what you do at present towards helping him and the others'. Charles wants to dine with her on the following Wednesday but in any case she doubts 'much whether even during the time when your main work will have to be private study of your own – you will ever be as much shut out of the labatory [sic] and even the wards as you think you shall be'.[10]

For much of June and July, Booth was out of the country on business. By this time he had clearly heard about the possibility of using School Board evidence and had made, either personally or through his clerks, approaches to the authorities for permission to interview the School Board Visitors. When he wrote to Beatrice shortly after his return he explained, 'I lost no time in calling upon Mr Mather of the School Board but found that worthy just about to start on a holiday or some such diversion'. As a result of this and also of Maurice Paul's involvement in examinations, Booth determined to have a holiday from the inquiry himself and to begin work with the School Board Visitors on 1 September.[11]

Booth was, however, keen to encourage Beatrice in her present preoccupation – the essay on social diagnosis. Disingenuously he remarked in the letter of 27 July: 'I could not myself undertake a long course of reading of the authorities on any subject to save my life, but I must not undervalue the result to those who can – I think such work should be done by deputy as much as possible'. It is clear from the archive that Booth *did* to some extent live off the reading of his wife and his friends.[12] But, if he saw mileage for himself in Beatrice Potter's endeavours, he was prepared to help Beatrice in her task in a practical way. 'I found my secretary [Argyle] and his assistant

---

[9] *My Apprenticeship*, p. 237. In fact the *Report of the Mansion House Committee Appointed March 1885 to Inquire into the Cause of Permanent Distress in London and the Best Means of Remedying the Same*, December 1885, used the School Board returns as a prime source of information.

[10] Passfield, IIi(II), 6, Mary Booth to Beatrice Potter, 6 June 1886.

[11] Passfield, II i (II), 8, Charles Booth to Beatrice Potter, 27 July 1886.

[12] See references in Mary Booth's diary, cited in Norman-Butler, *Victorian Aspirations*, e.g. pp. 94, 97, 107, 120.

[?Arkell] sore distraught for lack of work . . . It has occurred to me that he [Argyle] might perhaps be of some use to you in looking up this or that – you being rather far from the British Museum. Can you make any use of him?'. One way that had suggested itself to Booth was in help with the interesting essay on social diagnosis: 'Could Argyle help to work up your sketch of the legislation of the last 50 years or did you get enough done yourself . . . to prove that "we are not governed by general principles" beyond controversy?'[13] Perhaps he knew that his wife's cousin was looking for a research assistant. Beatrice Potter's friend, Arabella Fisher, had suggested the name of the daughter of the scholar Toulmin Smith as a likely candidate for such a post in January 1886.[14] In any event, Beatrice was not about to look a gift horse in the mouth and readily accepted the offer. Four days later Booth wrote back to her, 'Argyle . . . took very kindly to the proposal of doing some work for you. I will write to him and set him agoing in the right direction'.[15]

In these letters to Potter, as part of a written conversation about social investigation, Charles Booth set down some of his own ideas. The first was an attempt to explain the complementary function of statistical information and personal observation. 'I think I should say that the statistical method was needed to give bearings to the results of personal observation or personal observation to give life to statistics.'[16] He came back to this subject in the letter of 31 July when he spoke of the relationship between facts and other facts. It is an extremely important passage because it forms the basis for Booth's theory of empiricism yet it has been more or less overlooked by scholars:

> It is this relative character or proportion of facts to each other, to us, to others, to society at large and to possible remedies that must be introduced if they are to be of any value at all in social diagnosis. Both single facts, and strings of statistics, may be true, and demonstrably true, and yet entirely mis-leading in the way that they are used. A framework can be built out of a big theory and facts and statistics run in to fit it – but what I want to see instead is a large statistical framework which is built to receive accumulations of facts out of which at last is evolved the theory and the law and the basis of more intelligent action.[17]

Much has been made of Booth's intent to describe things as they were. But it is vital that we note that 'describing things as they were' involved a framework built out of facts and reaching conclusions based on the identified relationship between facts. 'Amongst all the complicated relations of the

---

[13] Passfield, II i (II), 8, Charles Booth to Beatrice Potter, 27 July 1886.
[14] Passfield, II i (II), 6, Arabella Fisher to Beatrice Potter, 24 January 1886.
[15] Passfield, II i (II), 8, Charles Booth to Beatrice Potter, 31 July 1886
[16] Passfield, IIi(II), 8, Charles Booth to Beatrice Potter, 27 July 1886.
[17] Passfield, II i (II), 8, Charles Booth to Beatrice Potter, 31 July 1886

facts dealt with they must have one in common, which is their place in the framework – without this they are of no use for the purpose in hand.'[18] He went on to explore for his own and Beatrice's benefit the relationship he perceived between inductive and deductive methods – another indication of his appreciation of the problems involved in empirical investigation. 'As to deductive and inductive methods I seem to need both eternally and never could separate them in my mind nor decide which moved first', he told her. 'No induction is possible (I should say) without preceding deduction. Nor any deduction without preceding induction.' It was his conviction that, 'If induction does not promptly lead to fresh deduction it is barren' and 'if deduction be not very humble and modest leaning on induction past and demanding increasingly inductive proof for every step it makes forward it will assuredly go wrong'. This was, in his opinion, where political economy had gone wrong. It was an abstraction, what was required was 'actuality'. Booth was to found his own work on this belief. Its premises were clearly set out before he began serious work on the inquiry: 'by deduction, or the deductive method, I here mean having or finding a theory and looking for the facts, and by induction, or the inductive method, getting the facts and looking for a theory or law.'[19]

It is important to underline the fact that Booth, in his use of the combined techniques of personal observation, derived statistics and official statistics, from the first was concerned not so much with verification of facts as with placing 'demonstrably true' facts in proportion.[20] Time and again in the correspondence and in the printed works he returned to this theme. 'It is to me, not so much verification – the figures or the facts may be correct enough in themselves – but they mislead from want of due proportion or from lack of colour.'[21] It is only too easy for an academic working in the twentieth-century equivalent of an ivory tower to interpret this statement as an intention to enliven dull statistics with a bit of local colour. This was far from Booth's intent. He was a man who saw his research in the context of policy, of social action. His aim was to describe things as they are so that eventually a theory might be derived from this accurate picture and a policy produced which would eradicate the ills he described. Detailed personal observation brought home the meaning behind the statistics; the statistics lent proportion to the detailed personal observation. A proper statistical framework such as he constantly strove for would prevent either exaggeration or

---

[18] Passfield, IIi(II), 8, Charles Booth to Beatrice Potter, 31 July 1886.
[19] Passfield, IIi(II), 8, Charles Booth to Beatrice Potter, 31 July 1886.
[20] As the Simeys stated, see Simey, *Charles Booth*, p. 100.
[21] Passfield, IIi(II), 8, Charles Booth to Beatrice Potter, 27 July 1886.

diminishment while personal observation would make the reader feel the reality of the situation in which poor and rich, employed and unemployed, East Ender and West Ender, employers and employees found themselves.

When Beatrice Potter described the methods which Booth employed she concentrated on the way in which he sought to establish the relations between the detailed personal observation and the statistical framework.

> However accurate and comprehensive might be the description of technical detail, however vivid the picture of what was happening at the dock gates and in the sweated workshops, I was always confronted by Charles Booth's sceptical glance and critical questions: 'How many individuals are affected by the conditions you describe: are they increasing or diminishing in number?' 'What proportion do they bear to those working under worse or better conditions?' 'Does this so-called sweating system play any considerable part in the industrial organisation of London?' 'Thus . . . I became aware that every conclusion derived from observation or experiment had to be *qualified* as well as verified by the relevant statistics.[22]

Booth was rejecting the sensationalism of Mayhew, of Stead, of the *Pall Mall Gazette*, by insisting on proportion but he would not throw out the baby with the bathwater – the human aspect retained its importance partly because he was a man of compassion but also because in human experience lay 'actuality'.[23] A close reading of Booth indicates his profound and lasting awareness of the complexity of the human condition and the importance of noting detail and variety.

3. Not Probably a Perfect Instrument but a Usable One

Fortified by conversations with Potter and Paul in the spring and summer of 1886, and by the further reflections caused by his revision of the paper for the Royal Statistical Society, Booth concentrated on careful planning of his future work in early autumn. This was an essential process:

> I can and do believe that for some time the *method* of the Enquiry must be formulated and worked before the truths sought are considered, and that meanwhile the truths imagined must be laid aside.[1]

[22] *My Apprenticeship*, p. 339.
[23] See quote from *Poverty*, 1, p. 66 in Simey, *Charles Booth*, p. 103.
[1] Passfield, IIi(II), 8, Charles Booth to Beatrice Potter, 21 September 1886.

For this reason, he did not plunge into interviewing the School Board Visitors. Instead he worked out carefully what information he wanted to obtain from them, how such information would be collected and classified, and how it would fit into the broader framework of the inquiry. We can discover a good deal about this process through the correspondence between Maurice Paul and Beatrice Potter as well as through Booth's own communications with her. For instance, on 3 September Paul wrote: 'Booth was here yesterday. They [Booth and Argyle] have had two evenings with School Board Visitors and he is going to try and draw up a principle of classification of their information, which he will submit to you and me for criticism. Then next week we are to try together, with one of the School Board Visitors, whether his classification will hold water.'[2] Booth elaborated on this on 5 September 1886.[3] On the first meeting with the School Board Visitors 'we got a rough idea of what sort of information was to be had', whereas on the second evening they 'made a definite effort at the statement of the facts concerning certain streets'. He commented that the first evening 'dealt with very much more picturesque facts than the second' but that the sort of streets dealt with are 'probably more frequently to be met with than the sinks of iniquity and hells upon earth which were described to us by old Mr Orme, the first Visitor we met'. (Further evidencing his concern for setting facts in proportion and achieving the proper balance.) The second evening was spent with Mr Foote, School Board Visitor of St Paul's district. Booth sent Beatrice with the letter a table of the facts which he and Argyle had drawn up with Foote's assistance: 'We made a rough table to work on and improved as we went along'. Accompanying it was a list of the actual occupations named in Foote's material. It was accepted that this was but a first step: 'Our idea is that having made our classification we should note down *every* occupation we hear of, and so make this list in the end a dictionary of employments, classified for our purposes into 40 or 50 heads . . .'

Far from being blind to or ignoring potential methodological problems Booth shows that he was only too well aware of them. Would the School Board Visitors tell him all that he needed to know? In some accounts of Booth's work the impression is given that Booth was uncritical of his sources and that this led him to reach unfortunate and unscientific conclusions. For example, we are told that it was in criticism of his paper before the Royal Statistical Society in May 1887 that Booth was made aware of the difficulties involved in using the School Board Visitors as a source for establishing earnings.[4] Almost as an after thought, Booth's admission of this fact at the

[2] Passfield, IIi(II), 8, Maurice Paul to Beatrice Potter, 3 September 1886.
[3] Passfield, IIi(II), 8, Charles Booth to Beatrice Potter, 5 September 1886.
[4] E.P. Hennock, 'The Measurement of Urban Poverty: From the Metropolis to the Nation, 1880-1920', *Economic History Review*, 2nd. ser., xl (1987), p. 208.

planning stage is footnoted.[5] But this deep realisation came a little less than a year *before* the Tower Hamlets paper was given to the Royal Statistical Society. 'You will see that I have abandoned to some extent the division by earnings and have fallen back on that by trades.' He was acutely conscious of the difference between fact and opinion: 'We can get from the Visitors an opinion upon the earnings of each man and I should like to find some way of noting this down for averages; but I feel that at the end it is only opinion and I hesitate to make it the basis of our classification. The character of employment is at any rate a fact . . .' What could he do to supplement the information from this deficient source? 'I think that we may so arrange and deal with the information as to this [i.e. trades] as to make it yield the facts as to earnings, in a way that can be proved if disputed – I should like to have the School Board Visitors view as *one* item of evidence.'[6] 'What is needed is that the employments should be so arranged as to be capable of research by other means into the facts of income of each class and this will need a good deal of thought.'

He had already begun this work on creating a statistical framework by July 1886. This was characteristically the kind of work assigned to Jesse Argyle. Booth had contacted Mr Hey (who was later to work for him on the trade and industries inquiry) who would let him have figures for the Society of the Iron Founders based on the July returns by 15 August. Meanwhile Maurice Paul had obtained 'the figures for one large printing house from the Employers' side' so that Booth might 'get the Printers Societies done for the same time [15 August] and so have something in shape for a September start'.[7] Presumably good headway had been made and by 10 September Booth had confidence that he could obtain the information as to earnings from these and other sources because he had already decided that 'the district figures will be classified according to occupation – and the trade figures, starting naturally with occupations, will be classified according to earnings – but I shall try to get at the School Board Visitors opinions as to earnings also'.[8]

Would the School Board Visitors' information be reliable as a guide to conditions in the better districts? Already in September 1886 Booth was alive to the problem. 'The unknown element will be very considerable in better districts where it will cover families with children as well as those without.' He was comforted that, 'In the poor districts the Visitors know pretty well what the people are, children or not and in any case I think the character of the families with children will be similar in each street to that of

[5] Ibid.

[6] Ibid.; see also for reinforcement, Passfield, IIi(II), 8, Charles Booth to Beatrice Potter, 10 September 1886.

[7] Passfield, IIi(II), 8, Charles Booth to Beatrice Potter, 31 July 1886.

[8] Passfield, IIi(II), 8, Charles Booth to Beatrice Potter, 10 September 1886.

those who have none'. More challenging was the problem of the young and unmarried of either sex: 'We only deal with the heads of families but to separate them from the young persons and unmarried men and women, is an important step'. But he felt that they could obtain 'from the Visitors (and in many other ways) information as to the employments of these classes in each district'.[9]

It is appropriate to note that Booth, in seeking to 'measure poverty' was not attempting to measure earnings but rather to measure the condition of poverty which might be related to earnings but might also have its roots elsewhere. Clara Collet spoke truly when she much later described the Poverty Series of her mentor as 'a statistical record of impressions of degrees of poverty' but we should be careful to remember that Booth was himself well aware of the nature of his findings. Without prejudicing the issue, there might be as much to say for the evidence of the eyes (especially where corroborated by others) as of earnings.[10]

Booth argued that no false start should be made and informed Mather of the School Board that he would 'delay one or two weeks before beginning the work'.[11] Although Paul had told Beatrice in his letter of 3 September that 'CB has already found out that the committee is an incubus',[12] Booth nonetheless called a meeting of the Board of Statistical Research for the Thursday following to consider methodology. He despaired of anyone else attending other than Paul, but, while bewailing Alfred Cripps' absence and his own lack of knowledge of 'the others' (?Jones and Radley), urged Beatrice to do her best to 'come up for a day', relying on her at least to 'write her views' if she did not.[13]

When the meeting took place it consisted 'as I had expected, of Paul and myself and we have decided to go ahead'. He leaves us in no doubt as to the grand plan that was in his mind. 'We have slightly enlarged and improved the tabulation of employments and brought into such shape that each heading can easily be made the subject of a special series of trade enquiries. The two plans will thus become complete and every bit done will be so much towards the whole statement for London.' He was ever the optimist. 'I don't think the whole work is beyond our reach and I think it might be completed in three years.'[14] Five days later Paul wrote in jocular fashion to Beatrice: 'Booth's plan is to get Tower Hamlets done by May 1887, London done by

[9] Passfield, IIi(II), 8, Charles Booth to Beatrice Potter, 5 September 1886.

[10] Clara Collet, 'Some Recollections of Charles Booth', *Social Services Review*, i (1927), p. 384.

[11] Passfield, IIi(II), 8, Charles Booth to Beatrice Potter, 5 September 1886.

[12] Passfield, IIi(II), 8, Maurice Paul to Beatrice Potter, 3 September 1886.

[13] Passfield, IIi(II), 8, Charles Booth to Beatrice Potter, 5 September 1886. The 'others' probably included Arthur Acland, see Booth Correspondence, MS 797 I/1310 Charles Booth to Alfred Marshall, 18 October 1886, 'Mr Arthur D. Acland . . . who is associated in the present attempt.'

[14] Passfield, IIi(II), 8, Charles Booth to Beatrice Potter, 10 September 1886.

May 1888, and ALL ENGLAND done by May 1889. *Sic itur ad astra*. Of course he is only half serious.' Paul was less than convinced: 'I tell him, when he makes such startling statements as this, that we shall all have hair as white as snow before we get London done. He answers cheerfully. 'Ah I like to have some one with your sceptical spirit to keep the thing going, especially if he will really work.'[15]

'The information will have to be got by personal interview with each Visitor and a good many hours of it for each,' Booth told Beatrice. The School Board Visitors would have to be paid for their time.[16] Beatrice was warned that 'we shall relegate any female visitors to your care'.[17] The planning of the work would be such that 'any one of us might tackle his Visitors and thrash out his district filling up so many sheets of figures and so many pages of remarks'.[18] Next week 'He [Booth] and I and Argyle', said Paul, 'will set to work separately in the evenings we can spare in pumping the Visitors'.[19] By 15 September it seemed that more than just the four of them would be needed for the work. 'He and I and Argyle will divide forces, and, with as many people as we can get to help us, set to work on Tower Hamlets . . .'[20]

Work on Tower Hamlets had already begun in the form of a pilot study. Indeed the pace was now so fast that there was too much to do to think things out. According to Paul he thought 'about three times a day now for three minutes a time on the average . . .'[21] Paul told Beatrice that on the evening of 14 September they were at 'work on the statistical scheme. We are doing the district of St Paul's, which contains 20,000 people . . . I think we shall get it finished next week and then we shall tabulate it and see how the principle of classification has answered'. Interviewing the School Board Visitors would follow if the system of classification held water. Orme, 'the Visitor with whom we dealt last night', apparently gave them information about the employment of the heads of household in, for example, Cable

---

[15] Passfield, IIi(II), 8, Maurice Paul to Beatrice Potter, 15 September 1886.

[16] Passfield, IIi(II), 8, Charles Booth to Beatrice Potter, 5 September 1886. M. Bulmer *et al.*, *The Social Survey in Historical Perspective* (Cambridge, 1992) unaccountably quotes Booth out of context here ('lent themselves to my purpose', does *not* mean gave their services free!) and ignores the definite statement in Passfield, IIi(II), 8, Charles Booth to Beatrice Potter, 5 Sepember 1886 that is reprinted on p. 103.

[17] Passfield, IIi(II), 8, Charles Booth to Beatrice Potter, 5 September 1886; She had volunteered to undertake her own district Beatrice Potter to Mary Booth, early March 1886, Norman Mackenzie (ed), *The Letters of Sidney and Beatrice Webb*, i (Cambridge 1978), p. 56.

[18] Ibid.

[19] Passfield, IIi(II), 8, Maurice Paul to Beatrice Potter, 3 September 1886.

[20] Passfield, IIi(II), 8, Maurice Paul to Beatrice Potter, 15 September 1886.

[21] Passfield, IIi(II), 8, Maurice Paul to Beatrice Potter, 15 September 1886.

Street, detailing the nature and extent of the trades involved and providing material on wages. Orme contradicted Potter's published view that sack-making was now dead in the East End but opined that 'remuneration in the trade has much declined. A farthing a sack is the price now for making only and a quick worker can make four dozen, a shilling a day'. Paul commented, 'Looked at philosophically that sort of thing is purely abominable'.[22]

The close association which Booth formed with the Cambridge economist Alfred Marshall at this time must not be overlooked, for Marshall had considerable influence upon him. Marshall seems to have initiated the relationship with a letter of 15 October 1886, perhaps regarding the contents of the 'Occupations of the People' paper before the Royal Statistical Society. Booth lost no time in taking advantage of the friendly overture. 'I am now engaged (with some others) on an attempt to describe analytically the industrial & social status of the population of London: that is, to state the proportions in which different classes exist, with the actual present condition of each.' He asked Marshall for 'criticism, in advance, on the method adopted'. The intention was 'to piece together information from as many different sources as possible, so as to make the evidence check & complete itself so far as possible' but using data supplied by the School Board Visitors as a framework. Booth proposed sending Marshall his pilot study of St Paul's sub-registration district.[23] Marshall responded by return and Booth sent 'a mass of materials' post-haste. Unfortunately Marshall's replies are not present. That the two remained in reasonably close personal contact is evident from later correspondence and from Mary Booth's diaries. On 25 June 1889 G.B. Longstaff addressed the Royal Statistical Society on the subject of the forthcoming 1891 census. In the ensuing discussion Marshall made clear in a lengthy comment both his close association with Booth and the unanimity of their stance on the census and the need for a central statistical collecting body. 'Mr Booth and I were a pair', he declared, 'Mr Booth represented the skilled producers, and he the unskilled consumers of statistics'; because of this, it was Booth and not he who could comment more authoritatively on the precise requirements regarding a new schedule of occupations for the census. Of course, it well suited the Cambridge intellectual to allocate to Booth the role of 'producer' of statistics but this does not diminish the importance of this evidence of their working relationship.[24]

[22] Passfield, IIi(II), 8, Maurice Paul to Beatrice Potter, 15 September 1886.

[23] Booth Correspondence, MS 797 I/1310, Charles Booth to Alfred Marshall, 18 October 1886.

[24] *Journal of the Royal Statistical Society*, lii (1889), pp. 461-63.

4. Making the Dry Bones Live

For the next few weeks Booth, Paul and Argyle and a number of others interviewed the School Board Visitors, drew up in notebooks a tabulation of the households of the streets of Tower Hamlets in the East End and attempted to analyse what they had found. It is important to realise that the books in the Booth Collection are *not* the School Board Visitors' books but, rather, tabulated data collected by Booth, Argyle, Arkell or Paul as a result of interviewing the School Board Visitors and, probably, examining their books.[1]

What was the nature of the evidence supplied by the School Board Visitors and was it to be relied upon? School Board Visitors (later known as School Attendance Officers) occupied a responsible position. The job was coveted and reserved for those who could pass a competitive examination for short-listed candidates in arithmetic, composition, dictation and tabulation. The salary was around £100 per annum, placing them low down on the rung of middle-class, 'white collar' employment. Turnover in the job was low despite the fact that they were not especially well-paid for the job and according to the Royal Commission on Education of 1888 were known on occasion to take simultaneous employment in other areas – e.g. as relieving officers or rent collectors.

For the purposes of enrolment and attendance the School Board Visitors undertook an annual census of all school children within their division and in so doing acquired an intimate knowledge of working-class life. Under the powers of the 1870 Education Act the London School Board required each and every child to pay fees to the teacher each Monday. Non-payment of the 'school pence' led to exclusion of the child from school and eventual prosecution of the parents for the child's absence. There was much opposition to the system.[2] The School Board Visitors were charged to collect information about family economic circumstances from the parents, from neighbours and from employers when parents disobeyed the bye-laws regarding school attendance, were in arrears with 'school pence' or applied for remission of school fees. It was the School Board Visitors who served the parents with notices to attend a 'B' meeting of the divisional committee for cross-examination. Much depended upon the individual School Board Visitor's perception and penetration. None of them had a right of entry to the home or a right to inspect evidence of income. In relying upon their

---

[1] Confusion has sometimes occurred. See, for example, Jane Lewis, 'Parents, Children, School Fees and the London School Board, 1870-1890', *History of Education*, xi (1982), p. 302.

[2] See *School Board Chronicle* (December 1872).

evidence, Booth was effectively relying upon the assessments of the School Board Visitors which were based on 'externals'.[3] The School Board Visitors had their work cut out to collect accurate and full information about the children in their districts: the workload was crippling as each had between 3,000 and 6,000 children of school age on their roll and had an enormous number of tasks each week if the job were to be well done;[4] there was no legal obligation to supply the information required; there was no legal right to detain truant children in the streets; there was no certainty of 'catching' all the school age children when the population was so migratory; and the Visitors were intimidated by physical threat and disease. Indeed in 1887-88 the School Board appointed a special visitor to seek out children who had escaped the net of the existing machinery. Over 8,000 'vagrant' children were thus located.[5] At first sight then, Booth's reliance upon the School Board Visitors for data sounds overly confident. Was Booth right to extrapolate from a sample of the population (albeit not a random sample as it was confined to families with school age children) to the entire population? Only studies of mobility based on scrutiny of the census are likely to resolve the issue.

Between 1886 and 1891 the team covered 13,600 streets in London for the survey. In connection with the pilot study for the East End, Booth, Paul, Argyle and Arkell subjected each of the School Board Visitors to about twenty hours of intensive cross-examination regarding the information on individual families contained in their heads and in their own routine notebooks. Even in this context Booth did not rely entirely upon the School Board Visitors as a source of information. For example, one of the notebooks contains detailed information about model dwellings in Whitechapel, Shoreditch, Shadwell, Bethnal Green and the Minories, at least some of which was given directly by the managers and rent-collectors of the building themselves.[6] It is more often than not forgotten that Booth had connections with the world of philanthropy through his friendship (and that of his wife) with Canon and Mrs Barnett of Toynbee Hall. Ella Pycroft, manager of Katharine Buildings, near the Minories, was not only a close friend and colleague of Beatrice Potter but also one of the 'buttresses' upon which

---

[3] *Royal Commission on the Housing of the Working Classes*, qq 1437-78, 1481-83, 1525, 1544, 4346, 4365, 4858, 4913-19; Booth Collection, B10, fo.47.

[4] See C. Pritchard's comments in the *School Board Chronicle* of 1885; and R. Massey, 'Compulsory Education and its Difficulties', Address to the School Board Conference, May 1886; London School Board Records, 1886-1901.

[5] See David Rubinstein, *School Attendance in London, 1870-1906: A Social History*, Occasional Papers in Economic and Social History, 1, Hull University Press (1969), passim; Jane Lewis, 'Parents, Children, School Fees and the London School Board, 1870-1890', *History of Education*, xi (1982), pp; 291-312; see David Englander, 'Booth's Jews: The Presentation of Jews and Judaism in *Life and Labour of the People in London*', *Victorian Studies*, xxxii (1989), pp. 551-71.

[6] Booth Collection, B19.

Toynbee Hall relied.[7] It was she who gave Booth detailed information about the residents of Katharine Buildings (based upon her ledger of its inhabitants).[8] We know from one of Maurice Paul's letters to Beatrice Potter that Ella had been on the verge of working for Booth: 'Ella was going to help us in the statistical enquiry, by undertaking the lady schoolboard visitors in the Tower Hamlets' in October 1886.[9] Her father's disapproval of her relations with Maurice Paul rendered this impossible in autumn 1886 but, as she later became engaged to Paul, it is not entirely impossible that she did do some interviewing for Booth. Another rent collector who helped Booth with information was Miss Coe, a colleague of Ella Pycroft.[10] Mr Grimes, another acquaintance of both Ella Pycroft and Beatrice, provided information about Peabody Buildings (probably the Bethnal Green building).[11] A further notebook records the information given by Miss Busk, another of the rent collectors in the Toynbee Hall circle, for several model dwellings in Stepney.[12] It was of Miss Busk that Mrs Barnett wrote that she, at six feet high, was as 'brave and buoyant as she was big' while going about her visiting in London's roughest streets. It was she also who had supplied Miss Pycroft with Miss Coe as assistant rent collector when Ella was left on her own at Katharine Buildings.[13] Such material as this was used in the section of the Poverty Series treating model dwellings but it also formed part of the pool of information for the streets survey.

Other sources of detailed information are recorded in some of the notebooks. For example, missionaries gave detailed information on the residents of Felstead Street, Wick Road, Hackney Street, Robstone Road and Woolpack Place in the Hackney and Shoreditch districts.[14] Occasionally information is recorded about particular trades. For example, the Singer sewing machine collectors gave detail about a 'tailors workshop' and the categories of such workshops in Hackney.[15] As such entries are rarely dated or explained, it is entirely possible that they were added to assist Arkell and Argyle in providing material for 'The Tailoring Trade' and other special studies. The notebooks were used as convenient repositories for many categories of information: inside the back cover of B55 was inscribed a short list of the rents of clubs and a short list of 'streets occupied by tailors'. The

[7] Henrietta Barnett, *Canon Barnett* (London, 1921 edition), p. 427; Margaret Wynne Nevinson, *Life's Fitful Fever* (London, 1926), pp. 85ff.

[8] For the erroneous suggestion that Ella Pycroft was a School Board Visitor see M. Bulmer, *The Social Survey in Historical Perspective* (Cambridge, 1992), p. 81.

[9] Passfield, IIi(II), 9, Maurice Paul to Beatrice Potter, 5 October 1886.

[10] Passfield, IIi(II), Ella Pycroft to Beatrice Potter, 3 October 1886.

[11] Passfield, IIi(II), Ella Pycroft to Beatrice Potter, 19 February 1886.

[12] Booth Collection, B29.

[13] Henrietta Barnett, *Canon Barnett* (London, 1921) p. 133; Passfield IIi(II), Ella Pycroft to Beatrice Potter, 19 February 1886, 15 July 1886 and 3 October 1886.

[14] Booth Collection, B45.

[15] Booth Collection, B52.

Battersea notebooks are especially noteworthy for additional, often topo-graphical, data.[16] A continuation of the series beyond B68 definitely contains material collected in late 1890 and 1891 pertaining to the special streets survey.[17] For these reasons, it is unsafe to assume that all the material in the so-called street notebooks was collected for the original streets inquiry either of Tower Hamlets or the rest of London as surveyed.

There should be no suggestion either that Booth or his team were unaware of problems associated with overmuch reliance on the School Board Visitors' testimony. Within the notebooks themselves there are criticisms. For example, one of the interviewers, Charles Skinner, commented on the Chelsea School Board Visitors:

> With regard to these families – some visitors count all the families they can find in the streets, but others only count those with schoolchildren. Mr Ware says that the former way is the correct one, but I find that some of the Visitors hardly know themselves what to count as a family – too much reliance should not therefore be placed on these figures.[18]

Where a School Board Visitor was new to the district there might be a strong case for turning elsewhere for the required information: 'Mr Robert has only been on this district about 18 months. Mr Taylor will be able to afford information about this district . . . Fair amount of district unscheduled'. Especially problematic was the recording of information about school children who lived in dwellings scattered amongst well-to-do housing, where the School Board Visitor did not call at all.[19] The interviewer of Mr Matthews, School Board Visitor for Hare Street, Bethnal Green, accused him of exaggerating the poverty and degeneracy of those families to whom he could not gain access.[20] Others were said not to have good knowledge of the people.[21] Such reservations there were about the quality of the data and they must have made it more difficult to work. Booth placed more emphasis than ever upon double-checking the information. The data which Booth's team obtained was then entered into small notebooks. Those for the East End contained considerably more detail about individual streets than did the later books. In the early books the name of the street headed the page and there followed quite detailed information, in tabulated form, for each house and household or family. This information included occupation, probable income, number of children and the number of occupants in each room. Only after taking all this information, Booth and his associates

[16] E.g., Booth Collection, B60.
[17] See below for Booth Collection, B72.
[18] Booth Collection, B66, fo. 6.
[19] Booth Collection, B66, fo. 106.
[20] Booth Collection, B47, fo. 155.
[21] Booth Collection, B58.

themselves inspected the streets concerned.[22] Each of the families detailed was assigned to one of eight classes.

When Booth moved on to compare the East End with other areas of the metropolis he changed his method somewhat. The unit now became the street and not the family. Each family was still classified but there was no comparable material on income, occupation and poverty on a family basis. Additional information was secured from the police, from relieving officers, from school divisional committees and from district superintendents. The team were, however, now in a position to draw up a 'poverty map', on which each street was classified according to the general condition of its inhabitants and given a colour code.[23]

Table 1[24]

Class*	Description		Map Colour for streets	
A	The lowest class of occasional labourers, loafers and semi-criminals		Black	
B	Casual earnings: 'very poor' (below 18s. per week for a moderate family)		Dark Blue	
C	Intermittent earnings	Together 'the poor' between 18s. and 21s. per week	Light Blue	Mixed
D	Small Regular earnings	for a moderate family		
E	Regular standard earnings	Above the line of poverty	Pink	Purple
F	Higher class, labour	Fairly comfortable good ordinary earnings		
G	Lower middle class	Well-to-do middle class	Red	
H	Upper middle class	Wealthy	Yellow	

The colours represent the general complexion of the street in socio-economic terms. Purple and Pink streets include representatives of several classes
*Socio-Economic Class of People

An examination of the archive associated with this street survey, however, indicates that matters were not so simple. Argyle and Arkell drew up the notebooks in tabular form neatly enough but the manner in which they were filled out leaves much for the historian, bent on reconstituting the material and comparing it with the printed text, to desire. Notebooks B1 to B68 cover the materials collected between 1886 and 1889. In many cases class allocations do not appear to tally with the colour accorded the street or are simply

[22] See *Poverty*, 1, p. 25; Booth wrote that this policy was changed after the inquiry into the Tower Hamlets: 'But later we gained confidence, and made it a rule to see each street ourselves at the time we received the visitors account of it'.

[23] See Raymond Kent, *A History of British Empirical Sociology* (Aldershot, 1981), pp. 52-63, for an excellent description of Booth's methodology as outlined in the printed work and a discussion of its implications.

[24] The archive contains detailed listings of all the changes made to the maps in the light of comment from the police and others, see for example Booth Collection, D2, D3 and D4. This work is undated.

not given; it is often difficult to ascertain what was being enumerated and what the basis of the enumeration was.[25] While Booth and his associates were obsessed with accuracy, and there is certainly no suggestion that they consciously massaged their figures, it must have been abnormally difficult to construct the neat statistical tables of the Poverty Series from the notebooks. With few exceptions those who interviewed the School Board Visitors did not sign their work. Charles Booth, Charles Skinner and Graham Balfour sometimes appended their names. But in general the attribution of inter-viewing must depend upon that most unreliable of sciences, palaeography. Other hands do occur but are often impossible to identity positively. Three people were largely responsible for notebooks B8-B64, Booth, Jesse Argyle, and George Arkell, with relatively minor contributions from others. In the majority of cases, the book was clearly the work of more than one hand. After the street entries had been recorded, another scribe added street colours (more often than not Jesse Argyle), and yet another added letters of classification and totalled up the street children. There are some exceptions. For example, Clara Collet seems to have been responsible for the whole of B60 and for B64 apart from the colour classifications. The early notebooks are notable for their general legibility (although there is some significant difficulty in distinguishing E from F) but there is some drop off in presen-tation in the Battersea survey. Some of the early books were opened, headed and ruled by hand in pen by one of the secretaries, Argyle or Arkell. From B12 onwards the column heads were printed. The columns were typically filled in lead pencil, presumably to facilitate correction. Additional material, for example class letters, were added in either coloured or black ink or crayon. Apparent changes in the classificatory system, unremarked and unexplained in the text, do not assist interpretation. (For example, B33 is the first notebook definitely to use the letters C, F and H). The layout of the books, and the amount of detail included therein, also varies. For instance, from B65 onwards each page contains data for a large number of streets and a general character comment, presumably supplied by the School Board Visitor. A large part of B65 is in shorthand. This has tentatively been identified as George Arkell (on the basis of his highly distinctive '3'). This is interesting in itself. It suggests that, especially once the East End survey had been finished, the notebooks might have been completed at relative leisure some time after the interview. It would surely be unwise to assume that all the annotations were contemporary with the interviews or, indeed, with the original street survey.[26] Further work remains to be done to establish the

[25] See David Englander, Rosemary O'Day, *The Charles Booth Notebooks: Poverty Series. A Calendar for the Computer*, forthcoming.

[26] We are most grateful to Dr Judith Ford, an expert palaeographer, for her help in analysing the notebooks. Her researches suggest how very important it is to be cautious in attributing work to particular individuals.

precise correlation between the printed text and the tabulated data of the notebooks but it may be that it is on this level that the most telling criticisms of Booth's work with the School Board Visitors can be made.

In 1887 Booth felt himself in a position to present his findings relating to Tower Hamlets to the Royal Statistical Society, which he duly did in May 1887. While critical, the audience gave Booth sufficient encouragement for him to pursue his wider study of the whole of London. He was not, in any event, a man to be diverted from his purpose.[27]

In 1887 Mary told Beatrice Potter that 'Charlie' was 'really enjoying' his East End life because 'I think it rests him & makes a change from business thought' being 'worth more in its way than even Gracedieu's quiet and beauty'. But she was probably voicing her own rather than Charles' thoughts when she described it as 'plainly a second string to one's bow looked on as a holiday relaxation'. Certainly Charles liked 'the life and the people and the evening roaming and the food' but his interest was more than casual or personal.[28] It was part of that attempt to lift the curtain on East London to which he alluded in *Poverty*, 1, p. 172. Unfortunately little remains as a record of Booth's direct experience of East London streets other than the extracts which were later printed by his wife in the *Memoir*. The streets represented in these fragments do not appear in the special street survey of the Poverty Series.[29] Perhaps, as the writer of the *Memoir* intimates, he thought this would be a betrayal of personal trust as he had lived among them without declaring his purpose.[30]

Booth did not overestimate his personal knowledge of the East End. 'I have no doubt that many other men possess twenty or a hundred times as much experience of East End people and their lives.' Yet he was confident that 'what I have witnessed has been enough to throw a strong light on the materials I have used, and for me, has made the dry bones live'. With the same touching confidence as other slummers like Beatrice Potter, Booth believed that he had pulled the wool over the eyes of his landlords, convincing them that he was not who he was, and claimed to have lodged for several weeks apiece at each of three houses. Interestingly, he claimed to have experienced the life of Class E, who were those in good circumstances

[27] As we know from other sources, the studies of women's work, the docks, boot and shoe industry and tailoring were already under way in 1887: see pages 83ff below.

[28] Passfield, IIi(II), 6, Mary Booth to Beatrice Potter, 1887; Booth Correspondence, MS 797 I/1234, Charles Booth to Mary Booth, 11 September 1879.

[29] They were Chester Street, Eldon Street, Ferdinand Street and Dutton Street.

[30] Mary Booth, *Memoir*, p. 104; *Poverty*, 1, p. 158.

living in well-built and quite commodious houses. He described this experience as being of 'wholesome, pleasant family life, very simple food, very
regular habits, healthy bodies and healthy minds; affectionate relations of
husbands and wives, mothers and sons, of elders with children, of friend
with friend'.[31] He had some direct experience of life in Classes C and D but
his knowledge of Classes A, B and C was for the most part at second-hand.

While it has proved impossible to locate the original record of Booth's
sojourns in the East End, the synopsis in the *Memoir* is of great value to us.[32]
The account was clearly drawn up after the publication of the first volume of
Poverty,[33] and points infuriatingly to the one-time existence of a now-lost but
once meticulously kept Booth diary.[34] In this diary he kept a careful and
detailed record of his East End life. There is much interesting comment
upon family life among the working class in even the fragment that
remains.[35]

Observation was a skill which Booth spent much time perfecting. While it
is impossible to collate the observation with derived opinion, judgement and
analysis, it is evident that much of what he thought about the life of the
people was drawn from his own experience and observation. Personal
observation made him recognise that the boundaries between the classes
(rigidly defined by letters of the alphabet and colours from the palette) were
in reality blurred, softened and imperceptibly shaded into one another.[36]
This awareness carried over into his analysis of the seventy selected streets
in 1889.[37] 'I watched with much interest the relations existing between
Classes E and D in the persons of my landlady and her other tenants,' he
remarked. '*Mutatis mutandis*, they were not very different from those which
exist in the country between hall and village.' 'There was evinced', he
reflected, 'a keen sense of social responsibility not unaccompanied by a sense
of social superiority.' The landlady altered a dress to fit the daughter of a
Class D tenant; the landlady's daughter played with this girl but always
bought the sweets; the drunken father of the girl was told to amend his ways

[31] *Poverty*, 1, p. 158.
[32] Mary Booth, *Memoir*, pp. 105-30.
[33] Ibid., p. 109.
[34] Ibid., p. 114.
[35] The Simeys were mistaken when they declared, 'Much of what Booth recorded on the
journeys of exploration lies unused in his notebooks', *Charles Booth*, p. 105. None of this
material on Booth's lodgings survives outside the *Memoir* and the printed text, although there
are of course many reports of Booth's formal interviews.
[36] *Poverty*, 1, p. 159.
[37] *Poverty*, 2, pp. 40-235; especially p. 44.

or go. The humanity which is so apparent in his analysis, and which belies the columns of bald statistics and indeed his reputation, was founded upon this direct knowledge. He reflected on the ability of even bad parents to love their children and make them happy. He thought the 'simple, natural lives of working-class people' in some ways preferable to the 'artificial compli- cated existence of the rich', not because he romanticised their position or underestimated the strains of their existence but because he had felt this difference. The rich existed, the poor lived. Yet 'the uncertainty of their lot, whether or not felt as an anxiety, is ever present as a danger'. 'The health, habits or character of the man' are all important to the wife and family.[38] 'Or it may be the woman who drags the family down.' 'Or it may be that trade shrinks.' 'The lot falls partly according to merit and partly according to change . . .' It is this humane approach to the problem of poverty and the people who experienced it which was characteristic of Booth's approach. He was not sentimental about the poor, not sensationalist, but sensitive: 'In laying my ideas before my readers, I trust that if they are considered futile and visionary, the facts I have brought to life may not be discredited by being brought into company with theories . . .' It is a pity that his wish has not been granted by historians and social scientists.

Booth determined to bring this methodology of sensitive, detailed obser- vation to bear upon the problem of describing things as they are.[39] While it is possible that he drew directly upon his personal observations in this context, he appears to have relied heavily upon contributions from others. There was no house-to-house survey initiated by Booth or carried out by his secretaries or associates. The archive, however, does contain much material collected for the study of selected streets. There were seventy of these streets in the printed work in the main taken from the inner central London area.[40] The materials originated with School Board Visitors, district visitors, deaconesses, clergy and missionaries. For example, the Revd Mr Dodge of Trinity Square, Southwark granted an interview on 25 July 1889 and provided information on six of the seventy streets.[41] The streets were given

---

[38] *Poverty*, 1, p. 161.

[39] As intimated in the introduction and argued more closely below, this methodology was a firm refutation of the habit of the Political Economists of stating assumptions without the requirement of proof and disallowing the possibility, even the probability, of variety in human behaviour and conditions.

[40] *Poverty*, 2, pp. 226-29 is a tabular presentation of his findings; pp. 40-225 present the detailed findings. See Appendix I for tabular presentation of the archival material relating to this survey, including a list of the real names of the streets chosen.

[41] Booth Collection, A2, fos. 51-63.

the fake names of Chesterfield Street;[42] Ginger Street;[43] Hart Place;[44] Carver Street;[45] Rupert Place;[46] Little Tarleton Street.[47] Other information was sought from the Lady Superior of St John's Mission House, Smith Square, Westminster;[48] from the Eton Mission, Hackney Wick;[49] from the Revd Rupert St Leger, Curate of Holy Trinity, Shoreditch;[50] the Vicar of St Andrews, Thornhill Square and E. Rider of Barnsbury Park, Islington;[51] and an unknown source for Pond Street (probably Pond Terrace), Chelsea.[52] The book itself reveals some of the sources he used – information came from the City Missionaries;[53] a lady visitor;[54] and a male visitor.[55] While Booth himself visited at least some of the streets, he did not necessarily supply the information for the detailed survey even of these streets.[56] Sometimes the material was very much up-to-the minute: the account of Golden Place was dated 1890.[57] Information was supplied on Doon Street, King Street, Henry Street, Hotspur Street, Orville Street and others in November 1890.[58] In the event, it seems, much of this new information was never used.[59]

The annotated tables of selected streets in the archive suggest that the School Board Visitors supplied a good deal of the material used here also,[60] while Booth states in the printed text that the School Board Visitors' information obtained in 1886-87 was checked against that of the clergy

---

[42] Booth Collection, A2, fo. 55; *Poverty*, 2, pp. 214-19.

[43] Booth Collection, A2, fo. 56 (Gun Street) in the main taken from the inner central London area, *Poverty*, 2, pp. 139-41.

[44] Booth Collection, A2 (Fox's Buildings), fo. 57; *Poverty*, 2 pp. 142-43.

[45] Booth Collection, A2 (Doon Street), fo. 58; *Poverty*, 2, pp. 176-79.

[46] Booth Collection, A2, (Surrey Row), fo. 59; *Poverty*, 2 pp. 102-07.

[47] Booth Collection, A2, (Devonshire Place), fos. 60-63; *Poverty*, 2, pp. 84-85. For the real names see Appendix I.

[48] Booth Collection, A2, fos. 46-50, for Little Tufton Street and Romney Street. These are the real names.

[49] Booth Collection, A2, fos. 29-32.

[50] Booth Collection, A2, fos. 1-10, for Half Nichol Street.

[51] Booth Collection, A2, fos. 33-39, for Lyon Street (possibly Lyons Gardens).

[52] Booth Collection, A2, fos. 40-45.

[53] *Poverty*, 2, pp. 46-82, for Shelton Street, Parker Street, Macklin Street and Goldsmith Street and Smart's Buildings formerly 'The Coal Yard'.

[54] *Poverty*, 2, pp. 88-89, for Flint Street.

[55] *Poverty*, 2, pp. 188-89, for Peel Street.

[56] *Poverty*, 2, pp. 94-96, for his personal record of a visit to Summer Gardens, at the back of Fount Street.

[57] *Poverty*, 2, pp. 108.

[58] Booth Collection, B72, fos. 173-239.

[59] See list of streets on pp. 126-29 of *Poverty*, 2.

[60] Booth Collection, A2, fos. 17-24.

given in 1889-90.[61] A limited check of the archive data against the printed text shows that at least on some occasions, however, the printed text for a street was more or less entirely a reworking of the non-School Board Visitor source.[62] The clergy material often came from the district visitors' records.[63] This time-lag accounted for many discrepancies. We know from a letter of Mary Booth to Beatrice Potter in August 1889 that the work was being delayed because 'the authorities have happened to take in the schedules of the School Board Visitors for purposes of their own just at holiday time, which C had hoped to utilise, getting them to come to Talbot Court in the day time so as to save so much evening work for our man later on'.[64]

In offering this material 'noted with "running pen" for analysis Booth commented that 'those who gave the information did not know what use would be made if it, nor were they asked to decide in what class each family should be placed'.[65] Nonetheless, it is apparent from the manuscript materials that respondents to Booth's request for house-to-house information were expected to follow a pro forma. When Rider wrote about Lyons Street he specified that the information was organised as follows: 'Name of Street; No. of the House; Names of Occupants; Occupation or earnings of men No. of children; Employment of wife (if any); Her earnings; and those of Children (if any); Rent of House; General Condition of all [houses]'. This information was designed to be comparable with that earlier supplied by the School Board Visitors. Any other material supplied was a plus. In some of the materials supplied by district visitors and so forth to Booth and Arkell in late 1890 Class letters are entered against the individual households. It is, of course, possible that these letters were inserted by Booth or Arkell and not supplied by the respondents. We do know, however, that clergy and visitors were asked to comment on the accuracy of the map as respects colour of the individual streets.[66] Charity Organisation Society visitors also gave their views.[67] Policemen were asked 'to make general comparisons and give

---

[61] *Poverty*, 2, p. 230.

[62] Booth Collection, B72, cf. *Poverty*, 2, fos. 212, 215-18, p. 145; see Appendix I listing those streets which relied on a non-School Board Visitor source.

[63] *Poverty*, 2, p. 230.

[64] Passfield, IIi(II), 6, Mary Booth to Beatrice Potter, 11 August 1889; the office was on the third floor marked 'Charles Booth – Private', Booth Collection, A24, Letter to Trades Unionists, 22 October 1891.

[65] *Poverty*, 2, p. 230.

[66] Booth Collection, B72, see for example, fos. 246-47 and fos. 219, 251.

[67] Booth Collection, e.g. B72, fos. 179-82, 188-89.

particulars to places they knew well'.[68] This detailed analysis of seventy streets was offered to lend meaning to the statistics.

5. Head of the Statistical Tree

The work of analysing the special street surveys belonged properly to the years 1889-90, despite its origins in Booth's own observation of East End life in 1887. To 1887 and 1888 belonged the work of extending the East End inquiry to Central London, London North of the Thames, South London and specifically Battersea. The organisation of the work on these areas is to say the least a matter of conjecture. The work was much less detailed than that for East London.[1] This work was done with the collaboration of several associates who are rarely mentioned in connection with Booth's work. Graham Balfour, for example, produced the study of Battersea. He was a fellow member and sometime President of the Royal Statistical Society.[2] A committee consisting of E.C. Grey, R.A. Valpy, H.G. Willink, W.C. Lefroy, Margaret Tillard and Charles Booth conducted the inquiry into Central London.[3] In both these cases Booth notes that the methodology employed was identical to that for East London. Notebooks exist in the Booth Collection alongside those for the rest of London. These are full and contain much topographical information. An analysis of both handwriting and subject matter indicates that Clara Collet did much of the interviewing.[4] Jesse Argyle was responsible for the inquiry into London North of the Thames, which includes a study of Walthamstow.[5]

This is not the place to analyse and assess Booth's detailed study of life in London as expressed statistically and in comment.[6] The intention is to draw attention to the little-known parts of that study, for there can be no doubt that in emphasising Booth's work on the measurement of poverty scholars

---

[68] Booth Collection, e.g. B72, fos 191-98.

[1] Of *Poverty*, 1-178 pages deal with East London and about 120 on all of the remainder.

[2] *Poverty*, 1, pp. 291-99.

[3] *Poverty*, 1, p. 301; draft materials but apparently not notebooks by Tillard, Grey and Valpy still survive in the University of Liverpool collection.

[4] Booth Collection, B58, B60, B64.

[5] *Poverty*, 1, pp. 243-71.

[6] For criticisms of Booth's measurement of poverty see E.P. Hennock, 'The Measurement of Urban Poverty', pp. 208-27 J.H. Treble, *Urban Poverty in Britain* (London 1979), passim; E.H. Hunt, *British Labour History, 1815-1914* (London, 1981), pp. 117-22.

have neglected other aspects of the work. It will fall to others to assess this work but it is appropriate now to to indicate what we know of his concerns, methodology and approach. Such information is distressingly thin on the ground. Booth rarely mentions his reading or other influences upon him. There are one or two important clues to his working. Both Toynbee Hall and the Royal Statistical Society influenced his approach. One clue is that Toynbee Hall at this time provided him with a number of enthusiastic associates (Aves, Llewellyn Smith, possibly Stephen Fox), assistance with the collection of data both from their own case book and elsewhere, and a congenial milieu in which to discuss issues relating to East London and its problems. In early 1890 Henry Higgs was lecturing to fifty working men and women at Toynbee on Workingmen's Expenditure and 'holding them spellbound'.[7] This involved consideration of the work of Frédéric Le Play. On 13 January 1891 a Workmen's Family Budgets Conference was resumed at Toynbee. This seems to have been the sounding board for the work of Booth, Aves and Higgs on family budgets for the Economic Club.[8] Booth included thirty-nine family budgets in the Poverty series suggesting further his interest in Le Play's methods. Perhaps these budgets originally came from Toynbee cases. Other conferences at Toynbee Hall are mentioned by Beatrice Potter.[9] After initial doubts, Samuel Barnett offered Booth his keen support. This included valuable introductions to local government officials, trades union officials, businessmen, manufacturers and working people.

Another clue to Booth's thought during these years can be gleaned from the printed work itself. It has sometimes been intimated that Booth was unreflective about his methodology and, occasionally, that he was unaware of the distinction between fact and opinion. It is true that he sometimes found it difficult to handle the material he had collected and to reconcile fact with opinion but he was certainly well aware of the difference: where was the ever more deplorable condition of the poor leading, asked many social commentators, away from a Golden Past or away from today's Golden

[7] Collet MS 29/3/13/5/7, Henry Higgs to H.S. Foxwell 8 February 1891.

[8] Charles Booth, Ernest Aves, Henry Higgs, *Family Budgets: Being the Income and Expenses of Twenty-Eight British Households, 1891-1894* (The Economic Club, London, 1896). It is interesting to note that Miss Edith Collet, Clara Collet's younger sister, was credited with amplifying the scheduled budgets, abstracting the longer ones and 'the still more laborious task of summarising the accounts'.

[9] 'Women's Work and Wages', 16 November 1887, Diary; and 'Unemployment'. For more general discussions of the work of Toynbee Hall see the bibliography.

Age or towards a new Golden Era? Booth replied that an answer would depend upon one's premisses:

> Seen from without, the same habits of life, amount of income, method of expenditure, difficulties, occupations, amusements, will strike the mind of the onlooker with an entirely different meaning according as they are viewed as part of a progress towards a better and higher life, or of a descent towards a more miserable and debased existence.

Moreover, he reflected, 'we have also to take account of the relation of the present life . . . to the ideal or expectation'.[10] Where contentment ought to reign, measurement against an abstract ideal may induce discontent. To interpret the life of either an individual or a class, he emphasised, one must 'lay open its memories and understand its hopes'.

The problem of relativities greatly exercised him.[11] To understand the point of view 'we have to take unto account the condition of the onlooker's mind and of public sentiment generally, and the changes of feeling that occur, in this or that direction, by which it becomes more sensitive or more callous. On these three points – 1. The relation to past experience; 2. The relation to expectation; 3. The degree of sensitiveness of the public mind – we have room for great gulfs of difference in considering the same facts.'

To suggest that Booth was a mindless empiricist, is, in the light of such mature statements as these, clearly unsupported. In his chapter on poverty he discusses the question piecemeal, class by class. Although Booth's approach was not historical, he did not deny the importance of history or past experience while speculating on the extent to which each class made use of its memories. He had a knowledge of class composition and fluidity which allowed him to observe, for instance, that members of Class B, who were drifters from other classes, would tend to contrast their lives with those of others – often those that they had left behind.[12] Scholars should not examine just Booth's statistical tables. If these implied rigid separation between classes and occupations, Booth was well aware, from his personal experience, of relationships and interactions which became submerged in statistical tabulation.

[10] *Poverty*, 1, p. 173.
[11] See above, pp. 35-7.
[12] *Poverty*, 1, p. 175.

6. Trades of East London Connected with Poverty: Special Subject Inquiries

Even the first series of Booth's survey was a collaborative effort but little attention has been given to the production of the special subject inquiries produced in the main by his associates. The standard work by the Simeys scarcely mentions these trade and subject investigations, yet they formed an important part of the whole – occupying two full volumes of the four-volume first series. As we have seen above, they formed an integral part of the proposal from the first.[1] They were not an afterthought. The collaborators were not 'routine workers'.[2]

It is neither feasible nor desirable here to give a detailed description of how each of these investigations was organised nor to assess how the material collected was used. Relatively few notes apparently survive for this part of the survey. It is hard to be categorical on this point because the papers of the first and second series are not kept separately in the main archive at the London School of Economics. It seems probable that the Booth Collection A series, for *Poverty*, contains in the main the work done by Booth himself and his secretaries, George Arkell and Jesse Argyle. Notes taken by the associates such as Beatrice Potter, Llewellyn Smith, and Clara Collet – were personal notes and, as such, were retained by their authors. This conclusion seems to be borne out by the recent discovery at the London School of Economics of the David Schloss papers for his study of the Boot and Shoe Manufacturing Trade. These papers are entirely separate from the Booth Collection, which seemingly contains no mention of the investigation. Similarly, while there are quite extensive materials pertaining to Beatrice Potter's work for Booth, these are in the Passfield Collection, in her notebooks and in the manuscript diary for the years 1885-9.[3] The notes on the tailoring trade inquiry in the Booth Collection are those compiled by Booth, George Arkell and, perhaps, very brief reports by Collet and Green. Few remnants of Green and Collet's inquiry into women's work and wages survive other than in the form of George Arkell's interviews for the fur trade, and the match and box trades. Collet's diary is inconveniently silent

---

[1] Passfield, IIi(II), 8. See Charles Booth to Beatrice Potter, 10 September 1886.

[2] See Collet, 'Recollections'.

[3] Beatrice Potter's diary exists in three forms: a holograph diary; a typescript version (which in some cases modifies the holograph version or omits material from it); and an abridged, edited version. As the two later versions omit much of the interview material, we have normally cited the MS version. In general the date of an entry is given; in those cases where dates prove difficult to trace, volume number and page number are given. To add to the confusion *My Apprenticeship* often quotes rather inaccurately from the diaries.

for these years and an Alice Green collection does not seem to be extant. Because of the nature of these different archives, we have elected to examine in some detail what Beatrice Potter was later to describe as her investigation of the sweating system; to explore in rather less detail, to avoid repetition, the printed text and manuscript materials of the essay on women's work, attempting to deduce what sources Clara Collet used and how she used them; and to study the new material on Schloss in order to set out the basis of his chapter on the boot and shoe manufacture.

As we have seen above, Beatrice Potter was intimately involved in the beginnings of Booth's proposed survey of Life and Labour of the People in London. Heeding the advice of friends such as Herbert Spencer and Arabella Fisher that she should 'take up some line of inquiry', she had expressed a desire from the start to be an active participant in the quest for knowledge.[4] Early in March 1886 Beatrice wrote to Mary Booth: 'I think I shall have some time in London and should be glad to undertake my own school board district and the London and St Kath [Katharine's] Docks with the Royal Albert further down [? to run under the same Cd]'[5] Later Booth had intended her to undertake the interviews of female School Board Visitors.[6] This was possibly because Ella Pycroft was now no longer able to do the work.[7] In *My Apprenticeship* she writes, 'On the few occasions I attended these interviews it was enlightening to watch Charles Booth or one or other of his secretaries . . .',[8] making it reasonably certain that interviewing School Board Visitors was not part of her regular work routine. (She did interview one or more School Board Visitors in the course of her later work on the Docks, for example, but this should not be confused with her earlier involvement in the project in the autumn of 1886.)

Her real work for Booth was heralded in December 1886. She records that she spent 'two days in London with the Booths. Charlie is absorbed in his inquiry, working all the evenings with three paid secretaries. I have promised to undertake "Docks" in my March holiday. . .'[9] Although she was later to describe her work on the docks as part and parcel of a general inquiry into sweating,[10] and was of course first to publish the essay in the *Nineteenth Century*,[11] there is no evidence that, in its beginnings, this was any more or less than a discrete contribution to Booth's survey of trades

---

[4] 'I wish you would take up some line of inquiry', wrote Herbert Spencer to B. Potter, 8 October 1883 *My Apprenticeship*, p. 152; see also Passfield, IIi(II), 6, Arabella Fisher to Beatrice Potter, 24 January 1886, 6; Mary Booth to Beatrice Potter, 6 June 1886.

[5] Norman Mackenzie (ed.), *The Letters of Sidney and Beatrice Webb*, i, p. 56, Beatrice Potter to Mary Booth, early March 1886.

[6] Passfield, IIi(II), 8, Charles Booth to Beatrice Potter, 5 September 1886.

[7] Passfield, IIi(II), 9, Maurice Paul to Beatrice Potter, 5 October 1886.

[8] *My Apprenticeship*, p. 239.

[9] Passfield, MS Diary, 5 December 1886, *My Apprenticeship*, p. 300.

[10] *My Apprenticeship*, p. 314.

[11] Beatrice Potter, 'The Dock Life of East London', *Nineteenth Century*, xxii (1887).

associated with poverty. Since her father's stroke in November 1885 Beatrice Potter had been involved for most of the year in caring for him: investigation became perforce a holiday employment.

7. The Docks: Beatrice Potter

Let us establish how 'The Docks' was written. In late February 1887 Beatrice began the work which she had promised. She was not a complete novice, however, for she had busied herself in the last year or so with a study of the inhabitants of Katharine Buildings, where she was a rent collector, and with reading for her various articles on political economy and social diagnosis.[1] Her work on the inhabitants of the buildings may have fuelled her interest in the docks, as has been suggested, but this must remain a matter of conjecture. She drew on little of the material for her chapter.[2] She did not give *The Docks* her exclusive attention during those months: she continued beavering away on her article and she was simultaneously collecting some material for her 'sweating' industry work. She started with interviews with the Superintendents of the West India and East India Docks, establishing the *modus operandi* of the docks and ascertaining what other types of material she required. She spent time becoming acquainted with the contract system that had been in use for two years at the Millwall Docks. She accompanied Charles Booth in the West India Docks to pursue some lines of inquiry there and to interview Stephen Sim, the secretary to the Amalgamated Stevedores' Society. She contrasted the operation of the Millwall Dock with the West India and East India Docks.

On 30 March 1887 she recorded in her diary both her pleasure in the work and her dissatisfaction with the level of her knowledge of the subject:

> Thoroughly enjoyed the last month (I write towards the middle of my holiday). Have got statistical outline of dock labour for Tower Hamlets. Certainly, inquiring into social facts is interesting work: but it needs the devotion of a life to do it thoroughly. I feel that the little bit of work I do will be very superficial, and that, until I could take the inquiry as a life-work and not only as a holiday task, I should do very little good with it. But I need much preparation. A general but thorough

---

[1] BLPES, Coll. Misc. 43, Katharine Buildings.

[2] Deborah Epstein Nord, *The Apprenticeship of Beatrice Webb*, (London, 1986), pp. 144-47. Neither Epstein Nord nor Jane Lewis, *Women and Social Action in Victorian and Edwardian England* (Aldershot, 1991), add to our knowledge or understanding of Beatrice Potter's early investigative work and the conclusions that she drew from them. Nord confuses Potter's account of her work (written in 1926) with her actual work in 1886-88. It is not insignificant that Potter is referred to as Webb throughout. Lewis, while more conversant with the archive, occasionally makes similar lapses (e.g. p. 102).

knowledge of English history and literature . . . A theoretical grasp of the growth
of industry, and of the present state of industrial organisation. And a thinking out
of principles – of the limit of the subject nature, and the nature of the method . . .
This and a good deal more I need before I am fully prepared for direct
observation.[3]

[May 1887] 'I feel rather low about the proposed paper on Dock Labour. Besides
the bare statistics I want local colouring; – First I need clear distinction between
methods of employing men. Secondly between lives and characters of men
employed and where they live. Salaried men live out of the neighbourhood of the
work. Foreman live apart; are for the most part educated in the Docks . . . Must
realize the 'waiting at the gates', and finds out for myself the exact hours at which
the different classes are taken on.[4]

She determined to follow up several lines of inquiry as a result of this
reflection: the different classes of worker in the docks; the consequences of
the opening of the Suez Canal upon dock business; the work of the Tilbury,
Albert and Victoria Docks. Both Booth's opinion and that of the police were
to be canvassed. Further interviews were with, for example, a master
stevedore; with Mr Thomas, the School Board Visitor of the Millwall area:
with Kerrigan, the School Board Visitor for Limehouse (Stepney); with Mrs
Gibbs, the wife of a worker at the Cutter Street warehouse; with Mr Gibbs, a
worker at the wool warehouse; with Mr Bright, the manager of the South
Side Wharf at Millwall Docks; with Mr Coleman, a dock missionary; with Mr
Maulty, a chauvinist contractor; and with Mr Wight, manager of the Fresh
Wharf. Her brother-in-law, Daniel Meinertzhagen, obtained letters of introduction for her to the wharves. At a dinner at around about the same time
she had useful conversations with Mr Cox, Superintendent of the London
and St Katharine Docks, and Mr Beck, the Superintendent of the West
India Docks. Interspersed with reflections on the work of Herbert Spencer
in conversations with the Huxleys were walks in the dock areas:

This morning I walked along Billingsgate from Fresh Wharf to the London
Docks. Crowded with loungers – smoking bad tobacco and coarse careless talk,
with the clash of a halfpenny on the pavement every now and again. Bestial
content or hopeless discontent on their faces – the lowest form of leisure –
senseless curiosity of street rows, idle gazing at the street seller low joke – and this
is the chance the Dock offers.[5]

Thus she exaggerates somewhat when she writes in *My Apprenticeship*:
'Morning after morning I am up early, watching the struggle for work at the

[3] Passfield, MS Diary, 30 March 1887; edited version, *My Apprendiceship*, p. 300.
[4] Passfield, MS Diary; differently presented in *My Apprendiceship*, p. 301.
[5] Passfield, MS Diary, 6 May 1887; *My Apprendiceship*, p. 302.

dock gates; and observing the leisurely unloading of sailing vessels compared to the swift discharge of steamers'.

She also visited Peabody's dwellings and asked questions there about tenants who worked at the docks; toured a wool warehouse (Goudge-Cousin); spent an evening at a club in St George's Yard, talking to 'preferables' at the London and St Katharine Docks. One of these was Robinson, a socialist dock labourer. She consulted Charles Booth's notebook on the doss houses which served the docks and noted down interesting information. Unfortunately for us the diary entries relating to the period from 1 June to 11 August 1887 were torn out of the holograph diary.

Some of the reports of her work on the docks are wonderfully evocative. Witness her interview with Kerrigan, the School Board Visitor:

Describe his casuals, about 900, as hereditary casuals, London-born. The worst scoundrel is the cockney-born Irishman. The woman is the Chinaman of the place; drudges as the women of savage races: she slaves all day and night. Describes the communism of this class. They do not migrate out of the district, but they are constantly changing their lodgings: 'They are like the circle of the suicides in Dante's *Inferno;*' they go round and round within a certain area'. They work for each other: hence low ideal of work. They never see excellence in work. They never leave the neighbourhood. From the Dock-gate they lounge back to the street; 'treating' and being 'treated', according to as they have earned a few pence. Live chiefly on 'tobacco; which is a compound of sugar, vinegar, brown paper and German nicotine. The teapot is constantly going – bread and a supply of dried haddock which goes through a domestic preparation: dried in the chimney and acquiring a delicate favour by lying between the mattresses of the beds. They never read. Except the Catholics, they never go to church. On the Bank Holiday the whole family goes to Victoria Park. 'Permanent' men live outside the neighbourhood – Forest Gate, Hackney, Upton, some even at Walthamstow. Kerrigan does not think that corruption and bribery goes on in the West India Dock, as it does at the London and St Katharine's. 'Permanent' men might be classed just above the artisan and skilled mechanics. They read Herbert Spencer and Huxley, and are speculative of intelligent working men.[6]

or her visit to the docks:

Go to Docks early in the morning [records another May entry]. Permanent men respectable, sober, clean. Casuals low-looking, bestial, content with their own condition. Watch brutal fight and struggle: then sudden dissolution of the crowd with coarse jokes and loud laugh. Look of utter indifference on their faces: among them the one or two who have fallen from better things – their abject misery. The mass of the rejected lounge down to another dock to spread themselves over the entrance to the various wharves. About 100 of the lowest will

---

[6] *My Apprendiceship*, p. 303, which is a literary reworking of the entry for 18 May 1887 in the MS Diary.

congregate in the 'cage' in Nightingale Lane waiting for a chance of a foreman needing them as odd men. If a man weary of ennui and of an empty stomach drops off to sleep, his companions will promptly search his pockets for the haphazard penny.[7]

In many respects a poor note-taker (she occasionally comments that she has to interview someone again because her notes were too sketchy or nonexistent),[8] she had a flair for capturing the scene there and then, recording the vitality of the speech and observing keenly the life of the people, whether or not it had much relevance to the subject at hand. Thus the trip to Victoria Park with Kerrigan told her little about the docks but a good deal about the dockers and their community.

It is a pity that this facility did not transfer itself to her articles for the Booth survey for, despite the richness of the interview, Beatrice Potter drew directly on little of it for her chapter '*The Docks*'. It is perhaps understandable that she eschewed the style of Mayhew – after all she, like Booth, wished to avoid sensationalism. It is rather less obvious why, when she had such a flair for conveying the actual in all its immediacy, she rejected the real examples she had of what happened at the dock entrance in favour of rather strained and architected literary description.[9] On the rare occasions when she did refer to the views of real individuals she, oddly enough, elected to alter what they had said.

> I met Dartford, respectable tenant K[atharine] B[uildings], and he greeted me cordially. He is always in work, and complains that he never gets a holiday – says that many of the unemployed do not want to work, and get sacked for not turning up. I make a point of not mixing up with anyone. Women get thick together, and then there is always a row. The curse is the daily payment: it is always a mistake not to give the woman the money once a week instead of at odd times. Said [that] the worse a man is, the more work he will get at the docks.[10]

This conversation is clearly the origin of the passage on page 24 of the chapter referring to the few permanent men who chose to live near the docks and their subsequent isolation:

> If the temptation of cheap food and employment for the wife and children, induces a permanent man to inhabit St George's in the East or Limehouse, he will be found in a 'Peabody' or some strictly regulated model dwelling. He will tell you: 'I make a point of not mixing with anyone' and perhaps he will sorrowfully

---

[7] *My Apprenticeship*, p. 302, which is a literary reworking of the entry for 11 May 1887 in the MS Diary.

[8] See e.g. Passfield, VII, I, 8.62.

[9] See *Poverty*, 4, pp. 30-31 and compare with, for example, the Passfield, MS Diary entry for May 1887.

[10] Passfield, MS Diary, May 1887; *My Apprenticeship*, p. 302.

complain 'when the women gets thick together there's always a row' . . . 'In common with all other working men with a moderate but regular income, the permanent Dock labourer is made by his wife . . .'[11]

It is to be noted that she does not attribute the origins of the comment, although she had it carefully noted down in her diary and in fact knew the family well.

Sometimes, as with Dartford, she shows a distressing tendency to take over part of the interviewee's comment and present it as her own verdict. Documented examples were felt unimportant when she made her case. It was sufficient to say, for example, 'From my own observation as a rent collector, and from other evidence, we know that the professional Dock labourer earns from 12s. to 15s. a week, supposing his earnings were to be spread evenly through out the year',[12] without giving examples from her carefully kept Book of the Inhabitants of Katharine Buildings (1885-90) or saying just what that other evidence was. When she reported the activities of the dock police and the irritation it caused in the workers, she understandably neglected to report directly the views of Robinson, the socialist dock worker, who was the first to acquaint her with the views of the men themselves. 'Says he makes a point of secreting tobacco on his person to defy the rule.'[13] She had no statistical support whatsoever for her comment that women's work sapped the men's appetite and energy for work – its support was a comment from Cox of Millwall that, 'Sometimes have to sack men for not coming in time. Men depend on the wives' labour and only want to earn pocket money.[14] Despite her keen understanding of the personality of Mr Birt, General Manager of the Millwall Docks, 'a self-important man, who considers himself an authority on Dock Labour and comes out in a pompous manner with a set speech on the subject . . . the theme of which is the superiority of the labour employed by the Millwall Docks – and the comfort and respectability of their hands, all this in praise of the contract system', she was content to adapt his views and present them as her own unprejudiced opinion on page 19 of her account of Millwall Docks employment:

> It will be observed that the Millwall Docks employ relatively few hands. The trade is chiefly corn and timber, the discharging of which needs special skill and sinew. The Millwall Dock hands are therefore superior to the ordinary Dock and waterside labourers. And there are other reasons for excluding the majority of workers at these Docks from any general description of London labour. They are for the most part countrymen imported some years back to break a combination of corn porters. Cut off by their residence in the interior of the Isle of Dogs from

[11] *Poverty*, 4, pp. 24-25.
[12] *Poverty*, 4, p. 27.
[13] *My Apprendiceship*, p. 302.
[14] Passfield, MS Diary, 30 March 1887.

the social influences of the East End, they have retained many traits of provincial life . . . And the system of employment prevalent at the Millwall Docks appears to be efficient and satisfactory in its results to men and masters. The whole work is let out to large labour contractors. This form of the contract system is not open to the objection rightly advanced against the small working-man contractor . . .[15]

She was apparently comforted by the agreement of Mr Thomas, a School Board Visitor, that Millwall dockers were different.[16]

The chapter's useful description of the typical work of the docks was heavily derived from her detailed interviews with the superintendents, chairmen, general managers and occasionally foremen of the various docks.[17] Similarly the statistics of employees of the different docks came from this source and from, for example, the secretary of the Stevedore's Union. There is a close correspondence between the description of employment practices at the London and St Katharine's Company Docks and the interview Beatrice Potter gave to Mr Cox, Superintendent of the Docks, at the end of March 1887 and to one of the gangers at the same docks.[18] The statistics given on pp 18-19 of employment of this dock tally quite well with those given her by Cox, although she clearly made some changes (on what basis we do not know), adapting the quoted number of artisans, excluding clerks, and converting '4-500' preferables to 450. There is some evidence that she did try to check the figures she was given. When she visited Millwall Docks she 'secured the paymaster's sheets for 1886'.[19] She did see for herself the work of the docks.[20]

In the event her chapter on 'The Docks' was a somewhat colourless and contentless contribution. It combines the worst of two worlds: it contains few statistics and the results of poorly-documented personal observation. There is little exciting description and facts and opinions are rarely attributed. It contrasts most unfavourably with David Schloss's chapter on bootmaking, for example. The article offers few facts and offers assertion in place of proof. Clearly by the time it was published Beatrice Potter did have a good knowledge of dock practices – derived from her interviews, her notes on the tenants of Katharine Buildings, her personal observation and her reading – but the work itself was unsatisfactory. In reality she knew more about attitudes among managers and men to dock work than she knew about the work itself. She saw what the managers wished her to see; she heard what managers and men wished to tell her.

[15] *Poverty*, 4, p. 19.

[16] Passfield, MS Diary, 30 March 1887.

[17] See interviews at West India, East India, London and St Katharine's and Millwall Docks, entries under MS Diary, 25 February and 30 March 1887.

[18] *Poverty*, 4, pp. 21-22.

[19] Passfield, MS Diary, 22 March 1887.

[20] Ibid.

Yet, in the event, she chose to treat what she was shown and told as fact and she presented it to her readers with great authority. In later years she was to criticise the work on several grounds but not these. 'The essay on "Dock Life in East London" was, even in my own estimation, an inferior piece of work; the investigations had been scamped for lack of time, and my conclusions with regard to the disease of under employment and its possible prevention, though sound as far as they went, were neither exhaustive nor sufficiently elaborated to be helpful', she wrote in *My Apprenticeship*.[21] And in 1889 she bemoaned the fact that she had not picked up through her researches any inkling of the dockers' ability to organise. In fact it was not merely the extent of her researches which was deficient but her handling of the material she had collected. The investigative material she left would certainly repay inspection, yet seems to have been neglected.[22]

8. *The Tailoring Trade: Beatrice Potter and George Arkell*

It is possible to discover Potter's approach to work on the tailoring trade of the East End in even more detail. In early August she had 'settled with Charlie on the autumn's work. The sweating system is to be the subject of my next paper'. 'I have it in my mind to make it more of a picture than my article on "Dock Life".'[1] Her interest in this subject had been fed by her meeting in the spring with Mr Hoffman, a Methodist preacher and a foreman in a shoe factory who had 'made the sweating system a special subject of study'.[2]

By late August she had read Mayhew's *London Labour and London Poor* of 1851, which she described as 'good material spoilt by bad dressing – it is a mine of information – both of personal observation and of statistical enquiry – but there is no opening to it, nor any destination reached. It is overloaded with descriptive detail . . .'[3] She read it mainly for its entrée to the sweating system but her comments are revelatory of her approach to the work of investigation and writing itself. Immediately she mapped out an article on the sweating system which seemed to point her in the direction of a study of the boot and shoe industry. In October, just as she was embarking on the tailoring trade inquiry, she interviewed an Irish worker in the boot and shoe trade.[4]

---

[21] *My Apprenticeship*, p. 312.

[22] See John Lovell, *Stevedores and Dockers* (London, 1969), which makes no mention of the source and Gareth Stedman Jones, *Outcast London* (Oxford, 1971), which made no use of the archive.

[1] Passfield MS Diary, *c* 8 August 1887.

[2] Passfield, MS Diary, 24 March 1887.

[3] See Passfield, MS Diary; misdescribed as work of Makin in Typescript Diary.

[4] Passfield, MS Diary, 5 October 1887.

Work began in earnest in October 1887. Significantly, this time it began with close co-operation with Booth's office and specifically with George Arkell. She met with Booth frequently, sometimes two or three times a week.[5] George Arkell has received few if any bouquets from his contemporaries or from historians and social scientists. Yet such a bouquet is long overdue: his contribution to Booth's survey (and to the work of those who contributed to it) was enormous and important. It was he who was in charge of 'the map', for example. It was he who, with Jesse Argyle, prepared the statistical framework for the survey. He conducted interviews for several of the special subject inquiries of the Poverty Series and contributed largely to the second and third series also. He joined the team of secretaries early on (perhaps he was the young assistant for whom Booth had to find other duties in July 1886?) and remained with Booth certainly until the publication of the seventeen-volume edition of *Life and Labour* in 1903.

Booth's personal interest in the tailoring trade was important for the immediate direction of Beatrice's inquiry into sweating. A plan of campaign as to the investigation into tailoring by Booth survives.[6] In this Booth listed the names of the tailoring societies (including the headquarters and three branches of the Amalgamated Tailors; the Tailors' Mutual Association at the Black Eagle, Brick Lane; and the London Machinists). He observed that, when approaching the secretaries of the Jewish and German branches of the Amalgamated Tailors, Barnett's name should be used as an introduction. He then described the various types of workers in the trade (coat, waistcoat, 'trowser') and drew the divisions between the work in the West End and East End work, both in terms of craftsmanship and market, workplace and workers:

> – e.g. Coat – West End Work on premises by men only regular price
> Well paid
> Part of this in men's homes frequently
> East End – wife may help
> Good city middle class work (Hope Bros & Samuels)
> Workshops or through middle men in sweating shops.[7]

He was directing the campaign but under him Arkell and Argyle executed his general plans with flair and precision and exercised remarkable initiative. Arkell lent organisation to Beatrice's endeavours. First of all he produced a list of streets containing tailors' shops according to the factory inspectors' books and had it checked by Zeitlin of the Amalgamated Tailors.[8] Later he conducted a special street census for seven streets in White-

---

[5] See Norman-Butler, *Victorian Aspirations*, p. 91.
[6] Booth Collection, A 19, 'Tailoring', fo. 1.
[7] Ibid.
[8] Booth Collection, A19, 'Tailoring', fo. 14.

chapel (Fashion Street, Great Garden Street), Mile End Old Town Western
Part (Plumbers' Row, Jailor Street), Mile End Old Town Eastern Part
(Shandy Street) and Poplar (Leven Road and Glencoe Street) to check on the
accuracy of the lists.[9] These special street surveys were based upon the work
of the School Board Visitors and those for Shandy Street (by W.G. Harmier)
and Jailor Street and Plumbers' Row (by H.G. Bowsher), conducted in
October 1888, exist in tabular form in the archive.[10] More importantly, in
the present context, it was he who undertook to prepare statistics of the
tailoring trade in 1887 by obtaining a list of tailors' workshops in the East
End from Bradbury & Co's traveller presumably setting Beatrice Potter on
the trail of the Singers' Sewing-Machine agents. Then he obtained from
Zeitlin and Frecké (secretaries respectively to the Jewish and German
branches of the Amalgamated Tailors) the results of their house-to-house
inquiry on the workers and workrooms of the trade.[11] He personally
interviewed relatively large numbers of employers and workers in that trade
during the autumn and winter of 1887-88.[12] Fifty interviews, chiefly in
Arkell's hand, remain in the Booth papers at the London School of Economics as testimony to his active participation in this part of the investigation.
There may have been more originally – for the collection at the London
School of Economics is far from complete. Extracts from the factory returns
on women workers, labelled 'Miss Guiness's enquiry', and Board of Trade
returns provided information about women in the trade. Yet more interesting was the fact that Arkell contrived to interview no fewer than eighteen
women out of this number. All the interviews were detailed, perceptive and
full of information about the workshops concerned.

> Last Thursday, she commenced work at 6 a.m. and worked until 9.30 p.m. and
> did 8 pairs of these trowsers in the time. The children got the meals and she had
> hers as she was working. She finished 6 pairs by 4 o'clock and 2 more at 8.30 to go
> to shop next morning. These garments would involve a cost of 2d. for materials:
> thread, cotton 1d. and soap $\frac{3}{4}$d.[13]

Arkell, like later secretaries and associates of Booth, wrote detailed
reports of his findings on the trade which were presumably invaluable to
Beatrice and the others who worked on the tailoring trade for the first and
second series.[14] It was he who compiled the statistical tables and by a careful
process of analysis drew Booth's and the others' attention to lacunae and

[9] Booth Collection, A19, 'Tailoring', fos. 29-30.
[10] Ibid.
[11] Booth Collection, A19, 'Tailoring', fos. 33ff.
[12] Booth Collection, A19, 'Tailoring'.
[13] Booth Collection, A19, 'Tailoring', fos. 110.
[14] Booth Collection, A19, 'Tailoring', fos 178ff.

problematical areas.[15] In February 1888 he walked Beatrice through the East End.[16] Sometimes he challenged her ideas – a brave man![17]

This was in the future. On 3 October 1887 Beatrice Potter had Arkell to dinner and asked him to 'colour map so as to see exactly where the trades are localised'.[18] It was, she said, 'Arkell's idea to work the journeymen tailors first; and to go with a list of questions'.[19] At the same dinner he gave her details of rates of pay for tailoring work. Almost immediately Beatrice began interviewing workers in the trade. The first interview she records being that of a trouser hand named Connolly, who belonged to the Amalgamated Tailors, whom she interviewed on 5 October.[20] Throughout October there are references to interviews of workers in the trade.[21] These are interspersed with boot and shoe industry interviews. Probably all these were introduced to Beatrice Potter by the Barnetts.[22] Then she moved on to examine the Toynbee Hall casebook.[23] This supplied her with six cases, including one sweater who employed thirty workers, a man and wife engaged in making coats for the government, and three female coat workers. The details noted were those of sex, status in work place (e.g. tailor); place of work; nature of work performed (e.g. baster coat; breeches maker, all round sewn; makes waistcoats), hours of work; rates of pay; rhythm of work (e.g. 'customers work comes in late in the week – cutters are a "drunken lot" and won't come in until Thursday');[24] and stray comments, often very useful, about the life of the workers. There is every evidence that she had taken Arkell's advice to heart and taken a list of questions with her. He had lent system to her brilliance. On 14 October she questioned one of the School Board Visitors who proved to know nothing of the tailoring trade but regaled her with a vivid description of 'jew-life'.[25] 'The Levys came to tea. Mrs Levy promised me definite information about shop she worked in.

[15] Compare *Poverty*, 3, pp. 66-68 with Booth Collection, A19, 'Tailoring', fos 26-27.

[16] Passfield, VII, I, 8.63.

[17] Passfield, VII, I, 8.55.

[18] Passfield, MS Diary, 4 October 1887; Arkell was to show his mapping skills to great effect at a later date with the map of the Jewish East End for the Toynbee Survey, 1899, see C. Russell and H.S. Lewis, *The Jew in London: A Study of Racial Character and Present-Day Conditions* (London, 1900), and there are indications that he was contacted in connection with the New Survey of London Life and Labour, BLPES, NSOL, Parcel 9/1 20 May 1928: Letter from George Arkell to Llewellyn Smith referred to.

[19] Passfield, MS Diary, 4 October 1887.

[20] Passfield, MS Diary, 5 October 1887.

[21] Passfield, MS Diary, 5 October 1887 (Holt, worker on premises of Gardiner, who was also a 'sweater'); 6 October 1887 (Mackay, a breeches-maker); (Mrs Head, a waistcoat-maker); (Mrs Levy, 'my old friend', a machinist.

[22] Passfield, MS Diary, 6 October 1887.

[23] Passfield, MS Diary, 10 October 1887.

[24] Passfield, MS Diary, 6 October 1887.

[25] Passfield, MS Diary, 14 October 1887.

Also to get me in to small sweaters shop to learn part of the trade.'[26] Then there is yet another of those tantalising stray comments of hers that sets us wondering: 'Secured one of the Toynbee men to work for me.'[27]

On 20 October she completed this volume of her diary and declared at the opening of the next that: 'Now that observation is my work, I find it as necessary to have two books as when reading was my source of information. Otherwise the autobiography is eaten up by statistics of wages, hours of work, and names of employers – no room for the general history of a woman's life.' In the Passfield Collection is a book with seventy-nine written folios – in fact 158 pages of interviews and other material relating to Beatrice Potter's inquiry into the wholesale clothing trade in 1887, done while she was staying at the Quaker Devonshire House Hotel on Bishopsgate Street and dated 20 October 1887.[28]

A glance at this book demonstrates that she had determined not to repeat the mistakes of her dock inquiry. There was a deliberate attempt to interview a large number of both men and women and to ensure a fair spread across the trade. In her diary for 13 November 1887 she commented: 'Wrote out my notes and shall tomorrow decide on my plan of campaign with Charlie for the coming month in London.'[29] On 14 November 1887 she wrote some brief notes to herself (presumably with Booth) which show that she was aware of the need to do this: 'Will get at middlemen through Cohen R. Street, Darvin, Spiezel'; 'Jewish workers through A. Whathorn Clerg. from St Jermyn in the East and Madden'; 'Employers from Arkell's Book'.[30] The notes show that she deliberately interviewed the women workers and that she used George Arkell's interviews of women workers in trouser, vests and juvenile shirt sections of the trade also.[31] She planned and carried out interviews of her own of shopowners, middlemen and workers;[32] used interview material already collected by Booth's team (at least fifty interviews are extant); interviewed officials who might be able to give her privileged information; made it her business to find out through questioning and personal experience the processes of the trade; and searched such records as were available to her.

Mr Barnett's introductions were of great importance to her. Darvin, the School Board Visitor; Mr Lakeman, senior factory inspector for the East End in Home Office employment; a sanitary inspector; Mr Nash, a post office official; Mr [John] Burnett, who worked for the Board of Trade; Mr

[26] Passfield, MS Diary, 14 October 1887.
[27] Passfield, MS Diary, 14 October 1887.
[28] Passfield, VII, I, 8.
[29] Passfield, MS Diary, 13 November 1887.
[30] Passfield, VII, I, 8.21.
[31] Passfield, VII, I, 8.40; 8.69.
[32] Seventy-one are listed in the index to the volume.

[David] Schloss; Mr [Ernest] Aves (the last a resident of Toynbee Hall).[33] She also built up contacts with leading members of trades associations. Zeitlin accorded Arkell an interview in December 1887 and had earlier spoken in the Club of the Jewish Amalgamated Tailors to both Booth and Beatrice on 26 November.[34] Macdonald, 'a high-class journeyman tailor working in best West End shops', afforded her excellent descriptions of shop life.[35] William de Yonge, a collector for various societies, proved invaluable.[36] She interviewed the Singer's Sewing-Machine collectors.[37] She cultivated and exploited this network of contacts mercilessly but they did not always supply her with the information she coveted and expected.

David Schloss 'gentleman Jew . . . was quite certain he "knew all about it" gave me facts as to wages etc. . .', but this was to appear in print elsewhere. 'Had visited workshops in his capacity of sanitary inspector of Jewish Guardians.'[38] Yet, 'tho' he loudly proclaimed that he was most anxious to serve me could not introduce me to Agent of Jewish Board of Guardians because it would compromise his position at the Board'. Perhaps what he did offer, a meeting with the Chief Rabbi and his wife, was in the end to be more useful to her but not for her work on tailoring.[39] She completed her notes of the interview with a somewhat patronising comment: 'After the interview he seemed more genuinely anxious to help me than at the beginning. Ugly little swarthy fellow; with loud and familiar manners and very full of his own importance but a good natured little soul, I should think.'[40] This seems to be the first evidence we have of Schloss's knowledge of Booth's Inquiry. He was, of course, to contribute to the work himself.

Mr Lakeman, a factory inspector with the Home Office, a 'Square built man with general impression of checked shirt', welcomed her 'with a funny self-impressive air' when she called upon him at his house on the evening of 5 November 1887.[41] Any hopes she had of eliciting useful information were dashed, first by his anger at Burnett. ('He opened out in a bout of indignation against the Board of Trade and Burnett's Report. He thought it disgraceful stealing men's brains. That is what Burnett had done. He had come to him and cross-examined him and put all he said, without acknowledgement, into his report. . . What did the Board of Trade know about

[33] Passfield, VII, I, 8.22.
[34] Passfield, VII, I. 8.53-54.
[35] Passfield, VII, I, 8.47-48. Macdonald also wrote for Booth's Inquiry, see *Poverty*, 4, pp. 142-48 and see Booth Correspondence, MS 797, 11/27/7.
[36] Passfield, VII, I, 8.43.
[37] See her reference to interviewing these men, *Poverty*, 4 pp. 45-46; see also, Passfield, VII, also, 59.
[38] Passfield, VII, I, 8.27.
[39] See below p. 78.
[40] Passfield, VII, I. 8.27.
[41] Passfield, VII, I, 8.48.

sweating?') and then by his reluctance to provide a list of names and addresses of the East End sweaters.[42]

On occasion the services of a contact were, however, indispensable. On 22 October Beatrice interviewed C. Nash, a Post Office official, who had helped David Schloss and Mr Pattison set up a co-operative workshop among the workers.[43] Nash himself yielded useful information about the workshop and its problems. Then later he went with Beatrice to interview Mr Risenbury, lately manager of the co-operative, 'a fat, prosperous-looking Jew living in Ellen Street, Backchurch Lane'.[44] Beatrice Potter would not have gained admittance without Nash's introduction: it was difficult enough with his assistance to persuade Risenbury to let her in. 'This lady has nothing to do with the factory inspector I will take it on my responsibility that you do not get into trouble', urged Nash.[45] In the event a bribe sufficed. Beatrice noted wrily, 'Certainly he had reason to fear the factory inspector', after she had viewed Risenbury's workshop.[46]

As a woman investigator, of course, she was particularly dependent upon the company of others. Often the companion would be a contact such as Nash or Levy.[47] Sometimes she would entertain two informants together,[48] or she would meet a new informant at the house of another.[49] She toured the streets with Arkell.[50] On occasion Charles Booth himself was an active participant in her interviews. This is something which Potter underplays both in her diaries and in *My Apprenticeship* but is certainly worthy of note. All the more so because, according to her, Booth's presence was not necessarily advantageous. When he went with her to see Lakeman, Booth reacted with impatience to the factory inspector's tirade against Burnett. He 'cut it short by asking for districts and special information. Lakeman then gave me a general outline of the East End Trade . . . Then Charlie, rather unwisely, asked him bolt out "Would he give him his list of names and addresses of the Sweaters?" "No", said Lakeman, somewhat testily, "I can't do that".' Charles attempted to backtrack with an explanation of why the information was needed but it was too late. 'All this', lamented Beatrice Potter, 'was simply the result of the lack of sympathy C. had shown to the man's wounded vanity. Altogether I was sorry I had not been alone with him. I should have managed him better with softer and less direct treat-

[42] Passfield, VII, I, 8.48-49.
[43] Passfield, VII, I, 8.2.
[44] Passfield, VII, I, 8.18.
[45] Passfield, VII, I, 8.19.
[46] Passfield, VII, I, 8.19.
[47] See below; Passfield, VII, I, 8.6.
[48] Passfield, VII, I, 8.57: Hall and Macdonald.
[49] See Passfield, VII, I, 8.59: she met N. Joseph, a Jewish architect, at the house of the Chief Rabbi.
[50] Passfield, VII, I, 8.63.

ment. As it was we got nothing out of him, except the picture of a man smarting under the consciousness of another man reaping the fruits of that which he considered he had sown . . .'[51]

The book contains no questionnaire but one is often able to deduce from the notes the line of questioning. For example, in the interview of a middleman:

> Hansing Sweater Distributive, 206 Cable Street, Trouser Export for colonies chiefly. Shipper contract work First Middleman. This middleman brings cloth ready money, cuts out and distributes work to second middleman. Hansing's employer works for four or five shippers and distributes trousers (Hansing only knows about trousers) to nine other sweaters besides himself.[52]

Then there might be questions on issues which had recently been brought to her attention in some way. Thus: 'I asked him why he did not work direct for shipper – He answered, "I haven't got the head for business – I've often had the chance, but have got sufficient to do, to do my own part of the business",'[53] and 'Cross-examined him about foremen, whether they took bribes for employment or to conceal bad work – said the manager of the firm for whom he worked had dismissed three foremen for taking money to conceal bad work, and had now to look over the work himself . . .'[54] There were further questions about employers and workforce, condition of trade compared with that of twenty years previously; the Jewish sweaters; dishonest practices among the workforce; irregularity of work; demands of the market.[55]

Hansing proved co-operative. As a result he and his wife and three children, one of them a convent-educated girl, were later invited to tea:[56] 'The evening, tho' yielding me serious information, was not an agreeable one', wailed Beatrice, 'Hansing smelt strongly of brandy and in his anxiety to impress me with the fear that the whole of the End End was dissolute and drunken, breathed the brandy into my face', while 'His admiring wife cackled when he made a feeble joke and cried, "Oh! Mr Hansing you are getting impertinent!"' She 'could hardly get him out of the house, he went on repeating truism and commonplace'.

Her visit to the Levys (who lived in Katharine Buildings and later Wentworth Dwellings) produced a detailed report ranging from their family life to their employment and life style:

[51] Passfield, VII, I, 8.49: see also VII, I, 8.53-64. See Jane Lewis, *Women and Social Action*, p. 111 for an uncritical contrary view.

[52] Passfield, VII, I, 8.2.

[53] Passfield, VII, I, 8.3.

[54] Passfield, VII, I, 8.3.

[55] Passfield, VII, I, 8.3-4.

[56] Passfield, VII, I, 8.9.

They have four or five children; the eldest of whom, a boy, is a little scamp. The old Irish woman, dirty and incapable, looks after the home while Mrs Levy is out working. Levy is a gentle-natured man (a cigar-maker) earning little from the business of his trade. He and his wife have been lovers since they were children. Indeed according to Mrs Levy's account, their respective parents had to chastise them, because as mere children 'they would not leave one another alone'. Apparently the chastisement had not much effect, for at fifteen the young woman had to be married to her lover, for fear that the coming child should not be born in wedlock. Mrs Levy has had one child after another, losing about half of them. Levy treats his wife with courtesy, and is a fond but unwise parent. The joint earnings of the two come to about 30s a week.[57]

The Levy description is keenly drawn and bears the marks of a report written in retrospect (e.g. uncertainty of how many children they had). In writing this account Beatrice Potter had prior knowledge of the family, but the report is full of immediate personal observation and judgement: 'Their home is dirty and untidy and all the money is spent – but Mrs Levy says she must have plenty of food for her work is heavy. Levy is intelligent and glad to read books or newspapers. He has many friends of a respectable character and willingly talks on religion and social questions . . .'[58]

Through Levy, Beatrice Potter was introduced to a number of Jewish sweaters. Once again a thumb-nail sketch of the people and their home prefaces the account of their trade. Mrs Cohen, the 'small gentle Polish Jewess, with musical voice and pathetic accent', entertained her in a parlour which was 'untidy and without ornament or even sufficient furniture' in her 'damp and comfortless' house.[59] She 'bewailed the worry the employers had to bear. It is working from six o'clock in the morning to ten at night, and then worrying all the night'.[60] Similarly, when Beatrice was taken by Levy to meet Aarons it was noted that she was found 'at home in a well-furnished comfortable room' and was 'well-dressed and had the look of a good manager'. Her excellent dinner of 'meat and vegetables and a rolly polly pudding' clearly made Beatrice's mouth water. Only after this description did Beatrice report that Aarons had just left Cohen's employ because the work was too 'hard', sacrificing £2.8s.0d. a week. 'Gus', said Levy, 'had ruined his health by it' and was now seeking lighter work for much reduced pay (probably 25s a week) because 'handling iron' as a presser for Cohen 'of 14lbs for as many hours was too much for any man'.[61]

The Levys also provided another useful contact: Mrs Levy kept her

[57] Passfield, VII, I, 8.6.
[58] Passfield, VII, I, 8.6ff, Coll. Misc. 43, Katharine Buildings, passim; see Epstein Nord, *The Apprenticeship*, (London, 1985) pp. 144-47 for brief comment on this ledger.
[59] Passfield, VII, I, 8.7.
[60] Ibid.
[61] Passfield, VII, I, 8.8.

promise of 14 October and introduced Beatrice to her mother, Mrs Moses of
Oxford Street, Stepney, 'with a view to learning to be a plain hand'. After a
false start on 19/20 October, because there was no work, Mrs Moses, 'a fat,
cheerful Jewess' with 'low forehead, big jaw and greedy, good-natured eyes'
and her German Jewish husband, 'a rough, uncouth fellow' who 'looked as if
he had worked off the outer skin of mind and manners, constant sweating
reducing his patience with life to its lowest ebb', welcomed her on Monday
24 October into their workshop for four days. She commented at the end of
her stint as a plain trouserhand that when they parted it was as the best of
friends although their 'work must have been bad, for my sewing was too
good for the trade'.[62] Confusingly, she chose the name 'Moses' as the fake
name of her employer of April 1888 in her 'Pages from a Work-Girl's Diary'
but it was *not* the same employer.

The reports of the Potter interviews are reminiscent of many of those
later written up for the Religious Influences Survey.[63] Perhaps Booth
influenced Beatrice's reporting technique – we know that she on occasion
interviewed with Booth. On 26 November she went with Booth to interview
members of the Jewish branch of the Amalgamated Tailors.[64] We also know
that from the very early days Booth was convinced of the desirability of
making interviews conform to a pattern to ensure the ready transferability
of interviewers.[65]

Already in mid November Beatrice Potter was aware that she would not
obtain the necessary information for her essay from interviews alone. 'The
difficulty will be to get at statistical framework', she observed.[66]

She noted 'all the statistics we have to work on' on tailors in both East and
West Ends were:

	Men	Women
1871	111,843	38,021
1881	107,668	52,980
Difference	−4,175	+21,881

On 16 February 1888 she still did not feel that the deficiency had been
remedied: 'I have a good deal amount [sic] of loosely gathered material: CB
has a certain amount of statistical material – Remain to be done – a *complete*

---

[62] MS Diary, 19, 20, 24 October 1887, Passfield, VII, I, 8.11-16; MS Diary, 11-25 April 1888.
She worked as trouserhand again.
[63] See O'Day, 'Interviews and Investigations', p. 371ff.
[64] Passfield, VII, I, 8.53.
[65] Passfield, II i (II), 8, Charles Booth to Beatrice Potter, 10 September 1886.
[66] Passfield, VII, I, 8.22.

statistical basis; giving a proportionate statement of fact, an insight into the different forms of the tailoring so that I might give picturesque account.'[67]

Around this time she jotted down the 'Heads of Paper on East End Tailors',[68] which indicate the plan of the essay as it stood at that time. A reading of the printed essay will demonstrate that the plan was not adhered to. For example, the plan in February was to begin by criticising the whole concept of a 'sweating system' as too comprehensive and vague; the published version began with a seven-page discussion of the relationship between 'the new province of production' and the 'old-established native industry'.[69] The planned section on the Jewish community,[70] which did find a place in the version of this essay she published in the *Nineteenth Century*, was omitted in Booth's survey because she wrote a separate essay on the Jews. Great attention as planned was accorded the Jewish coat trade.[71] The February division of the coat trade into four types of workshop ('the best class of workshop doing bespoke work'; the 'large workshop doing slop and stock work'; 'the small men class'; and the 'lowest class grind for masters and grind for men workers') had by publication been converted into a more precise categorisation, complete with subdivisions, worked out in Booth's office, probably by Arkell.[72] Class C '(a class which unhappily forms 80 per cent of the East End Trade) – masters who, as Mr Burnett tells us, work as hard, if not harder, than their hands', dominates the text and she explains that it is here that 'we discover the most deplorable instances of noisome and overcrowded habitation'.[73] A complicated tabular presentation explains the subdivisions of the trade in this class and presents individual examples of workshops belonging to the higher grades.[74]

Her work was performed with the peculiar intensity characteristic of her. In part this was because of the pressure of time: it was an investigation which had to be fitted into. In part it was her holiday partly because of the background of personal misery. While more successful in many respects than the dock inquiry, the chapter on the tailoring trade of the East End is also a disappointment. She did not play to her strengths. In the event she shied away from a discussion of the concept of 'sweating'. There is little drawing up on the wonderful interview material she and Arkell collected; the 'picturesque' sections are grafted on to a colourless general argument. She signally failed to use observed detail to lend proportion to the scene she

---

[67] Passfield, VII, I, 8.53. Her spelling was dreadful.

[68] Passfield, VII, I, 8.60.

[69] *Poverty*, 4, p. 45.

[70] Passfield, VII, I, 8.60.

[71] *Poverty*, 4, p. 45-62.

[72] Booth Collection, A19, 'Tailoring', fos 2-6.

[73] *Poverty*, 4, p. 48.

[74] *Poverty*, 4, p. 50.

painted. The statistical infrastructure is more adequate than that of 'The Docks' but she does not appear comfortable with it.

9. *The Jewish Community: Beatrice Potter*

Beatrice Potter's work on the Jewish Community of the End End was undertaken as part of her investigation into East End tailoring. Initially it was not seen as a separate subject. When she published the article on tailoring in the *Nineteenth Century* it included a discussion of 'characteristics of the Jews'.[1] This was left out in the chapter when it appeared in Booth's survey and was replaced by an essay entitled 'The Jewish Community'.[2]

In consequence, much of the material upon which Potter drew for her study of the Jewish community was collected during the earlier inquiry on tailoring.[3] Here there is a wonderful description of a visit to a synagogue with Mrs Levy on 22 October 1887. She records that it was in a 'low quarter', 'with entrance as if into an ordinary house' and that they went 'upstairs into ladies gallery with trellis in fronts looking down into square hall with raised & draped platform in the midst'. Her precise description of the arrangement of the synagogue is interspersed with snapshots of its occupants: 'Scattered in these pews, low-class but apparently comfortably off Jews. Flung across their shoulders cashmere or silken scarfs. They were all sitting as if at ease, some in twos & three chatting in undertones, one now and again would offer his neighbours snuff . . . Presently a boy, with top hat & heavy gold watch-chain stepped up to the platform & taking his place at the reading desk, recited his confirmation with musical intonation.' Beatrice responded to the experience by comparing the service to a Christian service rather than by trying to understand it on its own terms. Admittedly Mrs Levy was little help. Unaccustomed to this approach to worship, Beatrice observed 'with the exception of an occasional burst of monotonous chanting from the congregation, there was little sign of attention, and to my mind, in the whole service there was no suspicion of devotional feeling. Even the boy, received into the church of his fathers, left the reading desk with an air of satisfied achievement – as if he had just passed the sixth standard.'

Perhaps even more marvellous for the historian are the recorded comments of Mrs Levy. It is a rare opportunity to hear a Jew, and a Jewish woman at that, of the time speak, albeit through a gentile intermediary. 'Mrs Levy explained that parents are proud if their son can show sufficient education to recite the Hebrew scripture and prayer to allow of his public

---

[1] *Poverty*, 4, p. 61.

[2] *Poverty*, 3.

[3] I.e., between October 1887 and April 1888.

recitation as a full-grown Jew.' Asides from Beatrice abound but do not diminish the value of the comments: 'Walking away, Mrs Levy, who seemed very ignorant of the meaning of the various acts of the service, explained that women were held of no account when they married. In the lowest-class synagogues, no places were provided for them. Their only religious duty in the way of attending services after their confinements'; 'The poor foreign Jews, male & female, seldom went to synagogue, tho' they were scrupulous to the law of Moses as regards the sabbath etc.' Mrs Levy herself 'thought it a mockery to go to synagogue, when she intended to break the law the following none [sic] by lighting her fire and cooking her dinner'. Accordingly, Beatrice notes, 'After we had watched Mrs Levy prepare the chickens for the Sabbath dinner, we walked to Rupert Street . . . '[4]

In the early encounters with Jewish tailors and their families, Beatrice showed herself acutely conscious of their housing standards and eating habits.[5] This applied to sweaters and workers alike. The Levys had a dirty and incapable Irish woman to look after the children while she worked, had a dirty and untidy home but ate well and had a caring if indulgent home life.[6] The description from the MS Diary in October 1887 of her training as a trouserhand with the Moses family of Oxford Street, Stepney emphasised detail about their housing: 'Four rooms and a kitchen, 12s., one room let, 3s . . . A small back yard. Three rooms on ground floor, two used as workshop . . . '[7] There was scant and inadequate furnishing 'for out of work days' and 'Mrs Moses dress was of the dirtiest and most dishevilled'.[8] Later she was to observe of Samuel Montague M.P. and his wife: 'They live in a luxurious but gloomy Kensington Palace Gardens mansion & are blessed with ten children – the ugliest & most depressed looking family I have ever set eyes upon.'[9] Her keen eye for detail was apparent.

In the early months of the tailoring inquiry Beatrice also became interested in what she was later to call the 'Jewish passion for gambling'. A trip to the club of the Jewish branch of the Amalgamated Tailors told her little about tailoring. 'Much more interesting was the conversation on gambling clubs which seem to be the great institution of East End life. Sometimes these are registered as workmen's clubs, but more frequently they are rooms rented in Eating Houses.' Zeitlin told her of one presser who saved £22 in nine years and lost it in one night at such a club. 'I asked what did these men do with the money when they had got rich.' 'Gamble it on races and on the stock exchange where they are devoured by larger parasites, suggested Charlie Booth', to which the rest agreed. Zeitlin suggested that the clubs

---

[4] Passfield, VII, I, 8.5-7.
[5] See above p. 73.
[6] Passfield, VII, I, 8.5-8.
[7] MS Diary, October 1887; *My Apprenticeship*, pp. 316-17.
[8] *My Apprenticeship*, p. 317.
[9] MS Diary, *circa* December 1887.

should be closed by the police but went on 'of course that's impossible because the police gamble themselves, or if they don't, they take money from the eating-house keeper'.[10] This information on the Jewish gambling clubs augmented that supplied by an interview with 'W.de Yonge plausible little Jew'.[11]

At this time she was proposing that her paper on East End Tailors would include a 'General picture of Jewish life in the East End'. She noted that the coat trade was 'in the hands of the Jews' and intended to compare the lives and prosperity of the Jews with the plight of the Christian population. 'They form a community', she observed. Also important were the *chevras* (foreign Jews congregated in synagogue-based confraternities), public opinion, the Jewish Board of Guardians and parental government. Her comment on the plan was telling: 'This must be the striking and graphic part of my article.'[12]

A note of her timetable for the last week of November and the first fortnight of December 1888 bears witness to a flurry of activity on this front. The Diary indicates that she had recently resumed work after a longish gap (roughly March-November 1888) when she reports 'a long morning at the British Museum reading up *Jewish Chronicles* and such like' on 19 November. On 28 November she is 'Hard at work at the "Jewish Community", seeing Jews of all classes, all day long'.[13] Meetings with Booth, Arkell, Ernest Aves, Stephen Fox, Llewellyn Smith and Clara Collet jostle for position with those with the Adler brothers and Blank and trips to Petticoat Lane and the Jewish Working Men's Club.[14] The meetings with Booth's other associates were, we think, significant. They indicate on the one hand the importance to her of being part of a larger concern with its wealth of expertise. The people she called upon were significant too. Fox was eventually to work on the tobacco trade, known as a Jewish trade; Llewellyn Smith was currently working on immigration into the metropolis for the Booth survey; Ernest Aves, a Toynbee man, had an intimate knowledge of the East End and of so-called 'Jewish trades', furniture making and boot making; and Clara Collet, of course, was to write the chapter on women's work for the survey. On 16 December Potter observed of Llewellyn Smith: 'He is formal minded – but has ability – and is generous in his helpfulness to others working on the same line.'[15] Notes on the interviews mentioned in this list do survive, and are most informative although totally unstructured.[16]

Already she was alerted to in the importance of the Jewish Board of

[10] Passfield, VII, I, 8.53-54.
[11] Passfield, VII, I, 8.43.
[12] Passfield, VII, I, 8.61-2.
[13] Passfield, MS Diary, 28 November 1888.
[14] Passfield, MS Diary, not in the typescript as far as can be ascertained.
[15] Passfield, MS Diary, 16 December 1888.
[16] Passfield, MS Diary, xii, p. 170.

Guardians.[17] She had interviewed David Schloss in October 1887. In late November 1888 she was making detailed notes on an article in the *Spectator* of April 1887.[18] In November she was recording detailed notes on the reports of the Board of Guardians in her Diary and in her note book of the investigation.[19] She noted, for example, the total number of apprenticeships sponsored by the Board in various trades – boot and shoe, tailoring, cigar, glazing, general dealing, hawking – in 1872[20] and 1878[21] – and the loans of implements for these trades arranged in 1875.[22] She observed that by 1881 the loans of sewing machines had fallen off but only because of 'commercial firms adopting the idea'.[23] A long extract from the report for 1884 pin-pointed the special problems which the influx of foreign Jews posed for the Board.[24] In 1885 she noted the continuing influx from Germany, Poland and Russia, the existence of the temporary shelter for immigrants in Leman Street,[25] and the precise way in which relief was distributed by the Board of Guardians. These notes justify the assessment that Potter was inordinately influenced in her sketch of the Jewish community by the viewpoint of Anglo-Jewry.[26]

She built upon this statistical information and comment by searching the records of parliamentary commissions and statutes,[27] and by acquainting herself with the Jewish calendar and its major feasts.[28] She seems to have interviewed the head of the temporary shelter on Leman Street and to have heard that there was 'no class feeling among Jewesses; this a disadvantage as there is not so much respect' and that prostitution among Jewesses was becoming a problem.[29] Adler, the Chief Rabbi's brother, gave her miscellaneous information about the customs of the Polish Jews from which she took tantalisingly brief notes: 'Wigs of Jewesses'; 'Cabalistic signs'; 'Wise women among the Polish Jews'; 'All the bones of the body shall declare it'; 'Respect of Jews for their religion tho' they do not observe it'.[30] And a visit to the Jewish Working Men's Club on Berner Street yielded a little information about the 'lower grade of foreign Jews who have neither the means nor the

---

[17] Passfield, VII, I, 8.62.
[18] Passfield, MS Diary, xii, p. 167-69.
[19] Passfield, MS Diary, xii, p. 160-62 and Passfield, VII, I, 8.62.
[20] Passfield, MS Diary, xii, p. 160.
[21] Passfield, MS Diary, xii, p. 161.
[22] Passfield, MS Diary, xii, p.160.
[23] Passfield, MS Diary, xii, p. 161.
[24] Passfield, MS Diary, xii, p. 162.
[25] Passfield, MS Diary, xii, p. 163.
[26] See David Englander, 'Booth's Jews', *Victorian Studies*, xxxii (1989), pp. 560-61 and passim.
[27] Passfield, MS Diary, xii, p. 169, 170.
[28] Passfield, MS Diary, xii, p. 171.
[29] Passfield, MS Diary, xii, p. 172.
[30] Passfield, MS Diary, xii, p. 175.

education to belong even to the small *chevras*' and who benefit from the free meals offered.[31]

Her interview with Joseph Blank, who was then a new employee at the *Jewish Chronicle*, provides one instance where she encountered the views of the son of poor immigrant Polish Jews who had made good. He told her about the condition of Jews in Poland where they 'live in far worse condition (acc to Blank) than they do in England'. 'When they come to England the Jews belonging to one city will form themselves in *chevras*: the base of a common religion – a common home', he informed her. 'They save enough money to rent a house,' he went on, 'take down the partition of the rooms, a strip light, a balcony (generally built like a workshop in the back yard), a grating with muslin curtains; horribly close and smelly . . . overcrowded.' They, he continued, 'choose and employ a minister for between £60 and £150 . . . [he] makes up the money by giving scripture lessons'.[32] There were forty to fifty *chevras*. Blank went on to discuss the role of the *chevras* as benefit societies and the attitude of Jews to worship within them: 'during services they will discuss business'; 'the Jewish religion a perpetual History lesson'. This was *all news* to her. Talking to him certainly set Beatrice thinking: 'Reading the Talmud', she noted down and, in parenthesis, 'What is Talmud?' With a relieved sense of being on more familiar ground she characteristically seized upon Blank's observations about Jewish appearance. The 'mean' appearance of the immigrant Jews gives place to the 'florid robustness of English Jews'.[33]

The Christian response to the Jewish community thereabouts was also explored. Beatrice already knew what English workers thought of Jews in their trades;[34] now she turned to the headmistress of an infant school in a Jewish neighbourhood who thought 'Jewish children much more alive than Christian children: quick witted – vitality . . .'[35] Jews shunned domestic service she was told, 'derivative of absence of class feeling'. An enquiry agent told her that Polish Jews were worse off in England than at home but were now 'free'.[36] She found much more material on her visit to the Revd Barraclough, Chaplain to the London Society for promoting Christianity amongst the Jews. She noted down the basis of the society's work and gave her views of the small group of children studying there – 'about half are the children of gentile women and Jew husbands. They look badly taught and

---

[31] Passfield, MS Diary, xii, p. 177.

[32] Passfield, MS Diary, xii, p. 174.

[33] Passfield, MS Diary, xii, p. 174. See also interview with the Chief Rabbi's brother, Adler, on p 175 for the emphasis and with Samuel Montague, M.P., pp. 182-83, for opinion on 'sharp intelligence' of the Jews 'trained for generations on the Talmud'.

[34] She may also have had access to the interviews of furniture-makers, see Booth Collection, A6 and A7 for this.

[35] Passfield, MS Diary, xii, p. 176.

[36] Passfield, MS Diary, xii, p. 176.

dull' – and the young men working there who 'have a hangdog appearance as if they were heartily ashamed of themselves'.[37] 'The impression of the chaplain is that all Jews are agnostic and all deceitful but he allows that they are a "moral people".'[38] She picked up from him the information that the men there were chiefly those who had once been Talmudic students in Poland, supported by charity and who once they came to England continued to study, as Christians, still supported by charity. They 'frequently became missionaries and clergymen. 200 Hebrew Christian clergymen out of 2000 Hebrew Christians'.[39] Beatrice was permitted to inspect their report. Her work here was continued at the Operative Jewish Converts' Institution.[40]

The meeting with Llewellyn Smith noted in her memorandum for Sunday 16 December 1888 was that famous 'Fiasco' when she and Llewellyn Smith, 'a Toynbee man and fellow statistician under the guidance of an official of the Jewish Board of Guardians', and agent of the Ladies Protective went down to see the arrival of immigrant Jews and consoled themselves when none came 'with "shop" over indifferent coffee and buns' at the refreshment room of Fenchurch Street Station. The more successful sequel to this meeting produced the well-known description in the book.[41]

The timing seems important. The published text owes much to the material which Potter collected in the last six weeks of her inquiry into the Jewish community – the only time when she was exclusively concerned with Jews themselves rather than their occupations. Perhaps the description of the Jewish immigrants' arrival owes what immediacy it has to the fact that it had been experienced a month or so previously – it was reporting rather than research. On 8 January she was 'Hard at work at the paper on the J[ewish] C[ommunity] and more than half through with it.' and on 23 January she confidently confided to her diary 'my paper not quite finished but in a hopeful condition. Think it will more than satisfy C. Booth and will prove one of the "attractions" of the book'.[42] On 11 February her triumphant entry reads: 'Finished and sent it off to be copied: it has taken me longer than the other two: I trust it is better(?)'

Thus ended an era for Beatrice Potter. Her close association with the Booths was at an end. Already in November she had been aware that 'C. Booth has no more work for me to do' and was looking towards working on her original idea – 'the actual nature of Economic Science'.[43] A study of co-operation 'under Benjamin Jones' was projected in December.[44] Her amic-

[37] Passfield, MS Diary, xii, p. 178.
[38] Passfield, MS Diary, xii, p. 179.
[39] Passfield, MS Diary, xii, p. 179.
[40] Passfield, MS Diary, xii, p. 180.
[41] See, *Poverty*, 3, pp. 182-85.
[42] Passfield, MS Diary, 8 January 1889, 23 January 1889.
[43] Passfield, MS Diary, 28 November 1888.
[44] Passfield, MS Diary, December.

able relations with the Booths, husband and wife, ended. She had broken with her dear friend and cousin Maggie Harkness over a silly argument. Now she looked briefly to the Creightons and to Professor Alfred Marshall for intellectual direction and stimulation, although Toynbee Hall still had its attractions.

In later years Beatrice Potter rendered a triumphal account of her time with Charles Booth's Inquiry as her 'apprenticeship', the years in which she received training in her chosen craft. Close examination of the existing archive, which has involved piecing together tiny fragments of information and sorting out the sometimes distorted account of her activities during the years 1886-89, indicates that Beatrice Potter certainly threw herself into the work with great intensity for limited periods (perhaps a total of eight months were spent on investigation for five essays during the three and a quarter years covered here), familiarised herself with both printed primary sources and sources of information available to the personal investigator, and had the opportunity to observe and draw upon the expertise practised by Booth and many of his earlier associates (largely drawn from Toynbee Hall). There can be no doubt that she was very intelligent, very eclectic and very willing to be 'an apprentice' despite her decidedly unhumble personality. Nevertheless, she was untutored and she remained untutored. She was uncomfortable with the sorts of material Booth, Arkell and Smith made available to her. She remained unable to organise her interviews to produce a systematic run of material, despite the excellent example provided her. She did not know what precisely she should do with the wonderful interview materials she collected. Where statistics were used, they were provided by others and analysed by others. She displayed at best hesitancy in manipulating them. Fundamentally she was dissatisfied with her efforts. It was essentially an apprenticeship which had left her, talented as she undoubtedly was, relatively unskilled at the craft she had chosen. While it is true that she sometimes made valuable points in her early work, there is a sense of profound loss when one reads the archive.[45] This is accentuated when one reads the study of women's work produced by Clara Collet. Even in Beatrice Potter's last and best essay for Booth, 'The Jewish Community', we have to laud her enterprise in seeking to open up the unopened to an English public and the richness of her sources (evidence of which survives) rather than her success in describing the community and detailing the dovetailing of secular and religious life within it. Nonetheless this was a much happier exercise in description that either 'The Docks' or 'The Tailoring Trade'.[46]

---

[45] See José Harris, *Beatrice Webb; The Ambivalent Feminist* (London School of Economics lecture, 1984), pp. 14-15 for an undocumented but opposing view.
[46] For a further treatment of Potter's apprenticeship see, Rosemary O'Day, 'Before the Webbs: Beatrice Potter's Early Investigations for Charles Booth's Inquiry', *History*, lxxviii, 1993.

10. Women's Work: Clara Collet and George Arkell

A chapter on women's work had long been on Charles Booth's agenda for his survey. There was a good deal of interest in the subject at the time. The work for it, however, was hampered on many counts. Not least, woman-power. In 1887 Alice Green, the widow of J.R. Green, was undertaking the investigation of 'women's work and wages' but it was 'rather at a stand'.[1] By early November 1888 Mrs Green had left the work and Booth suggested to Beatrice that she undertake the investigation and complete the essay by the following March.[2] As Beatrice was just getting into her stride again with the study of the Jewish Community (which was not complete until February) it is perhaps unsurprising that she did not take up the challenge. Since Clara Collet's name is actively associated with the study of women's work later in the same month, it would seem reasonable to suppose that she joined Booth's team during November 1888.[3] Perhaps she had met Booth through the Toynbee Hall conference on women's work and wages in the November of 1887 or through her membership since 1886 of the Council of the Charity Organisation Society. It is conceivable that Potter herself made the introduction through a mutual friend, Eleanor Marx.

Clara Collet's work for Booth's inquiry has, perhaps understandably, been eclipsed by the attention given to Beatrice Potter's contribution. Potter was altogether a showier figure and adept at self-advertisement. Her later eminence has made her apprenticeship famous. Her flair, however, was not for solid research and analysis, whereas Clara Collet's certainly was. Collet as an investigator, if nothing else, was more than a match for Beatrice Potter.

Clara Elizabeth Collet was born in 1860 the second daughter and fourth of the five children of Collet Dobson Collet and his wife Jane. Her father was editor of the *Diplomatic Review*. Her mother ran a small laundry in North London. The family was Unitarian. She was educated at the London Collegiate School (1873-78) under Miss Buss. Her first position was at Miss Buss's recommendation as Assistant Mistress at the newly founded Wyggeston Girls' School, Leicester (1879-85), at an initial salary of £80. At Wyggeston she was coached by masters from the boys' grammar school in Greek and applied mathematics and had to manage Latin and English 'by myself'. In 1880 she graduated with a B.A. degree from University College, London.

---

[1] Passfield, II i (II), 6 Mary Booth to Beatrice Potter, 1887; Passfield, II i (II), Margaret Harkness to Potter, Christmas 1887; Harkness complained that Booth had not employed her to do this work, 'I know more than his lady sec . . . .'

[2] Passfield, MS Diary, 3 November 1888.

[3] Passfield, MS Diary, November 1888.

As such she was one of the first women graduates of the University of London. In October 1885 Clara took up residence at College Hall, Gordon Square to study at University College and take an M.A. degree in Moral and Political Philosophy (which included psychology and economics). She also took a Teacher's Diploma. She (jointly with Henry Higgs, although by her account they had never spoken until 1890) was awarded the Joseph Hume Scholarship in Political Economy in 1886. She took the M.A. in 1887.[4]

Sometime in late 1888 Miss Collet (as she was habitually if incorrectly known) entered Booth's employ and stayed with him until at least late 1890. Among her first tasks was taking over the study of women's work in the East End from Mrs Green. She was also involved in work for Graham Balfour's Battersea Street Inquiry. Several of the Battersea notebooks were apparently written by her and, notably, one contained special comments on women.[5] This finished, in 1890 she undertook a study of the Ashby-de-la-Zouche workhouse for Booth's work on Poor Law Unions and began work on elementary scholars in higher schools. This was a period of uncertainty in Clara's life – of drifting, depression and sometimes despair. She worked for Booth to keep body and soul together, using what skills she had acquired, but with a lack of total commitment. In May 1890 she wrote, 'This investigating work has many drawbacks . . . I would give it up and will give it up whenever I see a chance of earning a certain £60 even by lectures on economics. Not that I do not like the work when it is done or that I do not feel a kind of enjoyment in the risk often involved in facing unknown people, but although I enjoy the personal contact with so many people I should never see otherwise, the work leaves no roots behind.'[6] This was a temporary slough of despond. 'All she did was done with zest.'[7] The Clara Collet fondly recalled in 1948 was of a lively disposition. She had a penchant for 'amusing, and sometimes surprising, anecdotes, racily told', a 'brilliant mind' which was 'extremely critical', 'a charming personality' and 'a keen sense of humour'. Her great-niece's childhood memory of her as 'a small, neat and formidable person, with an immense double chin and chilly ways' does not seem to relate to the person revealed by the diaries and the inquiry.[8]

Her investigating work for Booth was interspersed with casual lecturing at Toynbee Hall (when she stood in for Higgs), with coaching girls and other short-term jobs. Her prospects were uncertain: 'What I am going to live on

[4] Collet MS; the *Economic Journal*, December (1940), pp. 558-61 reprints items in Collet's diary about Higgs and Higgs' letters to Foxwell in 1890, which were in the possession of Clara Collet.

[5] Booth Collection, B58, B60, B64.

[6] Collet MS, 29/8/1/53, Clara Collet's Diary, p. 106.

[7] 'Two obituaries of Clara Elizabeth Collet, 1860-1948', *Journal of the Royal Statistical Society*, series A, cxi, (1948), pp. 252- 54.

[8] Jane Miller, *Seductions* (London, 1990), p. 70.

next year I don't in the least know.'[9] In the summer of 1890, however, on her initiative the Junior Economic Club was founded.[10]

Throughout her life she was interested in the position of working women. She was a Fellow of University College, London, a Governor of Bedford College, London and a Member of College Hall, London. She wrote and published articles and official reports on the economic position of women. Her publications included: (for Booth's Inquiry) 'Secondary Education; Girls'; 'West End Tailoring (Women)'; 'Women's Work' (and later) 'Report on the Money Wages of Indoor Domestic Servants' (1899); *The Economic Position of Educated Working Women* (1902); *Women in Industry* (1911); *Changes in Wages and Conditions of Domestic Servants in Private Families and Institutions in the County of London* [by C.E. Collet and Daphne Sanger, October 1930] and *The History of the Collet Family* (1935).

Despite her own dissatisfaction with the work she undertook between 1888 and 1892, with hindsight it might be alleged that during these years she acquired the skills and the personal connections which allowed her to make a successful career. Her friendship with members of the Booth team survived. She kept in touch with Hubert Llewellyn Smith, for instance, and was in fact responsible for providing him with the data for the study of domestic service in the *New Survey of London Life and Labour* (1931).[11] She was one of those who attended Booth's celebratory dinner at the Savoy in 1904. In her later studies of women's work she used Booth's work for the comparative purposes. As her 'Recollections', showed, she held Charles Booth and his work in lasting high regard.

In 1924 she lectured in India on Joseph Collet, a former Governor of Madras, and in 1935 she published, in association with H.H. Collet, *The History of the Collet Family*. Her friendship with the novelist George Gissing has become famous, less so her friendship with the Cornish economist, Henry Higgs, her attempt at a novel or her interesting approach to the social novels.[12] She died at Sidmouth in 1948.

In the absence of further documentation it seems improbable that we shall ever be able to say much more about the organisation of the women's work inquiry than is evident from Arkell's notes, Collet's printed text and

[9] Collet MS, 29/8/1/55, Clara Collet's Diary, p. 110.

[10] See above, pp. 12-13; 1891: President of the Association of Assistant Mistresses in Public Secondary Schools, 1891: One of the four Assistant Commissioners who reported on women's Home Work to the Royal Commission on Labour, 1894: Elected Fellow of the Royal Statistical Society, 1893-1903; Labour Correspondent in the Board of Trade, 1903-17: Senior Investigator at the Labour Department of the Board of Trade to replace David Schloss (see pp. 16–17), 1917-20, Incorporated into Ministry of Labour Retired 1920; 1921-32: Member of various Trade Boards, 1919-35: Member of the Council of Royal Statistical Society, 1920-41: Member of the Council of Royal Economic Society.

[11] *New Survey of London Life and Labour*, 9 vols. (London, 1931- 35), ii, p. vii.

[12] Collet MS, 29/3/13/5/1-7; MS, 29/3/13/4; Miller, *Seductions*, 1990.

the Royal Commission on Labour's minutes of evidence. Collet was scrupulous in her attribution of assistance. Lakeman the Factory Inspector was no
doubt placated by her fulsome flattery. She duly thanked the Secretary of
London Bible and Domestic Female Mission, and managers of Homes for
Girls (perhaps, for example, Hoston Hall), superintentents of clubs and
evening classes, and large numbers of the girls themselves. 'I am most
indebted to Mr Geo. E. Arkell, from whose notes a brief abstract has been
made with regard to the women making trousers, vests and juvenile suits,
and who collected nearly all the facts about the fur trade.'[13] Given our
knowledge of the investigations undertaken by Potter, Schloss, Arkell and
Argyle, there seems no reason to doubt that Collet's total inquiry was
thorough and based upon extensive interviewing and observation as well as
official statistics.

Booth's own account of the method and order of Collet's inquiry is extant.
Mundella quizzed Booth before the Royal Commission on Labour in 1892
about the matter in which the statistics about women's work were collected.
Booth said that he had taken the detailed sheets of the 1881 census as the
general basis. The Factory Department of the Home Office and the Factory
Inspectors provided a list of all the workshops and factories known by them
to employ women. Booth continued, 'I arranged these in a sort of directory
according to the trades and localities of the trades'.[14] Lakeman, who had in
about 1887 produced a Home Office report on women's work, had, said
Booth, proved very co-operative. The Factory Girls' Helpers Union and
other similar missionary bodies were approached so that they could 'obtain
introductions to the girls, to find a road, so that we might become
acquainted with them'. To this end 'Miss Collet took up her residence in the
East End and lived there for three months', during which time 'she was
continually engaged in trying to come in contact with the girls, and those
who were working amongst them'. Where factory girls were concerned she
would 'invite them to her house'. 'She found it very difficult to get information that was satisfactory' but, he thought, she did eventually succeed. Home
workers were more elusive and so the researcher went to the clergy for
introductions to home workers 'who might be expected with those introductions [to be allowed to see] . . . home workers in their homes'. The next step
was to send a circular letter to the employers of women seeking interviews.
Those who consented were visited by Miss Collet: 'We did not try any
detective work, or to go into a factory where we were not welcomed'; 'Many
of the employers were very frank and showed her their wages books'. Booth
added further detail on the manner of working:

She made full notes as she went long. At first I was sharing in the work, as long as

---

[13] *Poverty*, 4, p. 257.
[14] See below for Arkell's role in this work.

it was confined to interviews with the factory inspectors, and so on; and after-
wards Miss Collet went on alone, and wrote down almost everything that
happened in full, and those notes I read as they were written. she then wrote her
own chapter – it is entirely her writing. I simply revised what she had written to
see that it contained everything that seemed to be trustworthy.[15]

Arkell again did much of the ground work. It was he who compiled the
lengthy and detailed list of places of women's work mentioned in Booth's
evidence: individual furriers, artificial flower makers, box makers, match
makers, tie and cravat makers, brush makers, toy makers, makers of
feather-beds, sewers of corsets and stays, confectioners, umbrella makers,
milliners, hatters and cappers, shirt makers and seamstresses and so on.[16]
His listing of East End furriers provided a certain amount of basic detail –
name, address, grade, branch of the trade, number employed in and out of
the work place, ages, wages and general remarks. Next to each is a date –
probably the date on which a letter was sent out to or received from the firm
in question.[17] Against some of the firms listed is an asterisk. This may or may
not indicate that the firm was visited – this would suggest twenty-seven
interviews amongst seventy-seven furriers and eleven interviews among
twenty-nine artificial flower makers, for instance. They allow us to be quite
certain that most of the preliminary work for the survey was done in the
winter of 1888/9 as Booth claimed. Collet, on her own testimony, moved
from this subject to Booth's inquiry into Ashby-de-la-Zouche Workhouse in
1890.[18]

Booth's office also provided a comment on the 1881 census returns giving
the occupations of employed female adults in East London and Hackney.
These may have been annotated by David Schloss.[19] Arkell's work on the
tailoring trade including detailed manuscript reports, were also drawn
upon.[20]

The surviving interview materials for the study will repay further investigation. By this time George Arkell was a seasoned interviewer. His reports
of the fur trade interviews are detailed, perceptive and systematic. Each
begins with the personal details of the interviewee and a note of the
circumstances of the interview. For example, when Arkell called on Mr
Posner of Posner & Gluckstein, 3 Butler Street, Moor Lane, E.C. it was 'by
appointment'. Arkell 'had seen Mr Posner before having had introductions

---

[15] *Royal Commission on Labour Minutes of Evidence*, Group C [C. 6708-VI] PP. 1892 (xxxv), qq
8,909-61.
[16] Booth Collection, A2, fos. 1-75.
[17] See Booth Collection, A2, fo. 17 which lists Abrahams of Great Prescot Street and dates the
entry 4.1.89; the interview, reported on fo. 89, is dated 17.1.89.
[18] Collet, MS 29/8/1/55, Clara Collet's Diary, p. 110.
[19] Booth Collection, A2, 'Women's Work', fos. 114-20.
[20] Booth Collection, A19.

from Mr Ansell and Mr G. Williams of Leaf & Sons & Co. and he had promised to give an account of the trade'.[21] Mr Gluckstein was also present. When he visited Mr Gluckstein of 103 Sheperdess Walk it was on an introduction from Mr Ansell but 'he was evidently disinclined to enter into details respecting the trade and would not give any figures'.[22] Similarly, despite an introduction from Mr Ansell (probably in the form of a letter), Arkell 'found Mr A[brahams] very suspicious' although he was slightly reassured after 'a few minutes talk on election matters'.[23]

In most of these interviews a brief physical description of the interviewee(s) is also included. So we read, 'Mr Posner acted as chief spokesman, Mr Gluckstein listening and expressing his opinion on the various points as they arose occasionally confirming but oftener questioning his partner's statement'. 'They are both', said Arkell, 'young men under thirty, of medium height. Mr P. belonged to the fair type of Jew, his partner however was darker and sharper featured.'[24]

In part Arkell's brief seems to have been to describe the processes of the fur trade. His visit to Posner & Gluckstein produced details of the various workers required. 'A Furrier's workshop must have the following workers', he explained 'cutters (men: there are a few women cutters but only for the light work trimmings etc), nailers (lads) and sewers (women) sometimes in the East End you may see men – greeners – doing this work). Sewers are usually paid by piecework . . .'[25] Work practices as well as pay and conditions were his concern. Mr King of Aldersgate Street informed him on 16 January 1889 that 'When a new class of work was given out the forewoman, who was usually a medium-paced worker, would make the first article. If it took her 15 hours to do, the price would be fixed at 2s.6d. Thus the quick workers earn more than 2d. an hour, while the slow or inexperienced worker would not exceed 1d. or 2d. per hour'.[26]

The interview reports provide a veritable smorgasbord for those interested in the workforce, whether from the employers' or the workers' perspective. Even when ostensibly interviewing employers (as in the surviving interviews), Arkell relied heavily on personal observation and upon contact with the workers themselves. He made Clara Collet aware of the origins of his assessments. At Posner & Gluckstein, 'I asked to see the workshop' and 'there were two cutters (men) working at a bench under the window, this bench extending right over the room. Close to the cutters were

[21] Booth Collection, A2, 'Fur Trade', fo. 76; Ansell was a tailor engaged in second class bespoke work whom Arkell had interviewed for the tailoring trade inquiry on 7 February 1888, see A19, 'Tailoring Trade', fo. 58.
[22] Booth Collection, A2, 'Fur Trade', fo. 84.
[23] Booth Collection, A2, 'Fur Trade', fo. 89.
[24] Booth Collection, A2, 'Fur Trade', fo. 76-7.
[25] Booth Collection, A2, 'Fur Trade', fos. 79-80.
[26] Booth Collection, A2, 'Fur Trade', fo. 85.

three women sewing. They were seated at a low table and did not appear to be working very hard. They were all mature aged women, the youngest would probably be thirty and the eldest forty' and a youth nailing a cape into shape.[27] Arkell painted vividly the scene which met his eyes and ears at the workshop of Hyams the chamber-master of Mount Street on 4 February 1889: 'There was one cutter at work when I went up, who as I entered the room was shouting the words of a song at the top of his voice but stopped abruptly amid the laughter of three sewers when he became conscious of my presence. The sewers (two Gentiles and one Jewess) were sitting on low seats before supported on trestles on which their work was placed.' 'The women', he commented, 'seemed happy enough. The Jewess was the youngest and best looking and judging by her dress and appearance was in better circumstances than her Christian fellow workwoman. The two other women were over forty, poorly dressed; one looked like a labourer's wife and the other was a widow.'[28] Arkell was observant of the appearance of the women but was careful to indicate when what he observed was unusual rather than typical: 'She was a girl about twenty, slim and respectably dressed, looked like a city work-girl and totally unlike many of the women I have seen doing the fur sewing.'[29]

Sometimes he took the opportunity to converse with and question the workforce. Thus, when he visited the lofty but dirty lean-to workshop of Mr Solomon, Plumber's Row, he 'waited and asked some questions of a woman in the shop. There were two women, both Jewesses, one a stout elderly woman and the other a girl. The former was boiling a pot on the coke fire while the girl was sewing some dark rabbit capes.' From them he learned the prices fetched for fur boas. They discussed the girls' labour and the elderly woman here chimed in and said that she used to be able to earn 15s. a week but now she could not earn more than 7s. '(The cutter informed me that she was a slow worker at this point.) After the season was over the sewers had to put up with only 3s. or 4s. a week. Another drawback, they said, was that the sewers had to purchase their own cotton.'[30]

The employers themselves were drawn as to the nature of the workforce. The interviewee was encouraged to talk quite freely on the general topic and Arkell summarised their comments on a range of issues. Mr Haking of Messrs Jacob & Son, Jewin Crescent, who in the season employed as many as seventy sewers and chamber masters, was helpful. His knowledge of his workforce was, however, at best mixed, which might in part be explained by the reliance of the fur trade on formal and informal sub-contracting

[27] Booth Collection, A2, 'Fur Trade', fo. 83.
[28] Booth Collection, A2, 'Fur Trade', fo. 98; See Englander, 'Booth's Jews', for Booth's presentation of the East End Jews in the printed work and the archive.
[29] Booth Collection, A2, 'Fur Trade', fo. 100.
[30] Booth Collection, A2, 'Fur Trade', fos. 103-4.

practices. As he observed: 'Every cutter had his own sewers, who made up the material cut.' He 'found the Jewish workpeople were the best; if they had the work, he could depend on getting it to time. His working girls were all Gentiles, women of twenty and upwards, some quite elderly women. He thought most of them were married but did not know.'[31] The details of their habitation were equally unknown to the employer: 'As to the fur sewers, the women employed on the premises lived in St Luke's, Walworth, and a large number in Bermondsey. (Mr H. did not know this, but called a man who supplied the information). None came from the East End; the girls in that district would probably work there.'[32] Neither did he 'know what the sewers did in the slack season, thought they waited at home until the work revived' but he did know that 'when he told a cutter there was some work for him the morning, he would go out and get his girls together in an hour or so. The girls employed one season usually came back the following year'.[33] He was willing enough to hazard that 'he did not think the workers were (any of them) of a class that worked only for clothes or pocket money. They needed their earnings'. As far as he could see only immorality could explain the better circumstances of the occasional employee: 'One girl he had noticed dressed much better than the others: she always had a good mantle', but her weekly earnings could not support this.[34] Immorality among the sewers was emphasised by Mr Wiring, a cutter who had recently become a small master who, when commenting on the difficulties involved in making a living wage during the slack season, alleged, 'Many of them are obliged to adopt an immoral life'.[35]

Some of those he interviewed tried to explain the balance between Jews and Gentiles among the sewers. Mr Monk Junior of 45 Union Street claimed, 'The fur sewers were nearly all Gentiles, all his (Mr M. Junr) were. The Jewesses did not care about the work; they could earn more money button holing. The Jewesses who were in the trade would be those who had no home nor parents or friends to keep them while they were learning a trade; they were obliged to take to the fur sewing as by it they could earn a little money at once.'[36] When Jewesses did want the work they were sometimes not very popular employees because they insisted on the Sabbath off.[37] Mr Wiring of Pedley Street, Bethnal Green averred that the ethnic nature of the workforce depended on the region for 'in Whitechapel the

---

[31] Booth Collection, A2, 'Fur Trade', fo. 91.
[32] Booth Collection, A2, 'Fur Trade', fo. 90.
[33] Booth Collection, A2, 'Fur Trade', fo. 91.
[34] Booth Collection, A2, 'Fur Trade', fo. 91.
[35] Booth Collection, A2, 'Fur Trade', fos. 109, 112.
[36] Booth Collection, A2, 'Fur Trade', fo. 100; see also fo. 90 for further comment on the lack of skill necessary for fur sewing.
[37] Booth Collection, A2, 'Fur Trade', fo. 97.

Jewesses preponderate, in Bethnal Green the Gentiles'.[38] He offered an explanation for choosing this trade which was not specific to either Jews or Christians. 'Some of the girls', he said, 'take to this trade because they cannot do any other. If a girl is near sighted, she cannot go to the tailoring.' Thus his own wife had given up button-holing in favour of fur sewing. Moreover 'a girl that cannot afford to be apprenticed would go to the trade as she could earn something at once. The trade used to be good and then girls went into it. And now they are obliged to stay in it because they could do nothing else. Mr W. would leave the trade but could not give the time to learn anything else'.[39]

Some volunteered opinions on the potential impact of the introduction of machinery. Mr Monk 'thought it would be a very good thing when the machines entirely superseded the sewer. It would be better for the girls as they could go and have a good dinner when they earned 14s. a week, not have to cook an herring in the workshop as they did now.'[40] Mr Benjamin of Wood Street, Spitalfields thought it would be excellent from his point of view to do as his father-in-law had already done and introduce machines because 'he employed one machinist and a number of learners and when these learners could use the machines properly he discharged the good hand and got another learner. By this means his father-in-law got his work done cheap but for himself he 'could not afford to do this'.

The reports were Arkell's way of communicating with Collet and he was painstaking in making clear the distinction between the materials supplied by his sources and his own opinions and observations. He offered some assessment of his sources.[41] Occasionally, also, he noted down intellectual points which he deemed worthy of further consideration. When he visited Jacobs & Son of Jewin Crescent and heard Mr Haking's opinion that his own fur sewers were mature women, Arkell inserted a comment of his own: 'are the fur sewers mostly elderly women, if so is this because the fur sewing is not so remunerative as other trades which girls can enter and which they consequently prefer, leaving the industry to the married and elderly women, who may be compelled to do this work by want?' And he felt free to challenge the statements of respondents.[42]

It is far from our intention to give the impression that George Arkell was responsible for the women's work inquiry. Even a glance through the printed text will convince that this was an extensive inquiry and one which was more than usually intelligent. Collet was not only thorough but creative. Look at her genealogy of shirts.[43] She was not only knowledgeable but

[38] Booth Collection, A2, 'Fur Trade', fo. 112.
[39] Booth Collection, A2, 'Fur Trade', fo. 112.
[40] Booth Collection, A2, 'Fur Trade', fo. 100.
[41] See Booth Collection, A2, 'Fur Trade', fos. 109-13.
[42] See Booth Collection, A2, 'Fur Trade', fo. 97.
[43] *Poverty*, 4, pp. 261-64.

highly critical of her sources. Look at her treatment of the machinists employed in the East End branch of a City firm. 'But this is only an inference.'[44] Look at her excellent treatment of home work as a general issue – delving in to discover its economic roots (pp 297-98) and the problems peculiar to married women who must earn a living.[45] Look at her mature use of comparative techniques to make general points.[46] Look then at her study of factory work and the interesting suggestions she has to make as to explanations of high infant mortality amongst the children of women factory workers;[47] and her unabashed challenge to the employers to decide whether half a loaf was better than none in times when trade is slack.[48] Even this is sufficient to convince that at this time her skill as an investigator and as an analyst was much greater than Beatrice Potter's. Small wonder that she was snapped up by the Board of Trade as a Senior Investigator in the Labour Department on Booth's advice in 1903.[49]

What the archive does do is help us to see how Booth's office supported her quest for information, Booth was personally involved in the early data collection and in continual touch with her work and George Arkell lent practical help and the benefits of his experience. We can also see how very incomplete the surviving archive is and the additional rich resources available for scholars wishing to look at the subjects covered therein. In the minutes of his evidence before the Royal Commission on Labour 1892, scholars have valuable data concerning Booth's awareness of the problematic nature of his information. In reply to the question, 'What was the general reception that you met with from the employers?', Booth answered, 'Our reception was most excellent generally where we were invited to go; but naturally we had to allow for the fact that those who asked us would be those who would be most likely to take a pride in showing us their places, and we had to discount that'.[50] Moreover, the reception was warmer in some trades than others.[51] He thought that a sub-commissioner would have great success in obtaining access but would have to guard against all putting 'their houses as much in order as possible' before her visit.[52] In addition, 'they must get personally acquainted with the workers by whatever means they can, and not expect to get much accurate information on the first inquiry or the first set of questions or conversation'.[53]

---

[44] *Poverty*, 4, pp. 261.
[45] *Poverty*, 4, pp. 299, 301 and passim.
[46] *Poverty*, 4, pp. 299-311.
[47] *Poverty*, 4, pp. 325-26.
[48] *Poverty*, 4, pp. 314-15.
[49] Booth Correspondence, MS 797 I/4803.
[50] *Royal Commission on Labour* Group C, q. 8,921.
[51] Ibid., q. 8,922.
[52] Ibid., q. 8,939, 8,940.
[53] Ibid., q. 8,941.

11. *The Boot and Shoe Industry: David Schloss and Jesse Argyle*

David Frederick Schloss, who we met in Beatrice Potter's tailoring trade inquiry in his guise as member of the Jewish Board of Guardians, has not received much attention from historians. In his day, however, he cut quite a figure in intellectual as well as Jewish circles. David Schloss was born in Manchester on 5 April 1850. He was educated at Manchester Grammar School and Corpus Christi College, Oxford and in 1875 was called to the Bar of Lincoln's Inn. It is not as a barrister that he is first drawn to our attention but as treasurer of the East London Tailoresses' Union in 1887. He was active both in the movement promoting the formation of women's trades unions and as the supporter of a short-lived experiment in a co-operative tailors' workshop. He was also active as a member of the Jewish Board of Guardians. In this capacity he had regular contact with the Charity Organisation Society and was led to write a number of articles for the *Charity Organisation Review* on sweating. In 1887 he attended the discussion of Booth's paper on Tower Hamlets on the Royal Statistical Society. It is not entirely surprising to find Booth assigning work on one of the sweated trades to him.[1]

In the late 1880s Schloss became one of Booth's core team for the first series. (This core team also included Paul, Potter, Collet, Ernest Aves and Llewellyn Smith, although Paul seems to have dropped out completely by the end of 1887.) He was, responsible for the chapter on the boot and shoe manufacture in the printed work but, as we have seen, he contributed in one way or another to other parts of the inquiry.[2]

Until recently there were thought to be no papers pertaining to the boot and shoe inquiry. The Booth Collection at the London School of Economics Library contains no office papers whatsoever. Now, however, the Schloss Papers themselves have been found to contain material collected by Schloss and others for this study.[3] This material is about to be properly listed. It clearly belongs to the Booth survey: there are six stiff-backed notebooks of

---

[1] Schloss was employed by the Labour Department of the Board of Trade in various capacities from 1893 until 1912, notably as Director of the Census Production Office 1907-8; he produced Board of Trade Reports on Foreign Immigration into the U.S. (1893), Profit-Sharing (1894) and Gain-Sharing. Published on his own account *Methods of Industrial Remuneration* (1892) and *Insurance against Unemployment* (1909), which were widely used in universities and public life. He was an active member of the Royal Statistical Society, the Royal Economic Society and the Economic Club.

[2] 'Tailoring' (as interviewee and researcher); 'Jewish Community'.

[3] BLPES, Coll. Misc., 0002552/A/0004, Schloss Collection.

the same type used by Booth and one small notebook. The contents span the years 1887-89.

These papers add considerably to our knowledge of the study of this trade. First of all, the work appears to have been begun by Ernest Aves. The notebook contains ten concise but detailed reports of interviews of 'shoe-makers visited in the autumn of 1887' by Aves. Aves did the work methodi-cally. A typical interview report lists name, marital status, age, address, job, prices, workplace, training, where/who the respondent worked for, earn-ings, views of general conditions in the trade.[4] Even then Aves displayed the perceptiveness and sensitivity which he was later to demonstrate as Booth's right-hand man on the Religious Influences Series. When he visited the mother of the shoemaker, Joseph Way, he commented on the difficulty even the sympathetic had in 'making principle and practice coincide'. She was 'a mission woman and knows a little about women's work in the district. Spoke about the small earnings of tailoresses . . . While expressing commiseration she fetched a little Ulster from an inner room that she had bought for her child for 2s.9d "wondered" what the worker got, but still had bought it, – and naturally, it being apparently very "cheap".'

Whether this was the extent of Aves' contribution to the boot and shoe survey we shall probably never know. Schloss makes no mention of his contribution although the book was certainly in his possession. Perhaps he felt that the work was too minor to be used or felt unable to use information collected in a different way from his own.

Perhaps more serious is the lack of acknowledgement to Jesse Argyle, Booth's 'senior secretary'. Two of the five notebooks contain material largely collected by and reported by Argyle.[5] Clearly he was to the boot trade what Arkell was to tailoring and women's work. As with Arkell, Argyle made exceptionally full notes because of his need to communicate with Schloss. He too was evidently a practised interviewer, accustomed to recording not only what happened and when but also the circumstances of the occasion, the appearance of the people involved and his own views of their testimony. When he visited Ben Nicholson's leather shop on Bethnal Green Road, and was told of the family industry which the rivetters, wives and children engaged in, making ladies' and children's shoes 'right through at home', he noted that 'the shop was full of men & women, mostly very poor looking, buying leather to make up at home in small parcels'.[6] Sometimes he showed considerable initiative in obtaining information. For instance, when he saw an advertisement in a sewing machine shop on Hackney Road for machine girls he records: 'Enquiry of woman in shop – Learners give time for 6

---

[4] See Appendix II.
[5] Schloss Collection, 'Bootmaking I' (of ninety-one pages, Schloss was responsible only for eleven) and one unmarked book beginning 'Carter, Ringland Road'.
[6] Schloss Collection, 'Carter' Book, p. 43.

months, then get 2/6 for 6 months, & 5s. for second year. After 2 years are improvers until fit to call themselves full hands. Some always remain improvers, being stupid . . .' and told them all about her 'career' to date.[7]

At least one other assisted in the inquiry. An unidentified interviewer contributed material, especially to the chapter on bootmaking. This was possibly Stephen Fox or Llewellyn Smith. Some of his interviews were in the company of George Mace, collector for Jones' sewing machine company. Schloss himself took detailed and informative notes of his interviews and visits. On one occasion he reports a visit to the workshop of Mr Fox of Ogle Street who employed fifty men on three floors. He described how the men paid £1 per week for a seat and subscribed for coal 'and find each his own lamp, seat & tools'. The acquaintance with this shop was prolonged: 'I was in & out of this shop all week & only saw one man drunk; said to be a very superior workman when sober; he did not work all week.' Schloss avidly observed the work of four individual workers for six days – Messrs Collins, Bean, Mahoney and Roberts – noting their exact hours, the way they worked, when and how often they wiped their noses, their breaks for lunch and tea, their enthusiasm or lack of it, their pace, what they made and how many they made. The reports contained in the notebooks confirm the impression given by the printed chapter that Schloss relied less on interview alone than upon close, personal observation based on repeated visits, multiple interviewing techniques and collection of written actual evidence. He based much of what he wrote upon the books kept by his respondents, for example.[8]

This said, it will be apparent that the figure of 221 interviews for the bootmaking inquiry is very much a minimum. On many occasions Schloss or Argyle were conversing quite freely with and certainly observing workers of all categories in the shops where they lingered. They were able as a result to speak confidently of the various divisions of the trade, the workers engaged in them, and the processes involved therein. The researcher interested in women's work, for example, will find Schloss's comments on women in the boot trade an illuminating adjunct to Collet's essay and, moreover, will know that the individual examples were drawn from personal experience and critically examined by the author in the light of what he knew and understood.

It is impossible to do justice in one paragraph to Schloss's work on bootmaking, which, despite its merits, has received little or no critical acclaim. It is not a showy, architected piece like 'The Jewish Community', yet it is written from a basis of knowledge and understanding far exceeding that of the would-be George Eliot. Eschewing the sensationalism of Mayhew, Schloss nonetheless made good and discriminating use of his contacts with

---

[7] Schloss Collection, 'Carter' Book, pp. 5-6.
[8] See Schloss Collection, 'Boot Trade IV', p. 44; *Poverty*, 4, p. 107.

employers and workers, union men and subcontractors, men and women to lend depth and perspective to his statistical material.[9] He used it not, as Beatrice did, to make a name, but as the stuff of the inquiry, on a par with the statistical evidence, as Booth had always hoped it would be.

12. Conclusion

Closer inspection of the archive pertaining to the special subject inquiries of the Poverty Series enable us to see Booth's survey for what it was – a well-planned and well-researched collaborative effort to describe and analyse the trades of London associated with poverty and a number of distinct topics, such as women's work, immigration, sweating and the Jewish community. It shows, dimly, Booth at the helm co-ordinating the enterprise and, more clearly, his dedicated secretaries organising both the office and the associates to expedite the work in hand. The characters of the secretaries and the associates emerge out of the shadows, stamping their various personalities on the work: Arkell and Argyle, the powers behind the throne; the youngish Beatrice Potter, an aspiring writer and social commentator torn between the models held up to her by George Eliot and Charles Booth; Clara Collet, the young and talented London graduate, weary of the school teaching for which she was trained and in search of a meaningful career; David Schloss, a prominent member of the Jewish community, involved in organising the workers of East London, intent upon describing the boot manufacturing trade and bringing his considerable analytical powers to bear upon it. Their personalities are important: if this was a collaborative work, if certainly was not one written by research assistants and then overwritten by Booth. Each of the essays discussed bears the distinctive mark of its originator. Booth allowed them considerable flexibility of approach and style – not altogether to the advantage of his total plan.

The archive, taken together with the printed essays, raises some important issues. Booth certainly had an overall plan for this part of the inquiry from the beginning. Trade inquiries were planned as early as September 1886 and, for example, we know that women's work, the docks and the boot trade inquiries were all under way during 1887. From the start these inquiries relied heavily upon interviews of large numbers of workers and employers. There is evidence that the style of the reports of the interviews mimicked those printed in Mayhew's *London Labour and the London Poor*.[1] The brief physical descriptions, the verbatim quotation, the choice details of the archive reports are found also in Mayhew. These are characteristic of all

---

[9] See 'Poverty', 4, pp. 89-93, for examples.
[1] Henry Mayhew, *London Labour and the London Poor* (London, 1861).

the interviewers, from Aves to Schloss, from Arkell to Potter, from Argyle to Booth. It is as if Booth directed his collaborators to report in this way. Beatrice Potter confided to her diary her criticisms of Mayhew's approach.[2] Perhaps Booth had suggested she read it before going further but this is mere surmise. Booth and the others were silent about their opinion of Mayhew's work. Much later Aves was to comment that it was interesting that critics believed Booth to be building successfully upon this earlier work. Perhaps initially Booth intended to model his printed work on Mayhew. If so he changed his mind.[3] While this is true of the archive, no hint of this approach is transferred to the printed text, where there is no sensationalism or demotic quotation.

[2] Passfield, MS Diary, late August 1887.
[3] See below pp. 156-58.

II

The Industry Series

*'My Beloved Trades of London': The Unknown Booth
and the Industry Series*

The Industry Series

Booth as a social investigator cannot hold a candle to Henry Mayhew. Such, at any rate, is the argument of Eileen Yeo and E.P. Thompson. Mayhew's inquiry into the London manufacturing trades and London street people has been presented as an empirical poverty survey which, conceptually and methodologically, stands head and shoulders above Booth's social analysis. 'Booth', writes Eileen Yeo, 'never put himself in a position where he could explore social attitudes and stumble onto sub-cultures. From the beginning he crudely equated qualitative evidence with sensationalism.' Karel Williams, writing from a different perspective, is no less critical. 'Booth', he tells us, 'talked to those set in administrative authority over the poor while Mayhew talked to the poor.'[1]

Neither claim can be sustained. Williams, who is primarily concerned with the role and nature of language in historiographic knowledge, operates a curious restriction of reference in his construction of the textual canon. What kind of semiotic mode of analysis is it, one may reasonably ask, which largely excludes seven of the seventeen volumes of the *Life and Labour* survey? And what kind of 'reading' is it that fails to address the interviews and investigations, the raw data, upon which the published text was based? The Thompson-Yeo version is equally deficient. Their attempt to rehabilitate Mayhew at the expense of Booth leads to judgements based on opinion rather than research. There is, in fact, only one examination to date of who Booth talked to or what was talked about. This account of his field work, the use of structured interviews and data-processing in relation to the neglected 'Religious Influences' series, has advanced our understanding of survey methods in social investigation. Booth is revealed as a careful critical analyst conscious of the defects of his methods and the limitations of his respon-

---

[1] E.P. Thompson and Eileen Yeo, eds, *The Unknown Mayhew* (Harmondsworth, 1973), p. 107; K. Williams, *From Pauperism to Poverty* (London, 1981), p. 313.

dents.[2] That he chose to say so little about them has been a cause of much misunderstanding. The interview notebooks, which are readily available for scholarly inspection, do however present us with a Booth who was not only aware of the significance of social attitudes but set out to explore them through personal interviews with representative workers. As we hope to show, there is an 'Unknown Booth' whose work is every bit as significant as that of the 'Unknown Mayhew'.

The Industry Series was not a success. Contemporaries were respectful rather than enthusiastic, admiring its thoroughness, breadth of view and perspective. The dense text and positivist presentation did not, however, strike the public imagination. The detail was overwhelming; the pace numbing. And there were five volumes of it. Even the Booths found the going tough. 'Some parts, we think, are a little dull', wrote Mary Booth, who also complained of the 'dreariness that comes over one as one plods through the account of trade and trade.'[3] Posterity has been equally unkind. For some the Industry Series is a flawed masterpiece; for others a work of reference and a scholarly resource.[4] Such assessments, reliant as they are upon the bloodless prose of the printed text, undervalue the achievement and underestimate the possibilities for further historical inquiry. Closer inspection of the notebooks indicates a process of investigation that was dependent upon the testimonies of real flesh and blood people; all sorts and conditions were included and all sorts of attitudes and experiences recorded. The irrepressible individuality of these notebooks, moreover, not only forms a striking contrast with the published account, but is a forceful reminder that it is possible to do for Booth's 'characters' what Mayhew did for his. We can go further. Whereas Mayhew's methods have to be taken on trust, Booth's procedures are open to inspection. We know who Booth interviewed and how he and his associates wrote up their findings; Mayhew's journalism, by contrast, supplies no such basis for comparison.

The Industry Series generated an awful lot of paperwork. For purposes of classification the whole population was grouped by trade and divided into sections. Lists of employers and trade unions were compiled from local directories and the Factory Inspectors' notebooks, forms were devised for the

[2] Rosemary O'Day 'Interviews and Investigations: Charles Booth and the Making of the Religious Influences Series', *History*, lxxiv (1989), pp. 361-77.

[3] *Industry*, 5, p. 335; *Economic Journal*, iv (1896), pp. 602- 5; T.S. and M.B. Simey, *Charles Booth: Social Scientist* (London, 1960) p. 129. Quotation from UL, Booth Correspondence, MS 797 1/3821, Mary Booth to Ernest Aves, 27 February 1901.

[4] A. Fried and R. Elman, *Charles Booth's London: A Portrait of the Poor at the Turn of the Century. Drawn from his 'Life and Labour of the People in London'* (London, 1969), p. xxxiii; Belinda Norman-Butler, *Victorian Aspirations: The Life and Labour of Charles and Mary Booth* (London, 1972), p. 123. One scholar who claims to have compared the published with the unpublished account concludes, erroneously, that 'most of what is valuable' in the latter is included in the former: see Charles More, *Skill and the English Working Class, 1870-1914* (London, 1980), p. 59.

earnings survey, schedules prepared, pencils sharpened and interviewers dispatched. A very large body of this material is preserved in the Booth archive, along with cognate correspondence, notes, and printed documents.

The archive is difficult to describe. It is a maverick collection, ill-formed, eccentric and unpredictable. Materials located in the Industry Series frequently belong to its predecessor. Individual trades and occupations are not listed. Booth's system of industrial classification included 'every employment recognized by the census' but at present access is only obtainable by hit and miss methods.[5] The Booth archive is in consequence something of a pot-pourri – exciting but frustrating.

The Industry Series papers falls into two broad categories. Group A fills some twenty-eight large folio volumes of loose-leaf materials and includes the lists of trade societies or firms approached, replies to questionnaires, wage returns, correspondence, reports and a large number of interviews conducted principally by the casual members of the research team. Group B consists of eighty-one octavo notebooks. In addition to the interviews transcribed by Booth and his secretariat, these include miscellaneous notes on industrial process, work-design and health risks, as well as assorted press-cuttings, digests and summaries. Institutional analysis fills many pages. There are fairly extensive notes on the origins, structure and function of selected trade and benefit societies often with supporting documentation pasted in.

Booth's concern to represent the whole of the population within his scheme of industrial classification found expression in the seven notebooks devoted to inmates of institutions. These consist of some 1,457 case-histories transcribed from the relieving officers' records of the Stepney Union. Booth, allowed privileged access to these records, obtained particulars of the name, age, status and occupation of applicants for relief together with details of their personal circumstances and family histories. These transcriptions from the official record often include statements from the applicant or their kin. If not a direct expression of the voice of the poor, these testimonies must be considered a very loud whisper. Booth himself used the material to create a powerful and moving portrait of pauperism which underscored the significance of sickness and old age as causes of poverty. As he was aware, his use was by no means exhaustive.[6] In this, as in virtually all other spheres of the inquiry, only a fraction of the material collected found

---

[5] The Harvester Microfilm edition of these papers is, alas, a facsimile of the current and inadequate listing compiled by the BLPES with the assistance of the Booth family nearly seventy years ago. The introduction to the Harvester Microfilm should be handled with caution. It is partial in coverage and inaccurate in particulars. Items located in Group A are not described and, contrary to assertion, George Duckworth did not write on dock labour, Ernest Aves never became Chairman of the Board of Trade and Clara Collett (sic) took no part in the Industry Series.

[6] *Industry*, 4, pp. 311-80.

its way into the published text. Charles Booth himself drew attention to the potential importance of the unpublished data for further study. His widow, with greater candour, predicted that the historian of the future, 'if he dives into the mass of note-books from which the pages of *Life and Labour* were gleaned, will find himself repaid by revelations more vividly true and lifelike than have found their way into the book.'[7] Her prescience, as will be shown below, was fully justified.

1. Interviews and Impressions

The Poverty Series addressed the social situation of the metropolitan poor. The Industry Series, though concerned to develop measures of convergent validity, differed in emphasis. 'The first inquiry', Booth explained, 'had been an attempt to describe the inhabitants of London, especially the poorer part of them, and their social conditions, as they lived street by street, family by family, in their homes.' The aim of the Industry Series, by contrast, was 'to review the people as they work, trade by trade, in their factories, warehouses or shops, or pursue their avocations in the streets or on the railways, in the markets or on the quays; to consider their relations to those whom they serve, whether employer or customer, and the remuneration they receive; and finally, to examine the bearing which the money earned has on the life they lead.'[1] The primary focus, then, was upon production and distribution – upon London as an industrial, commercial and trading centre; upon the multiplicity of its traders; the characteristics of its workers; the structure and organisation of the labour market; the work process and the social relations arising therefrom. From the classification and enumeration of its industries and workforce Booth moved to a description and analysis of London's working life. The salient features included the localisation of trades and the systems of production under which they operated; the supply of labour, its training, conditions and rewards; the sphere of trade unions; and the prospects for peace and progress arising from the relationship of employer and employed.

The work-centred approach of the Industry Series made the research interview central to the survey strategy. The absence of a cadre of officials who occupied a position in relation to the workforce, comparable with that of the School Board Visitors to the general population, was an important constraint which precluded a simple replication of the data-collection methods of the previous series. But, while compelled to create his own interview measures, Booth was not required to make bricks from straw. The tradition

[7] Mary Booth, *Charles Booth: A Memoir* (London: 1918), p. 105.
[1] Charles Booth, *Life and Labour of the People in London*, 9 vols (London, 1897), 9, p. 159.

of Blue Book investigation supplied information on questionnaire design and interview technique as well as substantial serial data for purposes of comparison. The tradition of private inquiry was equally informative. Booth was aware of Mayhew and was himself associated with the circular-based investigations conducted by the Mansion House inquiry into unemployment.[2] There was also the experience of the Poverty Series itself to build on.

Booth's contemporaries were curiously unaware of the character of the *Life and Labour* inquiry. Critics fastened upon the mass interview in the enumeration of poverty; the personal interview as a fact-gathering agent was barely noticed.[3] It was, however, the principal means by which information was acquired. Difficulties revealed in the Poverty Series were corrected in its successors. Mrs Hayes, an elderly trouser-maker who was terrified by Arkell's visit, underscored the importance of proper accreditation. 'I had noticed that the old lady seemed uneasy as I was talking to her', he wrote, 'and eventually I found out that she had heard that sewing-machines were to be taxed and she thought I had come to find out how many machines she had for the purpose.'[4] The need for greater uniformity in reporting procedure was also acknowledged. The latitude displayed in the early notebooks of Aves and Schloss, for example, diminished markedly in subsequent investigations.

The Industry Series, like its predecessor, drew heavily upon the resources of Toynbee Hall. The services of Aves,[5] Fox and Llewellyn Smith[6] were enlisted once more and its network of contacts again made available.[7] As with the previous inquiry the survey team included a mix of gentlemen and professionals. Chief among the former was Ernest Aves, apart from Booth himself, the single most important influence upon the organisation of the

[2] Mayhew was a standard reference sometimes consulted by Booth's secretariat or recommended to them by respondents: see BLPES Booth Collection, B144, fo. 88; B97, fo. 17 and see above pp. 21, 65, 96-7.

[3] See, for example, L.L. Price, 'Labour and Life of the People', *Economic Journal*, i (1891), pp. 565-70; Clementina Black, 'Labour and Life in London', *Contemporary Review*, lx (1891), pp. 207-19; F.C. Huntington, 'East London', *Quarterly Journal of Economics*, iv (1887- 88), pp. 83-96. Booth Collection, A58 also includes a useful selection of reviews and press-cuttings.

[4] Booth Collection, A19, fo. 125.

[5] Ernest Aves (1857-1917); born and educated at Cambridge; resident Toynbee Hall, 1887-97; sub-warden 1890-97; married Ermengard (known as Eva) Maitland, daughter of the historian, in 1897; contributed to *Economic Journal*; appointed Special Commissioner on wage boards and compulsory arbitration in Australia and New Zealand, 1907-8; Chairman of British and Irish Trade Boards 1913.

[6] Hubert Llewellyn Smith (1864-1945), Commissioner of Labour, Labour Department of Board of Trade 1892; Permanent Secretary to the Board of Trade 1907-1919; Chief Economic Adviser to Government 1919-1967; Director *New Survey of London Life and Labour*, 1928-35.

[7] Asa Briggs and Anne Macartney, *Toynbee Hall: The First Hundred Years* (London, 1984), pp. 17-18, 37; Standish Meacham, *Toynbee Hall and Social Reform, 1880-1914* (New Haven and London, 1987), p. 105.

research and analysis of the data.[8] Tall, loosely put together, somewhat slouching in his gait and preternaturally grave, Aves was of that generation that combined citizenship with commitment, action with knowledge, in a battle against ignorance and indifference. He had energy, intelligence, wide sympathies and sound judgement. A man of progressive outlook, he supported the extension of democratic association among producers and consumers. Apart from the material aspect, the trade union and co-operative movements were perceived as character-forming agents in which the values of discipline, duty and service might be acquired. In short, trade unions and co-operatives were the public schools of the working class. Like Llewellyn Smith, Aves welcomed the New Unionism,. He sided with the men in the dock strike of 1889, became the first president of the Trafalgar Branch of the Dock, Wharf, Riverside and General Labourers Union and was also a significant figure in the anti-sweating agitation. He was a believer in good sense, decency and in the fundamental harmony between social classes. 'Breaches of the industrial peace', wrote a contemporary, '. . . filled him with quite personal sense of pain.'[9] He remained a tireless exponent of the co-operative ideal and a firm believer in a rational and orderly form of trade unionism.[10]

Hubert Llewellyn Smith was like-minded. He was born into a Quaker family in comfortable circumstances. Educated at Bristol Grammar School and Corpus Christi College, Oxford, he obtained a first class in mathematics in 1886. After leaving Oxford, he became a lecturer for the Oxford University Extension Delegacy and the Toynbee Trust. He was a sometime resident of Toynbee Hall and also lived elsewhere in the East End. The New Unionism found in him one of its most energetic and able defenders. Co-author of the first, and still serviceable, history of the dock strike, Llewellyn Smith exemplified all that was best in late-Victorian social radicalism.[11]

---

[8] Aves contributed the whole section on the building trades, which he spent three years researching and writing, was consulted on all stages of the survey and was responsible for such attempts as there were to draw comparisons and formulate conclusions. Although he appears as Booth's assistant on the title page of the final volume, he wrote the lion's share of the text and might reasonably have claimed it as his own: Simey, *Charles Booth*, pp. 123-24; *Select Committee on Distress from Want of Employment: Minutes of Evidence* [365] PP. 1895 (ix) qq. 10,874-11,004; Booth Correspondence, MS 797 I/3935, Charles Booth to Ernest Aves, 12 June 1903.

[9] Obituary 'Ernest Aves', *Economic Journal*, xxvii (1917), pp. 292- 97; Obituary, *Toynbee Record*, xxix (1917) pp. 57-64.

[10] There is a revealing interview given by Aves as Sub-Warden of Toynbee Hall in Booth Collection, B227, fos. 197-239; otherwise the most accessible statements of his ideas are in the 'Labour Notes' which he regularly contributed to the *Economic Journal*, his articles on 'Wages' and 'Hours of Labour', contributed to *Encyclopaedia Britannica*, and in his book, *Co-operative Industry* (London, 1907).

[11] On Smith's early career, see Roger Davidson, 'Llewellyn Smith, the Labour Department and Government Growth, 1886-1909' in G. Sutherland ed., *Studies in the Growth of Nineteenth-Century Government* (London, 1972), pp. 239-45; and Alon Kadish, *The Oxford Economists in the Late Nineteenth Century* (Oxford, 1982), pp. 18-30, 70-75.

Beveridge, who knew him well, described him as 'one of the most constructive practical minds' he had ever encountered. Llewellyn Smith was also genial. He was, a contemporary wrote, 'a man of simple tastes, generous-hearted and free of all conceits and pretences.'[12] Beatrice Potter cast him for the role that Sidney Webb was destined to perform; the Booths considered him a possible suitor for their eldest daughter. In short, he possessed the intellect and the temperament of an outstanding social investigator.[13]

G.H. Duckworth, too, was of singular importance to the Booth inquiry.[14] Duckworth, when mentioned at all, is nowadays remembered as the incestuous half-brother of Virginia Woolf. The charge is unfounded.[15] George Duckworth was a capable and industrious man who for ten years was educated at Eton and, like Aves, went to Trinity College, Cambridge before proceeding to a successful career in the public service. He was a man of distinguished presence, exceptionally companionable, a delightful talker and a connoisseur of good living. H.A.L. Fisher, who knew him well – they were first cousins – wrote that he had 'a genius for happiness.' Booth thought well of him. Duckworth, he wrote, 'has a quick eye observant of details, a cool counsel, judgement, plenty of determination and very conciliatory manners.'[16] Put briefly, Duckworth was a sociable man who was curious and responsive to Londoners and their problems.

Esmé Howard, also a newcomer, was the old Harrovian son of an aristocrat who was likewise drawn to the Booth survey out of interest rather than need.[17] Howard, a man of advanced views – he was presented to the

[12] BLPES, Beveridge Collection IXa, 110.

[13] Booth Correspondence, MS 797 I/1369, Charles Booth to Mary Booth, 12 July 1895.

[14] George Herbert Duckworth (1868-1934), elder son of barrister Herbert Duckworth whose widow married Leslie Stephen; educ. Eton and Cambridge; married (1904) Lady Margaret Herbert, daughter of 4th Earl of Carnarvon; Secretary to the Royal Commission on Historical Monuments 1908-18; Deputy Director Munitions Finance 1915-18; Controller of Labour Finance 1918; Controller of Munitions Housing Scheme 1919-20; Chairman of Irish Land Trust for Re-settlement of Ex-Servicemen in Ireland 1924-27; Member of Advisory Committee on *New Survey of London Life and Labour* 1929; knighted 1927.

[15] The allegation made by Virginia Woolf against Duckworth has been treated as fact by her biographer and nephew Quentin Bell, *Virginia Woolf: A Biography* (London, 1972) and repeated by others in book-length studies: Louise De Salvo, *Virginia Woolf: The Impact of Childhood Sexual Abuse on her Life and Work* (London, 1989). The standard of proof required to reach such a devastating conclusion seems to fall far short of those customarily applied in historical scholarship.

[16] Obituary, Sir George Duckworth, *The Times*, 28 April 1934; Appreciation by H.A.L. Fisher, *The Times*, 30 April 1934; Booth Correspondence, MS 797 I/1504 Charles Booth to London County Council, January 1901.

[17] Esmé Howard (1863-1939), born Greystoke Castle, Cumberland, fourth son of Henry Howard of Greystoke; married (1898) Lady Isabella Giustiniani–Bandini; entered Diplomatic Service in 1886 and retired in 1892; Assistant Private Secretary to Earl of Kimberley, Secretary of State for Foreign Affairs 1894-95; returned to the Diplomatic Corps after war service in South Africa; Ambassador to U.S.A. 1924-30; created baron 1930.

electors of Worcester as a 'Socialist-Salvationist' – was in fact recruited by Duckworth, a close friend.[18] He was open-minded, understanding and industrious with a good deal of energy and enthusiasm. But although he found the work rewarding, his interests lay elsewhere. Social investigation was an interlude, albeit an instructive one, in a career in the Foreign Service. In this respect he differed from Aves, Fox and the others who were fast gaining recognition as authorities on social questions.[19]

Most of Booth's associates were paid for their services. George Arkell and Jesse Argyle, who each made substantial contributions to the project, were full-time salaried staff. There were other fee-paid workers, like Harold Hardy, a man of letters and free-lance writer, who was brought in to investigate and report on street sellers and mineral water makers.[20] Booth, though he surrounded himself with young Oxbridge-educated gentlemen like Llewellyn Smith and the barrister A.L. Baxter,[21] also valued the specialised knowledge of trade unionists and those connected with the world of labour. Fred Maddison, editor of the *Railway Review* and a future Lib-Lab member of Parliament, was, for example, commissioned to interview officers of the rail workers unions,[22] while W.H. Hey, a former secretary of the Ironfounders Union, was considered a suitable replacement when Baxter left the inquiry in 1894.[23]

Maddison had 'Toynbee' connections. So had Clem Edwards. A confidante of Mann, Tillet and Thorne, and a significant figure in the New Unionism, Edwards investigated the port transport industry and assisted

[18] Esmé Howard, *Theatre of Life,* 2 vols (London, 1935), i, p. 143.

[19] Duckworth, for example, received a short-term appointment as private secretary to assist Sir Henry Campbell-Bannerman with the work of the parliamentary committee on unemployment to which Aves and Llewellyn Smith also gave evidence; Fox made informed contributions to various journals. Duckworth's writings include 'The Work of the Select Committee of the House of Commons on Distress from Want of Employment', *Economic Journal,* vi (1896), pp. 143-58, 650-53 and 'The Making, Prevention and Unmaking of a Slum', *Journal of the Royal Institute of British Architects,* xxxiii (1926), pp. 327-37. See, too, Stephen N. Fox, 'The Factories and Workshops Bill', *Economic Journal,* x (1900), pp. 258-61; also his contributions to R.H.S. Palgrave ed., *Dictionary of Political Economy,* 3 vols. (London, 1899).

[20] Harold Hardy (b. 1864); educ. Keble College, Oxford; playwright and author of technical studies on copyright law and clergy discipline.

[21] Arthur Lionel Baxter (b. 1860); educ. University College, London; barrister-at-law, Inner Temple 1887.

[22] Fred Maddison (1856-1937) son of a hotel worker; educ. Adelaide Street Weslyan School, Hull; editor *Railway Review* 1889-97; M.P. Sheffield (Brightside) 1897-1900 and Burnley 1906-10. For his career, see *DLB,* iv, pp. 119-22; for his work with the Life and Labour Inquiry, Booth Collection, A23, fos. 49-76; for his connection with Toynbee Hall, *Toynbee Record,* vi (September 1894), pp. 54-55.

[23] William Henry Hey (1839-1907) was general secretary of the Ironfounders Union 1886-94. He was, Booth confided to Mary, 'trustworthy and needs employment badly', Booth Correspondence, MS 797 I/1367, Charles Booth to Mary Booth, pencilled note, 1894.

Aves with the building trades interviews.[24] In this connection, he worked with fellow journalist, H.W. Nevinson, another 'Toynbee' type, who at this stage of his career was living in Petticoat Lane 'among bugs, fleas, old clothes, slipper cods' heads and other garbage.' Nevinson, who described himself as a man of conservative tastes and revolutionary convictions, combined membership of Hyndman's Social Democratic Federation with an equal commitment to Luke Paget's Christ Church Mission in Poplar. Notwithstanding an unfortunate manner – Brailsford described him as 'a singularly handsome man who carried himself with such distinction that his friends nicknamed him "The Grand Duke" – Nevinson was sharp-eyed, curious and genuinely interested in the people among whom he lived.[25] There were other Toynbee men, lesser luminaries perhaps, but all of them curious and competent.[26]

While there were gains there were also losses. The Industry Series, unlike the previous inquiry, was written and researched entirely by men. With Beatrice Potter's departure went a sparkling intelligence and a certain verve. Beatrice, who had outgrown the Booth Inquiry even before socialism and Sidney made her position impossible, was not, however, interested in the gendered nature of work and its attendant issues. Alfred Marshall's assurance that these were fit subjects for a women to study served to convince her that female labour was unworthy of her talents, and that women were better suited as observers than observed.[27] The loss of Clara Collet was less painful but more damaging. Although she lacked Beatrice Potter's flair and confidence Clara Collet was ambitious, persistent and just as capable. Studies of women's work in east London and secondary education for girls, written for the Poverty Series, were significant contributions towards feminist sociology. Her departure left the Booth Inquiry without a specialist interest in

---

[24] Clem Edwards (1869-1938), English trade unionist and Lib-Lab politician. Brought up in comfortable circumstances, he dabbled in journalism and was a founder member and senior official of the Dockers' Union. He was called to the bar in 1899 and entered Parliament in 1906. He moved increasingly to the right thereafter and lost his seat in the general election of 1922: see Barbara Nield, 'Clem Edwards', *DLB*, iii, pp. 69-78; Booth Collection, A3, fo. 41. 'Building Trades: Wage-Earners Interviews'.

[25] Henry Woodd Nevinson (1856-1941). English war correspondent and man of letters; educ. Shrewsbury and Christ Church, Oxford; worked for *Daily Chronicle*, *Daily News* and *Manchester Guardian;* author of *Neighbours of Ours* (1895), a series of short stories, written in Cockney dialect, which had considerable merit but few sales: see H.W. Nevinson, *Changes and Chances* (London, 1923), pp. 78-118; H.N. Brailsford, 'Henry Woodd Nevinson', *DNB*, pp. 619-21; P.J. Keating, *The Working Classes in Victorian Fiction* (London, 1971), pp. 199- 206.

[26] The building trades interviews, for example, relied upon the services of Percival Burt Allen (Resident 1892-93), Arthur M. Price, A.R. Dyhurst and others.

[27] Beatrice Webb, *My Apprenticeship* (Harmondswoth, 1971 edn), pp. 349-54; also see S. and B. Webb, *Industrial Democracy* (London, 1902 edn), p. xiii. See, too, Royden Harrison, *Beatrice Potter and Robert Owen* (forthcoming).

women's employment or social conditions, and the Industry Series was much diminished in consequence.

Information was obtained by interview and personal observation. Employers and trade union officials were circularised and follow-up visits arranged with those willing to give further assistance. Separate schedules were issued which indicated to both parties the central concerns of the investigation – trade organisation, wages and the operation of the labour market.[28] The interview was critical. One of Booth's assistants explained:

> 'With regard to printed questions addressed to working men, the necessity for rendering assistance in filling in answers . . . is . . . obvious. For the most part, the labour of writing is highly distasteful to working men; they are not accustomed to receiving communications of this nature, and they are often incapable of giving precise expression to their thoughts with the pen. Even the experienced officials of the most highly-organised trade unions 'shy at' the task of replying to circulars.'

The personal interview was no less important in improving the coverage and quality of the information imparted by employers who were likewise more willing to talk than write. In his own words, 'No one who has ever had to ascertain facts in relation to labour will deny that there are very many cases in which for the purpose of getting at the truth, "half an hour's straight talk" is worth a ton of inquiry forms.'[29]

The interview itself was carefully structured. Investigators received precise and detailed guidance as to the information required. The questionnaire, prepared by Booth himself, was partly descriptive and partly evaluative. Instructions were given to report on the extent of organisation in particular trades and assess the influence exercised by trade unions. Investigators were asked to find out what class of person became a trade unionist, who resisted membership and why; to identify those branches of a trade and those localities in which trade unionism was strongest; and to describe employer response in terms of attitude and company policy. The social value of trades unions was equally significant. Information was collected on the social relations of workers, their sectional rivalries and divisions so as to estimate the degree to which unions 'cause friendship and increase good feeling amongst those who join.' Finally, interviewers were asked to supply a brief account of working life 'with full details where likely to be of general interest bearing in mind that to me and to most of those who will read my book have no ideas or the very vaguest ideas about the actual daily life of working men [sic].'[30]

The Industry Series, it should now be clear, was something more than a

---

[28] See below, Appendices III-IV.
[29] David F. Schloss, 'The Reorganisation of our Labour Department', *Journal of the Royal Statistical Society*, lvi (1893), pp. 49-50.
[30] Booth Collection, A23, fos. 49-50, memorandum for Mr Maddison 1892/3.

simple survey of industrial relations. Booth's interest extended beyond formal trade unionism or the purely descriptive aspects of the labour process. In consequence, information was acquired on the character of workplace organisation, the place of custom and ritual in relation to the working community and the influence of certain trade-specific practices upon the control of production. Booth was equally concerned with the ways in which work and work-culture informed everyday life. Investigators were thus directed to probe some possible connections between work, home and family. In the course of the interview questions were raised about residence, meals, dress, family income and expenditure. Respondents were also invited to comment on housing and rents and given the opportunity to supply aspects of industrial biography.

Booth was pleased with the response to his inquiries. 'Nothing could exceed the kindness with which our troublesome quest has in most cases been met', he wrote. 'Factories have been opened to us, wages books have been shown, and particular and elaborate returns have been especially prepared for us setting forth in the most accurate way the hours worked as well as the pay received in busy and slack weeks, and the exact terms of piece and time employment.' Trade unions were no less obliging. 'Particulars of every Trade Union or Society of importance has been obtained', wrote our triumphant inquirer.[31] In one area alone was there disappointment. From the outset the evidence of ordinary workers was seen as critical. 'From the individual workmen', wrote Booth, 'we wish if we can to get as vivid pictures as possible as these alone will make the book readable.'[32] Such testimony, though difficult to obtain, 'adds much to the life of the picture.' Although Booth felt that the biographical material fell short of expectations, the evidence of the notebooks suggests that the failure was one of presentation rather than substance.

The field work for the Industry Series began late in 1891. The bulk of the material, though, was collected in the next two years. The first volume appeared in 1895; the final volume in 1897. In that time Booth and his associates had interviewed hundreds of people. Who were they and how were they selected? Apart from remarkable figures like Thomas Okey, the Spitalfields basketmaker who became Professor of Italian at Cambridge, or Frederick Rogers, the literature-loving labour leader, the majority of respondents were unknown.[33] Most interviews were obtained as part of the follow-up to the questionnaire previously issued to interested parties; some informants were recommended by employers and foremen; a fair number

---

[31] *Industry*, 2, pp. 27-28.

[32] Booth Correspondence, MS 797 I/1320, Charles Booth to Ernest Aves, 24 February 1892. Cf. Simey, *Charles Booth*, p. 129.

[33] See Thomas Okey, *A Basketful of Memories* (London, 1930); Frederick Rogers, *Labour Life and Literature: Some Memories of Sixty Years* (London, 1913).

came through the informal network of contacts which had been built up in the course of the earlier inquiry. Within the survey population, women, children, the unskilled, the unorganised and white-collar workers were underrepresented. The bulk of those interviewed were working men. Some were self-employed; but most were wage-earners.

No attempt was made to obtain the age of respondents. Unless the information was volunteered, investigators relied upon their own judgement. Howard, for example, was sceptical when told by the foreman of an East London chemical works that he was forty-five. 'He was already much grizzled so that he looked over fifty.'[34] Two women book folders, interviewed at the Club and Institute Union, Clerkenwell, were likewise carefully scrutinised. The older woman was reported as 'slovenly in appearance' with 'the look of one who has worked hard but is getting beyond it now. Probably between fifty and sixty.' The younger respondent, 'a quiet unassuming woman . . . who has undergone some privations which have left their mark on her face', was 'Probably between twenty and thirty [and] neatly dressed.'[35] Booth, one suspects, had a preference for experienced individuals who could supply a certain perspective on trade developments, like, for example, the Bermondsey tanner who recalled when, fifty years earlier, 'the sheds used to be occupied by small middle-class men whose dress was always a blue frock and top hat.' In those less specialised days, the respondents continued, the men 'could do any part of the business, it was then more of a skilled business than it is now because everything was done by hand.'[36]

Interviewers invariably took account of the knowledge, expertise and judgement of their informants. The survey population seems to have included a large, possibly disproportionate, number of workers who were well-versed in their trade and active in its societies. Old trade unionists, like George Oliver and William Jeffrey, who led the Bermondsey leather workers in the strike of 1865, spoke authoritatively about the labour process and the pattern of industrial relations that arose from it.[37] William Hewit, a portmanteau maker, was 'a lord of the trade' who lived in 'a good middle class street' in Battersea.[38] Some were men of unusual culture. Mr Dumfries, a Bermondsey leather worker, 'who can talk beautifully for hours about Shakespeare and politics', was indeed recommended less for his knowledge and more for his conversation.[39] Jackson, the journeyman book binder, 'a man of about 30 who can do all branches of the trade', was also impressive. 'Mr J.', wrote the interviewer, 'is a very intelligent man and has a

[34] Booth Collection, B93, fo. 63.
[35] Booth Collection, B101, fo. 119.
[36] Booth Collection, B96, fo. 41.
[37] Booth Collection, B95, fos. 8-11, 190-22.
[38] Booth Collection, B96, fos. 50-56.
[39] Booth Collection, B96, fo. 7.

small library of which he is proud. Most of the books are leather bound and many of them elaborately tooled.'[40] Pinder, a builders' labourer, was also proud of his small library. The respondent, who was interviewed in the basement sitting room where he lived, was reading Burke's *Reflections on the Revolution in France*, and explained that 'he had been led to read Burke through having read Carlyle and wanted to know what the other side has to say.'[41]

Some interviewees, though, were in a shocking condition. The impoverished gas fitter, whose wife regretted not having had more children 'as they would have then have had them to look for assistance in hard times', was amongst the poorest of respondents. The one-roomed home into which the interviewer was shown was unfurnished except for a broken chair and a bed without any bedding. 'Everything they told me had been pawned to keep up the home.' The couple were neither rough nor vicious. He was a hard-working chap; while his wife wished to work, and would have done so, 'only that she had no clothes left to go in.'[42] Mr Powell, though employed, was scarcely better off. A casual jobbing hand in the newsprint industry, he was a respectable middle-aged family man, who worked and starved. 'I found', wrote Arkell, 'that the man had nothing to eat since breakfast (it was 4 p.m.) so I asked him to come and have something. He replied that there were others worse off than him upstairs who needed food more than he. I asked him to bring another with him.' Arkell watched them eat. 'After we had finished our tea, a slice of bread and butter was left. This Mr Powell wrapped carefully in a piece of paper and placed in his pocket.'[43]

From the outset investigators were required to check the accuracy of the information received. The verification process applied to people as well as to statements. Informants and respondents were frequently appraised, as much for their moral worth as their substantive knowledge. Nevinson, who with Clem Edwards undertook some of the building trades interviews, described the bricklayers of the Workmens' Institute, Stratford, as a capital set of fellows. 'Was greatly impressed by the respectability and keenness and straightforwardness of nearly all of the men I saw', he wrote, 'with several of whom I had separate conversations while Edwards was taking down schedule particulars.'[44] Mr Fitzpatrick, a dock labourer interviewed by Booth, presented himself as a big powerfully built man in his late fifties. 'Slow and awkward in his movements, his mental characteristics partake of the same qualities; and are united with a dogged determination nearly akin to obstinacy which when he got into a groove would keep him there.'[45]

[40] Booth Collection, B101, fo. 61.
[41] Booth Collection, A3, fo. 193.
[42] Booth Collection, A3, fo. 187.
[43] Booth Collection, B99, fos. 94-98.
[44] Booth Collection, A3, fo. 41.
[45] Booth Collection, A24, fo. 24.

Political opinions were noted, though more as a source of bias than as the basis for further exploration. John Nash, a Bow joiner, was summarised by Nevinson as 'a keen Radical politician, but reserved and silent, having a reputation among his fellows of being 'opposed to everything.'[46] The place of politics in relation to institutions was equally unclear. The socialism of the gas workers' union, for example, was seen largely in personal terms. 'Mrs Aveling is one of the leading spirits of this organization,' wrote Argyle, 'which probably partly accounts for its Socialistic character.'[47] Sub-political attitudes, too, found their way onto the page as respondents surveyed their working lives and the prospects that lay ahead. 'I have been nearly twenty-five years with my present employer and I feel I am that much nearer the workhouse', said one embittered trade unionist.[48] Others, particularly craftsmen, vented their anger on the upstart New Unions with their endless demands for levies and assistance in the name of a class solidarity to which they did not subscribe.[49] Trade questions rather than political issues were indeed the dominant interest of the survey population. Although the majority of those interviewed were probably members of trade unions, Booth discovered varying levels of commitment, some hostility and a good deal of indifference. Those like the masons' labourer from Somers Town, who had never got round to joining the union, or the unemployed marble polisher, who refused to enrol because the union 'would prevent him taking little jobs on his own account in the evening', were recorded by Booth's investigation along with more skilled, though equally unpredictable, types.[50]

It was interesting and exhilarating work. It also left a mark. Beatrice Potter's resolve to work in the service of Humanity, as is well known, was fortified by her unforgettable experiences with the Booth inquiry. Even in moments of depression when, as she put it, 'I get so sick of those ugly details of day work and piece work – overtime and shop rent – and the squalid misfortunes of defaulting branch officers or heckling and unreasonable members', her strength of purpose was sustained by the consciousness of poverty, waste and inefficiency which Booth and his co-workers had revealed. 'Who', she wondered, 'would choose to imprison their intellect in this smelly kitchen of social life – if it were not for that ever-important 30 per cent – with the background of their terrible East End streets. The memory of those low cunning brutal faces of the loafers and cadgers that hang about the Mint haunt me when I feel inclined to put down the T.[rade] U.[nion] report and take up a good bit of literature.'[51] Esmé Howard too found the

[46] Booth Collection, A3, fo. 130.
[47] Booth Collection, B144, fo. 14.
[48] Booth Collection, A9, fo. 158.
[49] Booth Collection, A3, fo. 172.
[50] Booth Collection, A3, fos. 252, 280-81.
[51] Beatrice Potter to Sidney Webb, 8 December 1891, *Letters*, i, p. 345.

work an eye-opener. Investigation into carriage builders, musical instrument makers, dyers and cleaners, brush makers and floor-cloth manufacturers, he recalled, brought contact with 'a totally new world' and a much better understanding of the deficiencies of a market economy.[52] Arthur Baxter was more deeply affected. He quit the inquiry in 1894 to go into the cab-owning business. Baxter put up the money and a 'working class friend' the experience. 'It seems a very odd thing to do', wrote Booth, 'but he seems soberly in earnest about it.' Clara Collet, who was also uncommitted, liked the work and felt 'a kind of enjoyment in the risk often involved in facing unknown people.'[53]

The Industry Survey encompassed the whole spectrum of production: from large establishments, like breweries and locomotive engineering works, to back-street braziers, self-employed printers and knife-grinders leading a hole in the corner existence in sheds, outhouses and lean-tos. The variety was extraordinary: foundries, workshops, warehouses, depots, building sites, railway works, gas works, chemical works, shipyards, brickyards, bakeries, refineries, distilleries, saddleries, binderies, tanneries, fruit markets, fish markets, meat markets – all were visited. In each case the work process was carefully monitored. The stages of production were noted and the organisation of work reported. Simple line drawings sketched into the note books served as an *aide memoire* and visual record of labouring London.

Booth and associates were shown over print shops, book shops, engineering shops and drapers shops. they recorded silversmiths, goldsmiths, coppersmiths, blacksmiths and tinsmiths. They saw wet coopers at the block warming, bending, hooping and heading, and watched tilers cut, punch and fix slates. They described barge builders filling joints with hair and pitch, and riggers fixing ships' running gear. They observed paper stainers flocking, bronzing, metalling and embossing, and looked on as smuttermen, silks-men, roller-men and purifier-men ground wheat into flour. They watched boot-makers, brush-makers, box-makers, whip-makers, rope-makers, mat-makers, mantle-makers, stay-makers, flower-makers, glove-makers and stick-makers. They spoke with dealers, drapers, hosiers and silk mercers; saw potters and piano-makers, tinkers and tailors: described bottling, corking and sighting operations in a mineral water factory, cutting operations in a cork factory and puddling operations at the white-lead works, where conditions were so bad that none was allowed to work more than three days in one week. They saw slaughter-house refuse turned into the finest toilet soap and the scraps and parings of hides turned into glue. They watched candle-makers dipping, rolling, pouring and moulding, and

[52] Howard, *Theatre of Life*, i, pp. 171-75.
[53] Booth Correspondence, MS 797 1/1367, Charles Booth to Mary Booth, 24? April 1895; MRC, Collet MSS 29/8/1/53, Diary 18 May 1980.

saw isinglass made from fish bladders. It had all been done before, but never with such system, comprehension, clarity and control.[54]

Booth's investigators marvelled at the creativity and energy of industrial London. Their reports convey an almost childlike delight in seeing things made, mended, moved or sold and a sense of wonderment at the resultant spectacle. Everyday commodities took on a new aspect when viewed from the point of production. Thus with Esmé Howard we find glassware shifted from the routine to the unexpected:

> A glass furnace at night is one of the most picturesque and weird sights imaginable. As you approach through a dark passage the furnace apertures are seen in the distance glowing like cat's eyes. On reaching the end an extraordinary scene bursts into view. In front of the furnace half a dozen or more dark figures hurry to and fro, now digging long tubes into the red molten glass, which itself provides all the light required; now drawing them back with a fiery mass at the end, to be first rolled into shape and then waved backwards and forwards in the air, taking a duller and yet duller tint of red as it expands and cools at the end of the blower's tube.[55]

Interviews were arranged for the convenience of the respondent. Locations varied. Some were held in office hours, a few in private homes, and a fair number were conducted in pubs; for notwithstanding the progress of the temperance movement, society business was often transacted on licensed premises. Booth's investigators spent many Saturday nights in pubs and clubs recording the observations of trade unionists and their representatives. Unions often displayed very distinctive styles. The vellum binders, for example, seemed relaxed when Booth's assistant stopped by. The society, founded in 1823, occupied two rooms on the second floor of a building off Houndsditch. The outer one, used as a club room, was full of strikers who were smoking and talking or playing cards.[56] Duckworth's experience with the Royal London United Riggers' Association was very different. 'The President, Treasurer and Secretary', he wrote, 'were . . . seated at one table facing the audience and I was given another.' The riggers, though down at heel, continued to do things in a right and proper manner.

> The proceedings were opened by the President – all standing up with their hats off while he read a sort of solemn prayer except that there was nothing religious about it or mention of the Deity; adjuring all . . . to . . . behave as brothers and support the authority of the chair. This the President read out from a well-

---

[54] The earliest survey of the trades of London which is, in any sense, comparable is George Dodd, *Days at the Factories* (London, 1843).

[55] *Industry*, 2, p. 84.

[56] Booth Collection, B101, fo. 15.

thumbed printed paper pasted onto a wooden tablet – like the college grace tablet at the university . . . He knew it very nearly by heart but not quite.

The meeting concluded in like manner with 'a vote of thanks . . . to me for having come down to see them 'out of working hours.'"[57] The strange and irregular movements of the Jewish cap-makers, by contrast, were quite unlike anything previously encountered. Arkell, who attended their Saturday evening meeting at the 'Duke of Clarence' in the Commercial Road, found the proceedings difficult to follow. 'The composition of the meeting', he wrote, 'changed constantly, newcomers entering every few minutes, whilst others strolled out. At times the number in the room rose to about 80 and the region near the door was congested.' The comings and goings were not the sole distraction. 'The women', he noted, 'were without exception well developed and plump, without the least indication that they had ever suffered privation of any kind.' The men – 'thin and undersized with sallow complexions and sunken cheeks' – seemed rather less interesting.[58]

Interviews were time-consuming. Some took two hours; others longer. Notes were sometimes made, but not always. John Edey, Secretary of the Patent Leather Dressers' Society, for example, 'gave information with great hesitation' and only on condition 'that nothing should be put down on paper while he was there.'[59] The transcripts are not, then, verbatim reports of proceedings. They are reconstructions written up from notes or from memory. The interviews were of two kinds: those conducted by the permanent members of Booth's secretariat were recorded in octavo size notebooks that were subsequently numbered, paginated and indexed; interviews filed by assistants were written on loose sheets of varying sizes. All followed the order of the schedule, usually under heads borrowed from it.

There was some variation in interviewer technique. Most interviews were face-to-face encounters conducted in private. Some, however, developed into a dialogue between interviewer, respondent and the respondent's friends or associates. Duckworth, set to interview a hoop maker, was unexpectedly referred from the office to the workshop. 'The following', he wrote, 'is therefore an interview with the foreman and the six men working there who joined freely in the discussion'.[60] In other cases a public meeting was required to complete the questionnaire. Where a trade union officer did not feel able to provide information, or where he was unable to approve the written-up report, the matter might be referred to the membership. The riggers, for example, held a special meeting to consider their replies. 'About

---

[57] Booth Collection, B85, fos. 63-72.
[58] Booth Collection, B110, fos. 83-84.
[59] Booth Collection, B96, fo. 66.
[60] Booth Collection, B84, fo. 1.

40 or 50 men came to the meeting', Duckworth remarked, 'and were very attentive during the discussion of the question on the Trade Union form'.[61] The cap-makers, too, insisted upon a collective response, and it was arranged for Arkell to meet with eight of the members chosen from different shops for that purpose.[62] The shipwrights, by contrast, sent a five-man deputation to consider the report of the interview with their secretary. 'They heard the report in silence', wrote Duckworth, 'and though taken through it point by point refused to say whether they (the points) were true or the reverse.' With their trade in decline, and themselves getting on in years – two members of the deputation 'were certainly 50 years old and two over that age and I prob[ably] between' – the shipwrights were cagey and indeed hostile to further inquiry. 'What right had Mr Booth or his employees to go prying into other peoples' business?', they grumbled. 'Much better to leave other people alone.' The investigation, it was felt, should be abandoned forthwith. 'What right had anyone to write about people without the consent of the people themselves.'[63]

The state of the trade and the age of respondents were not the only influence upon the supply of information. The effects of class and gender were equally significant. The Industry Series, unlike its predecessor, reserved no space for a special consideration of 'women's work.'[64] Women workers in the trade by trade survey were presented in descriptive rather than analytical terms; and there were too few of them. Booth's female respondents also occupied a lower position in the social hierarchy than the male interviewees; being drawn largely from the unorganised and depressed sectors of the labour force.

Once their confidence had been gained these poor women found their voice. Their statements, as recorded in the notebooks, present a powerful portrait of life at the margins. Women workers in general spoke of long hours and low pay, of methods of remuneration and of their place in the division of labour. Sweated labour was not always experienced as oppression. Married women, who assigned priority to the end rather than the act of production, sometimes considered the social value of the wage packet greater than the content. However small, the contribution to family income gave the contributor a claim to greater autonomy within the family. A former fur sewer, who worked at home with a machine, explained how she regretted her forced withdrawal from paid employment and the 'pleasure of making your own money.' 'When her husband was better off', she told Duckworth, 'he sold her machine, said that the work was too hard for her

---

[61] Booth Collection, B85, fo. 63.
[62] Booth Collection, B110, fos. 83-84.
[63] Booth Collection, B85, fos. 80-82.
[64] *Royal Commission on Labour: Minutes of Evidence*, Group 'C', [c. 6708-vi] PP. 1892, (xxxv) q. 8,932.

but she has regretted ever since the little extra of her very own earnings'. Mrs Benton, a widow from Limehouse, also found Duckworth easy to talk to. In her circumstances work was a necessity. A fur cap liner, she earned 7s.10½d. a week, lived on bread and cheese, supported an unemployed son and was at odds with his married sisters. 'Her daughters', she explained, 'spoke uppishly last time she saw them and she is not "a one to knuckle under to her children", they must come to see her first or she will never see them again'.[65]

Timing was important. The seasonality of production, for example, seems to have discouraged would-be respondents in certain consumer industries. A well-disposed Blackfriars hat manufacturer, who found participation inconvenient, wrote to explain: 'As ours is a piece work business and as no two persons ever earn alike it will be impossible for me to fill up your form, without I went into a lot of calculation [sic], for which being the busy season I have not time.'[66] The status of the survey, and above all the confusion of Charles with William Booth, made some informants unduly circumspect. Mr Palmer, a Bermondsey leather manufacturer, might, for example, have been more forthcoming had he appreciated the distinction. 'He was', Duckworth recorded, 'most unwilling to give me any information, and as he said goodbye asked me how long I had been working with the "General" – he seemed much relieved when he found I was no connection'.[67] The use of the data and the effect of publication were important considerations; for then, as now, the expectation of reward, and the extent of which the research interview might contribute towards it, was a key influence upon respondent participation. The depressed shipwrights, who could see no advantage in Booth's disclosures, were most uncommunicative. Leather workers, reassured by the reception of the Poverty Series, were more talkative. 'He asked', wrote Duckworth of their spokesmen, 'if this enquiry was likely to do anything for the workman, and on being told of the first volumes on London Labour said, "Oh if it is the same chap as did those then it is certain to do some good".'[68]

Employer response was influenced by similar considerations. Those who could see no immediate return were often unwilling to commit time and energy to the advancement of knowledge. 'Sorry I cannot assist you', wrote a Holloway linen draper. 'My business is carried on by self, wife and children. All we ask is legislative non-interferance'.[69] Sam Burns was equally blunt. A

[65] Booth Collection, B96, fos. 62-65.

[66] Booth Collection, B110, fo. 11.

[67] Booth Collection, B96, fo. 5.

[68] Robert L. Kahn and Charles F. Cannel 'Interviewing: Social Research', in David L. Sills ed., *International Encyclopaedia of Social Sciences*, 18 vols. (New York, 1968-79), viii, 149. See, too, Herbert H. Hyman, *Interviewing in Social Research* (Chicago, 1954). Quotation from Booth Collection, B95, fo. 47.

[69] Booth Collection, A20 [section 41]. fo. 32.

busy leather factor, he declined to see Duckworth, 'as he . . . did not see how he could gain anything by it and would do nothing for nothing.'[70] Others thought disclosure detrimental to business interests. These were of two kinds. On the one hand were employers who feared to divulge trade secrets to industrial competitors; on the other were those who considered the very act of inquiry subversive. 'I would certainly have the time expended to work up the figures you require if I thought that any useful purpose for the advantage of the poor or the increase of the peace and happiness of the country generally, could accrue from the publishing of the figures you desire to issue', wrote one such employer. "Do not those statistics tend to foster discontent among the poor, and instead of directing them to exercise the discipline, industry, and thrift by which their condition might be bettered, rather suggest that while such multitudes are poor, and so few are rich, the many might plunder the rich . . .'.[71]

Least co-operative of all were the small masters, merchants and proprietors engaged in the sweated trades. Reviled in press and parliament, harassed by Factory Inspectors, and subject to growing demands for the more effective regulation of their activities, these people were defensive and hostile to further scrutiny. Notwithstanding Booth's attempts to avoid prescription, the testimony of Beatrice Potter before the Select Committee on the Sweating System, together with the tendency to treat the Poverty Survey as a tract for the times, may well have compromised the investigation for this section of the community. Interviewers found them unhelpful and sometimes unpleasant. Arkell, for example, reported, 'a fruitless attempt' to assuage the fears of a tight-lipped tarpaulin manufacturer 'who was very suspicious and did not see why he should given any information.'[72]

Where the employer was a foreigner, these difficulties were magnified tenfold. Duckworth, who called upon a Whitechapel furrier armed with a letter of introduction from Canon Barnett, was mistaken for a Factory Inspector and sent off with a flea in his ear. Mr Koenigsberg, 'a Jew, small and evil-looking', created a most unfavourable impression. 'He was angry at my coming and told me to go in a mixture of German, Yiddish and English'. The son and daughter, though more amenable, were unreliable. 'Miss Koenigsberg', wrote Duckworth, 'contradicted herself a very great many times during the interview, the different members of her family who looked in from time to time made statements directly contradictory, so that the following interview is only an attempt at the exact truth'.[73] Arkell's experience was similar.

[70] Booth Collection, B96, fo. 14.
[71] Booth Collection, A8, fo. 616, Thos. H. Simmons to Charles Booth, 6 March 1893. Simmons, proprietor of the Export Perambulator Manufactory, did subsequently offer some information: see Booth Collection, A8 [section 18], fos. 30-31.
[72] Booth Collection, B105, fo. 39.
[73] Booth Collection, B96, fos. 47-48, 70.

The shipwrights, who had 'refused absolutely to state average earnings or to say whether the report was wrong', expressed a general resistance to the public discussion of wages and income.[74] Employers were no less reticent. Still-tongued sweaters were the most difficult. 'In all trades in which low wages are prevalent', Arkell concluded, 'the reluctance to give information is sinister'.[75] Even when informants were readily forthcoming, as was Mr Wiseman of the West India Dock Cooperage Company, the difficulties were considerable. Duckworth, though given access to the wage books, came a cropper on complex payment systems in which time rates and piece rates were combined. The 'collective bonus system', a sort of collectivised version of the butty system favoured, until quite recently, in the Durham coalfield, caused Duckworth chaos when encountered in London's dockland. 'The Piecework money is paid them in a lump and divided among themselves so that it is impossible to fill up the "further wages return".'[76] The point was also frequently made that analysis based on total wage costs might obscure significant differences in the position of different individuals within the same factory or work group.[77] The suggestion that the wages data for the Industry Series was obtained from employers without close inquiry is wrong. Booth had no illusions about the reliability of London employers or the unrepresentative character of those who were willing to answer his queries. The evidence of the notebooks shows that questions were asked, statements scrutinised, comparisons made and all reasonable attempts undertaken to verify the information provided.[78]

It was not only in respect of the collection of evidence that Booth was careful. Questions of interpretation were handled with equal diligence. Drafts on particular industries or sections were not only subjected to meticulous collective examination but were often sent for external assessment. Booth himself was permitted no exemption. Thus Harry Gosling, commenting on a report on Thames lightermen, pronounced 'the work excellent', while the exacting Aves, having failed to obtain corroboration by independent investigation, took Booth to task for his unsupported statements about the adverse effects of strike action upon the regularity of dock employment.[79] The Booth Inquiry sought to combat prejudice, not least its own. It sometimes failed but its successes were not inconsiderable.

---

[74] Booth Collection, B85, fos. 52, 81.

[75] Booth Collection, B105, fo. 39.

[76] Booth Collection, B84, fos. 44-46.

[77] Booth Collection, B93, fos. 39-40; Booth Collection, A20 [section 48], Replies to Questionnaires, fos. 3, 7; [section 41], fo. 74.

[78] See Booth's evidence, *Royal Commission on Labour*, Group C [c- 6708-vi] PP. 1892 (xxxv), qq. 8,921, 8,936-8,940. Cf. Thompson and Yeo, *Unknown Mayhew*, p. 105.

[79] Booth Collection, A23. fo. 41, Harry Gosling, Secretary of Amalgamated Society of Waterman and Lightermen, to Jesse Argyle, 11 November 1895; Booth Collection, A39, [section 7], fos. 11-14, Ernest Aves to Charles Booth, 25 April 1902.

2. Work and the Workers

The prominence of work in the Booth survey reflected more than an interest in the production of goods and services. Equally significant was the effect of work on the worker and on his or her place in society. The notebooks are a mine of information on the expectations and aspirations of individual workers and on the interaction of work with the bonds created by kinship, gender, religion, ethnicity, recreation and locality. Whether useful and fulfilling or alienating and oppressive, work for the bulk of the survey population was the central feature of their lives. It provided an identity as well as an income. Craftsmen, in particular, appear to have developed a distinctive work-oriented culture. Neighbourhood and community – patterns of sociability, of language, dress and politics – often reflected the needs and norms of the trade. In other industries work could be just as intrusive but rather less rewarding. Spokesmen for the shop assistants' union, for example, complained that the total commitment required by employers forced their members into a Jekyll-and-Hyde existence. 'This', Booth was told, 'has led to secret marriages; men living in during the week and with their wives from Saturday to Monday.'[1]

The Industrial Survey was not only concerned with work in relation to society. The social life of the workplace, too, was logged. The notebooks indeed recreate the sights, sounds, and almost the smell, of Londoners at work. The work environment made a deep impression. Messrs Martin, Hood & Larkin, lithographic and general printers, had a custom-built printery at Trafalgar House, Great Newport Street, which was spacious and imposing. 'On entering it', wrote Arkell, 'a visitor can hardly help noting how well lighted all the rooms are, even in the basement there were few dark corners.'[2] Smith Bros' bindery at Paternoster Row, by contrast, was decidedly inferior. 'The lower floors were rather dark partly owing to the narrowness of the street and the close proximity of the surrounding buildings but more to the great piles of paper, books and machinery which scarcely left room to move about freely.' The noise of machinery was intolerable, the toilet facilities abysmal. 'The general impression left after passing through was that both in arrangement and in the lack of arrangement, the only object considered here was the greatest possible amount of work.'[3] Equally grim was the Commercial Street sweat-shop, visited by

---

[1] Booth Collection, A20 [section 41], fo. 16.
[2] Booth Collection, B99, fo. 28.
[3] Booth Collection, B101, fos. 106-9.

Duckworth, where there was much crowding, little ventilation and 'a good deal of the *pazza del prossimo*'.[4]

The milieu of the workplace, with its shop clubs and slate clubs and informal support systems, was also noted.[5] Among parliamentary printers were discovered 'men who act as money lenders, supplying their needy shopmates' and an army of tally-men offering credit facilities for all sorts of purchases. 'You can often see advertisements addressed to foreman and others inviting them to take up agencies', said one disapproving manager.[6] Besides mutual assistance, the workplace supplied an area for the formation of friendships and close ties that sometimes persisted outside working hours. The leather trade, for example, was said to be 'a very sociable one'. Shavers and tanpit men, Booth was told, never drank 'more than three halfpints of an evening'.[7] Whatever the quantity consumed, after-work drinking seems to have been widespread among the industrial workers of late-Victorian London.

Meal-times, and tea-breaks too, offered opportunities for socialising on and off the premises. Arrangements varied both within and between industries. In some trades workers brought their own food and sent out for supplements; in others facilities were provided either by the employer or by the workers themselves. Print workers, for example, sometimes contributed 2d. per week to pay an old woman to cook for them. The development of close workties was, however, a gendered process. Informants, discussing meal arrangements in the printing trades, noted that women workers were more likely than men to take their food on the premises. The difference was easily explained. Inferior pay and inferior spending power served to restrict worker sociability and class solidarity. One vellum binder speaking of the women, put it simply: 'They could not afford to go out'.[8]

In productive relations, as in all aspects of London life, it was the infinite diversity that Booth found intriguing. The enormous variation in trade union strength was particularly striking. In some industries unions failed to develop any foothold; in others the boss did as he was told. One of the largest employers of skilled labour in the book trade, for example, considered himself in thrall to the gilders' union. 'The men come in when they like', he told Booth's assistant; he claimed that he 'cannot say anything to them as they can go and get work elsewhere'.[9] Dressers and dyers in the fur skin trade, too, were not to be trifled with. 'All the best men are in the Union', said the manager of one East End concern. 'If you offended one they would all go out and it would be impossible to replace them.' The

[4] Booth Collection, B96, fo. 78.
[5] Booth Collection, B96, fos. 12, 19, 27, 42.
[6] Booth Collection, B99, fos. 107-9.
[7] Booth Collection, B96, fos. 26-27.
[8] Booth Collection, B101, fos. 60, 66-7, 98, 104, 109.
[9] Booth Collection, B101, fos. 90-1.

respondent claimed that, he 'has often almost to go down on his knees to beg them in busy times to let him take more men in to do the work'.[10] His experience was not unique. Small and exclusive craft societies, like the Spanish and Morocco Leather Dressers, guarded the mysteries of the trade to the bafflement of observers and employers alike. 'It's a marvel the leather trade', wrote Duckworth, 'it's that peculiar . . . The masters don't know how things are got up, and the men won't tell them.'[11]

Employers, though wary of trade union power, were not uniformly hostile. 'Union men are the best', declared an elderly print employer. 'Very exceptional to find a good man outside the Society.'[12] Some, like Messrs Connolly Bros, curriers, allowed their workers to belong to a trade union and paid union rates but would not permit a closed shop.[13] Others were more critical. George Unwin of Unwin Bros, the publishers, 'a pleasant white-headed old gentleman', described members of the London Society of Compositors as 'regular duffers'.[14] Not all proprietors were anti-compositor. Mr Franklin, a City print manager, felt just as strongly about the lithographers whom, he told Booth, were 'the laziest and worst lot in the trade'.[15]

The most objectionable feature of trade unionism was that it stifled initiative, restrained output and made industry and employment vulnerable to foreign competition. 'With the Union man', Booth was told, 'the object is to do as little as possible for his money.' 'In the old times, before 1889, if a man came in and worked quick he was 'led a life" by others . . . The Union discouraged men doing their best. There is a sort of unwritten law and you must not do more than "so much an hour".'[16] The indictment went further. The narrow instrumental approach encouraged by the unions, it was claimed, diminished craft pride and this eroded industrial employment. Progressive publishers, like J. M. Dent, thought that craftsmen with designer skills were an endangered species. 'It is difficult to get a man to understand artistic work', he complained.[17]

Employers dreamed of a world free of unions as inmates dream of a prison without gaolers. Germany, with its docile, ill-paid workforce, seemed like heaven to hard-pressed English employers. 'German workmen in chemical factories work much longer hours for lower wages, and owing, I believe, to their military service, are much more amenable to discipline', one

[10] Booth Collection, B96, fos. 30-31.
[11] Booth Collection, B95, fo. 45.
[12] Booth Collection, B99, fos. 13-14.
[13] Booth Collection, B96, fo. 11.
[14] Booth Collection, B99, fos. 22-23.
[15] Booth Collection, B99, fos. 55-55.
[16] Booth Collection, B99, fos. 4-5.
[17] Booth Collection, B101, fo. 96.

of them told Howard.[18] A master who had lost control of the supply of skilled labour was like a fly in a spider's web. 'If he had his way', said one imaginary resister, 'he would only employ married men as they are more reliable.'[19]

Management practices, in reality, were more varied than employer attitudes. Apart from the process of economic development and the level of technology, much depended upon the size of firm and its labour and product markets. The contest between capital and labour was conducted principally in workshops and petty manufacturies. The small master, the typical London employer, operated a simple management structure. In consumer goods industries, like footwear, furniture and clothing, where once-skilled crafts had broken down into a set of semi-skilled processes, workers were subject to close personal supervision. In family firms these supervisory roles were often shared among the proprietor's relatives. Duckworth, describing the machine room of an East London furrier's, noted the strict discipline enforced in such establishments. 'The men working machines', he wrote,

> were very small looking foreigners with sunken pallid cheeks. Of the women some looked ill and others tired, and all were working as if their very lives depended on it, as indeed they probably did. There was no looking up as you passed and the scowls and evident dislike of Miss K. [the governor's daughter] when we passed and she asked about the work were ill concealed. Never have I seen machines worked so fast or such hopeless faces. There was no talking and very little giggling even when Miss K. was called away and I was left to walk round by myself. They seemed mostly too tired.[20]

In workshops other than sweat-shops effective management was generally vested in the foreman. Time and again it was the 'gaffer' to whom Booth was referred for information on wages and working practices. His role was critical in the organisation and allocation of work, in the fixing of wages and in the recruitment and discipline of the workforce. Training and promotion also depended upon his judgement. The foreman, who had usually 'worked his way up' from the shop floor, knew that knowledge was power and used it accordingly. A lad to whom he had taken might expect to prosper. 'If you are smart and liked by the foreman', Booth was told, 'he may tell you things and show you dodges which it would have been very difficult for you to have found out by yourself.'[21]

Discrimination was central to the division of labour. Differences were applied to the regularity as well as the level of earnings. In industries in

---

[18] Booth Collection, B93, fo. 41.
[19] Booth Collection, B101, fo. 98.
[20] Booth Collection, B96, fo. 79.
[21] Booth Collection, B96, fo. 24.

which skills were in short supply the less accomplished were the first to be turned off during the slack season and the last to be reinstated. Thus fleshers and shavers were kept on while less valuable yardsmen were dismissed.[22] The regulars, though, were not necessarily the best-paid workers. A vellum-binder, employed in a Bishopsgate printery, explained: 'They did not pay the highest wages not do they cut up the work and employ lads and girls to the extent that the large shops do. The old hands have many privileges.'[23] Within the workshop they enjoyed greater autonomy and job control. Though once again the most privileged were not necessarily the most free. Indirect management, as in certain sectors of the building and leather industries, for example, allowed workers considerable latitude. In the Bermondsey tanneries, where work was subcontracted to the foreman, controls were minimal. Booth's assistant explained: 'Work is given to the foreman at a given price to do in a given time. He shares it among the men who get it done as they like provided it is done by the right time.'[24]

Larger firms developed more elaborate management strategies. Model employers, like Hazell, Watson & Viney, the printers, had facilities for clubs, savings and refreshments and made provision for the technical education of their apprentices.[25] Burroughs-Wellcome, manufacturing chemists, were equally solicitous. The company, apart from a profit-sharing scheme, introduced an eight-hour day on the advice of Henry George, who was also persuaded to open its Dartford Works in the presence of 10,000 people. Booth was informed that he and his associates were welcome to visit the new plant 'with perfect freedom to speak with any or all of our employees'.[26] Others were more cautious. Allen & Hanburys, the Bethnal Green-based druggists, who relied upon secret bonus payments to selected workmen, did not wish their management methods to be made public.

Howard, though irritated by their secrecy, was impressed with their efficiency. The firm, having discharged one third of their girl workers during the summer slack season, used the seasonality of production as a form of discipline. Notes were made on work performance and only those deemed satisfactory were rehired in the autumn. 'In this way', Howard remarked, 'the idle and troublesome are weeded out.' The regime was strict. No hanky-panky was permitted – a man caught kissing a factory girl was dismissed – drunkenness was exceptional and St Monday unknown. 'The whole staff', Howard wrote, 'are an unusually high class of working people, both women and men. The girls are neatly and quietly dressed. The men

[22] Booth Collection, B96, fo. 17.
[23] Booth Collection, B101, fo. 100.
[24] Booth Collection, B96, fos. 19-20, 260.
[25] Booth Collection, B99, fos. 40-43.
[26] Booth Collection, B93, fos. 30-31.

have as a rule quick and intelligent expressions.' 'There is', he concluded, 'perfect amity between the firm and their employees.'[27]

The division of labour as described in the Booth notebooks was not a static one. Chief among the changes recorded was the decline of the London artisan. Competitive pressures, provincial and foreign, which had earlier led to the relocation of some crafts and the destruction or degradation of others, continued to erode the capital's manufacturing base. High overheads and falling prices intensified the search for cheaper methods of production. Cost-cutting measures within the existing division of labour included the manipulation of manning rations and wage payment systems, speed-up, overtime and casual labour. New technologies in some cases sharpened the contest for control. The mechanisation of typesetting, for example, led to turmoil in the print industry. The scene at the offices of the *Globe*, where machines had replaced men, was sombre. 'After the interview', Duckworth wrote, 'I went to the composing room with the foreman. It is a lofty room lighted from above with a gallery running around. In this gallery there were a number of empty frames – the piece hands used to work there. The Linotype machines were ranged along opposite sides of the room.'[28]

The profit squeeze also intensified efforts to improve labour discipline. In the building trades, as in engineering, 'speed' men, with extra pay, were also introduced to set the pace for other workers.[29] Renewed pressure was also brought to bear upon the irregularity of a task-centred work-culture with its drink customs and week-end excesses. 'There is often but little work done on a Monday', Duckworth was told. 'The men "take a Mike" and then have to slog it on later.' For Booth's benefit, he added that 'Mike' was the proverbial street pipe layer who merely looks at his pick and does no work.[30]

Shop floor responses were carefully documented. Some trades surrendered unconditionally. Clerkenwell watch-makers, in the face of American competition, vacated the mass market or shifted to repair work. Sail makers succumbed without a fight. Book binders, though more resilient, were still down-hearted. The eight-hours movement, contrary to expectations, gave them little relief from employer pressure. 'The eight hours has brought with it more over sight and time is more closely kept', said the secretary of the Vellum-Binders Society. 'The employers have gained by the change . . .'[31] The manager of the Bookbinders Co-Operative Society agreed:

> The conditions of employment are hardening. A man must be at his bench now ready to work when the dinner hour, or other meal time, is over, so he has to come in five minutes beforehand to put on his apron and slippers. Formerly men would

[27] Booth Collection, B93, fos. 69-71.
[28] Booth Collection, B99, fos. 83-84.
[29] Booth Collection, A3, fo. 256.
[30] Booth Collection, B96, fo. 56.
[31] Booth Collection, B101, fo. 27.

clear up their bench and wash their hands during the last five minutes but this is not permitted.[32]

Compositors were more combative. The issues raised by the introduction of the Linotype machine and the strategies pursued over its manning and regulation fill many pages in the Booth notebooks. Compositors, it becomes clear, were among the best organised crafts, with very high union densities. Print employers in the book and newspaper trades were less than keen to engage them. Arkell noted the stratagems devised to undermine craft control. Country compositors being considered more compliant than their Cockney compeers, steps were taken to replace the one by the other. 'When he wants a compositor', one master explained, 'he does not go to the Society House but advertises in the country newspapers and when replies are received tells the accepted applicant that he must join the Society.'[33] Others encouraged the formation of 'inner societies' of fifth columnists to regulate the supply of labour without recourse to the official union.[34] The Linotype made confrontation unavoidable. Booth's investigators record the opening phases of the battle.

In relation to the unskilled, however, it was the tail-end of the struggle with which the Booth Inquiry was concerned. The industrial survey, conducted during the economic downswing, when the shock waves created by the dock strike had subsided, supplies a unique portrait of the New Unionism in the depression of 1892-95. Comparing port employment before and after the strike, Booth was confident that the hopelessness and despair, reported in the Poverty Series, had been dispelled. The Dockers' Union made all the difference: 'What the men had achieved by organization', he wrote, 'was not to be measured solely by advantages obtained in pay or the conditions of employment. By organization they step into line with other more highly skilled and more highly paid labour, and so acquire a position of great practical value.'[35] The progress of realignment, however, seemed to depend not only upon the de-casualisation of dock labour, but also upon the cultural resources of the port worker. The difficulties here were formidable. Workers on the waterfront were not only inferior in market position and income; they also lacked the traditions, loyalties and values that enabled craftsmen to sustain effective trade unions.

The port transport industry was of great diversity in its occupational

---

[32] Booth Collection, B101, fo. 70; see also, Booth Collection, B101, fos. 87, 98.

[33] Booth Collection, B99, fos. 6-7.

[34] Booth Collection, B99, fos. 22-23. On the controversy aroused by these cliques, see H.A. Clegg, Alan Fox and A.F. Thompson, *A History of British Trade unions since 1889* (Oxford, 1964), p. 144; and for an attempt to set some of the general issues within a comparative context, see Royden Harrison and Jonathan Zeitlin, eds., *Divisions of Labour, Skilled Workers and Technological Change in Nineteenth-Century England* (Brighton, 1985).

[35] *Industry*, 3. p. 399.

make-up and employment structure. Port services were as varied as their providers. Small and specialised, port employers relied upon a reserve army of labour to satisfy their rapidly changing manpower requirements. The casual system of employment created an immobile but highly stratified workforce. Occupational distinctions based upon the assertion of a special skill, competence or aptitude, gave the riverside hierarchy an almost caste-like character. There were sharp divisions between ship workers concerned with the stowing and packing of goods, and shore-workers, responsible for discharging, dispatching and warehousing operations. Stevedores and lightermen, who considered themselves an elite among port workers, distanced themselves from mere quay labourers, as did the specialised handlers of bulk goods who regarded the work performed by the latter as unskilled, unmanly and unworthy. Tea porters considered dock labour beneath them. The Cutler Street warehousemen, Llewellyn Smith was told, 'pride themselves on not being as "dockers" are'. Specialists in the export department of the East and South Docks were called 'gentlemen dockers'. Unincorporated fruit porters were known as 'serfs'.[36]

The 'Teas', 'Wools', 'Lumpers' and 'Coalies' were both proud of their expertise and somewhat proprietorial in attitude towards their particular branch of employment. Some possessed well-established combinations. Fruit porters and lightermen, operating under the privileged jurisdiction of the City Companies, claimed preferential and monopoly rights in their respective spheres. Stevedores, corn porters, timber porters and coal heavers displayed all the exclusiveness and sectionalism of the craftsman without his bargaining power or external recognition. Small, compact and relatively highly-paid, these specialist hands were held up as archetypal dock workers. At the mercy of foremen and contractors, and constrained by custom and the localised work-sharing arrangements that were a central feature of dock labour management, the casual worker presented the union organiser with his greatest challenge.[37]

The Booth Inquiry devoted special attention to the character and condition of the waterfront unions. Riverside workers appeared democratic in spirit but conservative in practice, clinging to their customs and local privileges and suspicious of leaders who threatened to change them. 'Troublesome as were the discussions with the masters at the time of the strike,' wrote Booth, 'those between the men and their leaders were even more so, and, in this respect, the difficulties encountered after the battle had

[36] Booth Collection, B140, fos. 13-15, 27; B141, fos. 10, 42.
[37] On the condition of waterside labour, see John Lovell, *Stevedores and Dockers* (London, 1969); Gareth Stedman Jones, *Outcast London* (Oxford, 1971); Gordon Phillips and Noel Whiteside, *Casual Labour: The Unemployment Question in the Post Transport Industry, 1880-1970* (Oxford, 1985).

been won were greater than those met with during the strike or before it.'[38] His notebooks bear out this judgement.

Apart from the principals of the smaller societies, the survey included a good selection of the district and branch secretaries of the Dockers' Union as well as permanent officials like Mann and Tillet. Llewellyn Smith conducted the interviews with the assistance of Argyle and Arkell. Booth, as interviewer and analyst, contributed revealing life-histories of individual dock labourers and a detailed appreciation of the progress of their union.

Care was taken with the description and assessment of the New Unionism – its management and membership, subscriptions and benefits, policies and procedures and its relations with other unions. The quality of its personnel was also important. Thus Tom Mann, assessing the strengths of his executive, was reported to have said that, member for member, they were the equal of the Amalgamated Society of Engineers.[39] Subordinate officers, too, were noted for their energy and imagination. The strength of the union relied in no small part upon secretaries, like Mr Helps of the Export Branch (No. 3 District), who sustained the membership with a programme of concerts and 'free n'easies' held each month at Plimsoll Street School – the entertainment supplied by the men themselves on a borrowed harmonium. 'A great deal depends on having a vigorous chairman of Branch meetings', Llewellyn Smith concluded.[40]

Survival was indeed the basic concern. Impoverished dock workers found regular subscription difficult, increases impossible and levies loathsome. Trade union officers emerge from the interviews as a cadre that was more concerned with consolidation than advance. Whatever the principles and assumptions, the structure and procedures of the New Unionism were quickly adjusted to meet the circumstances and values of waterfront workers. Distant bureaucracies were singularly inappropriate. Thus the Coal Porters' Union – which eschewed an executive and referred all matters to the branches for approval – presented its exceptionally democratic arrangements as essential to the cohesion and commitment of the membership. 'It's here that most Unions go wrong', said Mr Brill, the president. Direct representation, he explained, acted as a brake on the impetuous, 'keeps up the interest of the whole body, and prevents suspicion of the Union officials which is the case of most centralised Unions'.[41] Direct election, Tom Mann argued, made a virtue out of necessity. 'In case of blunders', he explained, 'the responsibility can be thrown more directly on the men themselves, and hence there is less chance of disaffection.'[42]

[38] *Industry*, 3, p. 404.
[39] Booth Collection, B140, fo. 2.
[40] Booth Collection, B141, fos. 17, 43.
[41] Booth Collection, B144, fos. 65-66.
[42] Booth Collection, B141, fo. 4.

Stability and continuity were the watchwords of the New Unionism as they had been of the Old. Recruitment and retention were major concerns. Gasworkers, said Will Thorne, relied on moral suasion. 'Those who do not belong', he told Jesse Argyle, 'get such a heckling from their fellow workmen that they are generally brought in.'[43] Casual workers, facing aggressive employers in an overstocked labour market, were however, sceptical. 'Members', complained an official of the United Brickworkers and Brick Wharf Labourers' Union, 'seem to think that they are quite as safe for employment without paying to the Union, as they would be by paying.'[44] The regulars, by contrast, declined to place their privileges at risk. The Permanent Labourers' Mutual Protection Association, whose members' pensions were threatened by strike action, seceded from the more militant dock labourers' union. 'The pension', wrote Booth's investigator, concluding his interview with the Association's secretary, 'undoubtedly prevents strikes and causes both sides to be considerate with each other.'[45]

Unable to deliver wage improvements, general unions resumed functions which gave permanence and stability. The Navvies, Bricklayers and General Labourers' Union, for example, became a sick benefit society in 1894. Union officials, interviewed the following year, 'now claim that it is the mainstay of their society'.[46] The dockers had introduced funeral benefits some years earlier. Yet this essay in prudence and moderation was not a source of unqualified admiration.

The Industry Series was itself a response to the New Unionism. Booth was prompted to extend his inquiry in order to take account of the renewed signs of hope embodied in that extraordinary creative upsurge in the sweated trades and on the waterfront at the close of the eighties. His intention, from the outset, was that the inquiry would be union-led and worker-centred.[47] The unexpected capacity for organised and disciplined action displayed by hitherto unorganisable elements gave evidence of a peaceful outcome to the Labour Question. Booth wanted to know more about them and the possibilities which their action had created. That the downward extension of trade unionism was a progressive force he had no doubt. Booth, indeed, viewed organisation as an antidote to that 'helplessness' which he identified as a defining characteristic of 'sweating'. The diffusion of trade unionism, he told the Royal Commission on Labour, was among the most powerful of the convergent influences by which the social problem would be solved.[48] Over the course of the *Life and Labour* inquiry

---

[43] Booth Collection, B144, fo. 11.

[44] Booth Collection, B146, fo. 27.

[45] Booth Collection, B146, fos. 31-34.

[46] Booth Collection, B146, fo. 49.

[47] *Royal Commission on Labour*, Group C, [c-6708-vi] PP. 1892 (xxxv), q. 8,932.

[48] *Royal Commission on Labour*, Group C, [c-7063-i] PP. 1893-4 (xxxix), qq. 5,409. 5,418, 5,462-5,464, 5,608-5,611, 5,686-5,688.

his views changed, as it became clear that the New Unionists were as defensive and restrictionist in outlook as the Old.

3. *The Booths and the Webbs: Some Comparisons and Contrasts*

Ironically much of the experience acquired in the Poverty Series was to be appropriated by the Webbs for their trade union studies. Survey skills learned in the East End proved readily transferable when, in 1892, Beatrice Potter married Sidney Webb. A courtship accompanied by rule books, meetings and interviews, and a honeymoon spent investigating the trade societies of Dublin and Belfast, set the tone of their extraordinarily productive partnership. Its first fruits, *The History of Trades Unionism*, was published in the spring of 1894; it supplied the prologue to the scientific analysis of the structure and role of trades unions that was embodied in their magnum opus, *Industrial Democracy*, which appeared three years later.[1] These formative studies overlapped with the Industry Series but were very different in character. It is interesting and instructive to compare the Booth and the Webb inquiries in order to appreciate the significance of the material they gathered.

Industrial Democracy, Beatrice Webb recalled, relied upon the research undertaken for the *History of Trade Unionism*. The idea for such a study had been germinating before the estrangement from the Booths and arose directly out of her work on co-operation. That it would be a joint work was not at first apparent. Sidney Webb and Beatrice Potter were not at this point 'one intellect with two voices'.[2] Beatrice, a student of Spencer who wanted to study human beings 'just as if they were animals or plants', had developed an interest in institutional analysis. Her first thoughts were to organise a thoroughly up-to-date survey of trade unions in collaboration with other 'experts'. It was a course which the supportive Sidney encouraged. 'I think you would do well to take Ll[ewllyn] Smith into partnership in the T. Union book', he wrote in March 1891.[3]

The scope of the study, though, was clearer than the shape. 'I am beginning to see into the leading points I want to investigate in trade unions', she wrote in September that year. These, ranged under six heads, included trade union structure and administration; mutual protection; the standard of expenditure of the worker; monopolies and restrictive practices; and the skill, training and adaptability of the worker or, in her own phrase, 'the technical and moral gratifications of the worker as a pro-

---

[1] Beatrice Webb, *Our Partnership*, ed. B. Drake and M.I. Cole (London, 1948), pp. 25-32.

[2] A.G. Gardiner, *Pillars of Society* (London, 1916), p. 192.

[3] Beatrice Potter to Sidney Webb, 25 February 1891, *Letters*, i, pp. 257, 260.

fessional'.[4] The object of the investigation remained undefined. The contrast with the more sharply focused Industry Series was pointed.

Llewellyn Smith had preferred to remain one of Booth's associates rather than join with Beatrice and Sidney in an alternative project. Although the degree is not easily measured, there were evident tensions between the Booth and Webb inquiries. On the announcement of Beatrice's engagement, Mary Booth had taken her aside. 'You see Charlie and I have *nothing* in common with Mr Webb', she explained. 'Charlie could never go to him for help, and he would never go to Charlie, so that it would not be natural for them to see each other.'[5] Apart from anything else, there was a strong suspicion that her fiancé confused socialism with social inquiry. Booth, though, had taken against Sidney as much on social as political grounds. Llewellyn Smith had no qualms about Webb's pedigree but doubted his integrity. Beatrice's book, he felt, would be seriously compromised by any such association. A suggested exchange of information in respect of the London trade unions was coolly received. 'To my surprise', wrote Sidney 'he hummed and hawed; said he did not know how far he could use our material; and then asked me bluntly whether I was doing the work for science or for propaganda!'[6] Llewellyn Smith's comments suggest – albeit unwittingly – that a historical basis might serve to differentiate the two inquiries. Sidney, who had a well-developed historical sense, noted its absence in others:

> What seems to be most in the minds of Booth and Smith (and it is a hint to us) is to discover what part trade unionism plays in each man's mind. They are seeing more branch secretaries than general secretaries and cross-examining them. They have already begun . . . But they do not seem to be going *very* deeply into old records.[7]

Beatrice was not put out. The Booths would in due course come round. 'Do not trouble about it', she counselled. 'We have such stupendous advantages and good fortune in getting our information that we have no right to feel depressed on account of this stupid rebuff. We shall get the result of their enquiry – and probably the material before we want it.'[8]

Beatrice was right. Booth did come round and there was some subsequent pooling of information. Llewellyn Smith, who had on his own account undertaken historical research into port labour unions, was quick to mend fences. Sidney was delighted. 'He will . . . have got a mass of information

[4] Beatrice Potter to Sidney Webb, 2 September 1891, *Letters*, i, p. 286.
[5] Norman and Jeanne Mackenzie eds., *The Diary of Beatrice Webb, 1873-1892*, 4 vols (London, 1982-86), i, p. 359.
[6] Sidney Webb to Beatrice Potter, 24 October 1891, *Letters*, i, p. 313.
[7] Ibid.
[8] Beatrice Potter to Sidney Webb, 25 October 1891, *Letters*, i, p. 315.

about the riverside trades which will save us much work.'[9] Schloss and Fox,
too, were readily approachable. Clara Collet, by contrast, was thought to be
less obliging. 'Miss C.E. Collet, can tell him [SW] *everything*', wrote Isabella
Ford, 'but I don't know whether she will, of course.'[10] The information flow,
though, was not all one way. F.W. Galton, who had abandoned his craft to
become private secretary to the Webbs, was invited to lunch with Duckworth
at the Savile Club in order to discuss his trade and its conditions.[11] Even so,
the extent of co-operation was uncertain.[12]

The uncertainty made the learning process more difficult than it need
have been. Survey methods in both investigations were to some extent
experimental. The questionnaire administered to employers in the Poverty
Series interviews, for example, was revised and improved for its successor.[13]
But if the Booth survey found questionnaire design difficult, the Webbs
found it a nightmare. Imagining that their appetite for information represented the norm, the couple proceeded to construct a list of 120 questions,
displayed under twenty separate headings, on separate detachable sheets,
with spaces left for the answers. Beatrice, writing more than forty years
later, recalled the 'glum looks or stony silence' as trade unionists and
employers turned the pages of this elaborate and formidable document.
Notwithstanding the expense – they had in their enthusiasm ordered a
thousand copies to be printed – and the fact that the questionnaire represented a full week's work, the Webbs had made a mistake and knew it. 'When
the copies were circulated by post', she continued, 'the result, with a few
exceptions, was nil . . . Exceptionally intelligent trade union officials,
anxious to be helpful, ignored our questionnaire and posted to us their
current rules and annual report; a valuable result, but one which we could
have obtained more easily and more universally if we had merely asked for
these documents, without troubling the official with any questions.' Booth,
being more sensitive or far-sighted, included a request for these materials in
his interview schedules.[14]

The precepts which the Webbs were later to offer the prospective social
investigator are not so much an indicator of their actual practice as a

[9] Sidney Webb to Beatrice Potter, 9 December 1891, *Letters*, i, p. 347.

[10] BLPES, Webb Trade Union Collection, EA XXIV, fo.. 435, David Schloss to Beatrice
Potter, 6 April 1891; Webb Trade Union Collection, EA XLVII, fos. 73-77, Isabella Ford to
Dear Edward, 21 July 1891 and S.N. Fox to Sidney Webb, 28 February 1896.

[11] BLPES, F.W. Galton, MS Autobiography (1939-44), chaps 5-6, p. 20.

[12] Against certain of the Webb trade union interviews is written 'Mr Booth's books'. Whether
the annotation was included for purposes of comparison or demarcation is not clear: see Webb
Trade Union Collection, EA XLI, fos. 14, 37, 182, 208.

[13] Cf. Appendix I and II.

[14] Sidney and Beatrice Webb, *Methods of Social Study* (London, 1932), pp. 68-70. The abortive
questionnaire is reprinted as a caution on pp. 75-82; for the Booth Trade Union Questionnaire, see below Appendix III.

reflection upon its defects.[15] The centrality of the interview in relation to the Webb and Booth inquiries arose out of the uncertain status of the labour movement and its distance from the dominant literary culture. Oral sources were thus a necessary substitute for the written record. In the circumstances of trade union inquiry, wrote Beatrice, 'any adequate investigation . . . would be impossible without considerable personal intercourse with the leading personalities, and even with members of the rank and file'.

Booth and his secretariat relied upon the extensive network of informants available to them through Toynbee Hall, but also took pains to enlist the support of influential figures within the labour movement. 'They have a circular "letter of credence" from the [London] Trades Council which Ll. Smith seemed to think a great deal of', Sidney informed Beatrice in October 1891. The Webbs had their own network, created by Beatrice and enlarged by Sidney, which overlapped that of their rivals but grew wider as the character and scope of the Webb inquiry progressed. The formation of such connections was not without difficulties. The labour movement at the close of the eighties was a political minefield in which the prudent stepped carefully. Sidney was worried. One slip and their status as 'sociological adventurers' might be irreparably damaged. Not so Beatrice, who was confident that she had the measure of 'Old' and 'New' Unionists alike. Her good standing with the former ('it is the "Old" Unionists who have the records') did not make her unacceptable to their opponents, whose willingness to talk with anyone who would listen, made them, in her own words, '*very easy* to [interview] and to get at'.[16]

To get close to working people and their institutions required courage as well as perseverance and Beatrice possessed both. The Webb partnership, it is well known, relied upon a broad division of labour in which Sidney did the reading and the writing and Beatrice the inspiring and the talking. It was she who undertook the field-work, supervised their research assistants and conducted 'our innumerable interviews with trade union officials and members, with friendly employers and their foremen, and with the agents of employers' associations'.[17] Beatrice, who was both attracted and repelled by 'this somewhat ugly side of humanity', interviewed trade unionists in bars, hotels and even had them round for dinner when she was temporarily resident at Herbert Spencer's house in St John's Wood. 'Poor Herbert Spencer!' she confided to her diary, 'To think that his august drawing room is nightly the scene of socialistic talk, clouds of tobacco, aided with whiskey'.[18]

---

[15] See T.S. Simey, 'The Contribution of Sidney and Beatrice Webb to Sociology', *British Journal of Sociology*, xii (1960), pp. 112-15.

[16] Beatrice Potter to Sidney Webb, 25 October 1891, *Letters*, i, p. 316.

[17] *Methods of Social Study*, p. 133.

[18] *Diary of Beatrice Webb*, i, pp. 361-63.

She did not work alone. The bulk of the Webb interviews were under-taken by F.W. Galton a time-served engraver and trade union official, whom Sidney engaged at the beginning of 1892 for £100 per year plus expenses. 'Webb and Miss Potter', he recalled, 'had drawn up a sort of questionnaire for my guidance', and so armed he sallied forth on his first industrial tour. Galton was in many respects an excellent choice. Although pleased to escape the life of a journeyman engraver, he was neither uncomfortable with trade unionists, as was Sidney, nor uninterested in industrial processes, as was Beatrice. He soon fell into a regular routine, 'Each spring and summer was spent travelling about the country making investigations. In the autumn I returned to London and my time was spent mainly in dissecting the material gathered and arranging it and re-arranging it as required for the various chapters of the History of Trade Unions'.[19]

The Webb interviews differed from those of the Booth Inquiry in certain respects. In the first place, the survey population appears to have been of a more homogeneous character with the underrepresentation of manage-ment and its representatives being more pronounced than in the Booth survey.[20] In the second, the Webb interviews, though organised for the convenience of the respondent, lack the variety of location and enriching detail of the Booth notebooks. Visits to mines or potteries, dutifully under-taken by Galton, were useful and sometimes essential, but not engaging. Dissimilarities in interview technique were greater still. Beatrice likened the research interview to a form of cross-examination. Sidney, who had quali-fied as a barrister, was like-minded. Together they behaved like bewigged pugilists. Omitted from *Methods of Social Study*, but well-known to all who came into contact with them, was what Margaret Cole described as 'their devastating technique of joint interview, in which they battered from either side the object of their attention – sometimes a political opponent, some-times an official who had not devoted much thought to the underlying implications of his official actions – with a steady left-right of question, argument, assertion and contradiction, and left him converted, bewildered, or indignant, as the case might be'.[21] Interview skills, so central to the craft of the social investigator, were never acquired by the Webbs.

The recording process was also distinctive. Beatrice herself, a poor note-taker, relied upon secretarial support from Galton.[22] The Webb interviews, while structured, did not follow a standard format. Some were written up as

[19] BLPES, Coll. Misc., 315, F.W. Galton, MS Autobiography (1939-1944), i, chaps 5-6, pp. 9-18. See, too, F.W. Galton, 'Investigating with the Webbs' in M. Cole ed., *The Webbs and their Work* (London, 1949), pp. 29-37.
[20] Precise comparisons are difficult. Booth, we know, circularised all the principal London employers and declared himself satisfied with their response. The handlist of the Webb Trade Union Collection, by contrast, includes but a handful of employers.
[21] Margaret Cole, *Beatrice Webb* (London, 1945), p. 59.
[22] On Beatrice's inadequacies as an interviewer, see above, pp. 62ff.

a continuous narrative; others were no more than a series of discrete statements.[23] Booth's practice of taking telling phrases and striking quotation was not adopted. Neither was the data organised under various heads to facilitate comparison and analysis. As an information retrieval system their procedures were hopeless. But for Sidney's phenomenal memory, it is difficult to imagine how it could have worked at all. The conclusion is irresistible: the apostles of regulation would have benefited enormously from the guidance of a first-class project manager.

Notwithstanding some similarities – documentary analysis, interviews and personal observation – the Booth and Webb surveys addressed the labour question from different standpoints. Booth, a social reformer rather than a scholar, possessed a limited understanding of the historical process.[24] The *Life and Labour* inquiry, as he readily confessed, was a snapshot of London in the last decade of the nineteenth century. The retrospective element was personal rather than structural and derived from individual life histories obtained by interview. The Webbs, as historians and sociologists, operated a wider time-frame but a narrower vision. 'In spite of all the pleas of modern historians for less history of the actions of governments, and more descriptions of the manners and customs of the governed', they wrote in 1894, 'it remains true that history, however it may relieve and enliven itself with descriptions of the manners and morals of the people, must, if it is to be history at all, follow the course of continuous organisations.'[25] Sociology followed the same course. Organisation was central and continuity critical.

The Webbs, in short, were primarily concerned with the role of trade unionism in advanced industrial society. Progress, in their view, depended upon the expansion of industry and the effective use of productive resources. The superiority of factory production over domestic manufacture was taken as axiomatic. Besides the satisfaction of consumer wants, the factory system was also preferred for its character-forming discipline. The personal habits and injurious irregularity of the independent producer would soon be a thing of the past. The retarding effects of a drink-based work culture – so damaging to the supply of qualified officers and trade union leaders – might also be diminished. 'There is no longer a choice between idiosyncracy and uniformity', they wrote approvingly.[26] Big was beautiful. The future, as they saw it, lay with large-scale capital intensive industry, managed by professionals, and with trade unions that were national in scope, centralised in administration and serviced by trained

[23] For an example of the former, see Webb Trade Union Collection, EA XL, fos. 69-76, interview with J. Taylor of the United English and Scotch Carpet Weavers Association; for an example of the latter, see ibid., fos. 222-23.

[24] See obituary notice, *The Times*, 24 November 1916.

[25] Sidney and Beatrice Webb, *The History of Trade Unionism, 1660-1920* (London, 1920) p. viii

[26] Sidney and Beatrice Webb, *Industrial Democracy* (London, 1902), pp. 326-27.

experts. Coal and cotton were the paradigms. These federations with exclusively trade objects, which together accounted for a fifth of union members, formed a sharp contrast with the boot makers, brush makers and antediluvian handicraft workers in the 'archaic trades'. Trade unionists in these outmoded industries were said to be ineffectual and irrelevant and at odds with 'the more thoughtful workmen' who 'denounce the whole system of individual production . . . and . . . urge its supersession by the factory system, where collective regulation, both of wages and hours, would become possible'.[27]

The feeble condition of trade unionism in London gave substance to their analysis. As authors of the 'first complete census of Trade Unionism from one end of the kingdom to the other', the Webbs had no difficulty in showing the uneven distribution of trade unionists by occupation and district. Trade unionism was found to be most highly developed among colliers, cotton operatives and engineers; its strongholds lay in the mining and manufacturing districts, where in some cases it 'was practically coextensive with the manual working class'.[28] London, by comparison, was a desert. On this the Booth and Webb surveys were at one. Total union membership amounted to 180,000 equivalent to 13.5 per cent of the adult male population. These were divided among some 250 separate organisations. In few cases were the members of a single trade combined in a single society. Only thirty-five societies had a membership of more than 1,000 and these accounted for 112,000 (62 per cent) of the total. The remainder had on average just over two hundred members.[29] These tiny trade societies, with their non-protective benefits, their indifference to training, industrial impotence and idiosyncratic culture, were everything that the Webbs deplored. Their days, though, were numbered. In the Webbian world of the future, trade unions would surrender incidental 'friendly' functions so as to better perform their prescribed role as industrial bargainers, administrators, technical instructors and advisers to government.

Preoccupied with labour organisation, the Webbs were impatient of impediments to its perfection. Foremost amongst them was the disorganised labour market. None was more disorganised than the London market. Large-scale industry, killed off by provincial competition and the prohibitive costs of land and fuel, left a labour force deficient in semi-skilled factory occupations and encouraged resort to industrial alternatives that permitted large fluctuations in output without overhead cost to the employer: in other words, sweating. No advance was possible so long as outworkers, small masters and casual labourers were free to work under conditions that were incompatible with physical health or industrial efficiency. The Webbs

[27] Webb, *Industrial Democracy*, pp. 337-44.
[28] Webb, *History of Trade Unionism*, pp. 422-41.
[29] *Industry*, 5, pp. 143-46.

5555

indeed posited a fundamental antagonism between the organised and the sweated trades. The elimination of the latter, in all their degenerate forms, was vital to Britain's industrial ascendancy and to the progressive development of the labour movement. 'Home work', they declared, 'makes all Trade Unionism impossible.' Small masters and independent producers were equally injurious. Casual labourers were 'hopeless'.[30] In London, where the 'parasitic trades' were prevalent, there was no scope for the practical and sober-minded trade unionism of the colliers and cotton spinners. The unorganised masses of the metropolis, in short, presented themselves as a nuisance requiring discipline and control. London labour, apart from its negative effort on the trade union movement, was of little concern.

The Webbs were interested in policy rather than experience, in things as they might be rather than things as they are. Booth, though he shared certain of their assumptions, had different priorities. In the first place he was more age-sensitive. He too was concerned with continuous institutions but with him it was the family that assumed primacy. The Webbs, by contrast, were either hostile or indifferent. Sidney considered the family a nuisance. Beatrice was ambivalent.[31] The *Life and Labour* survey, from its inception, had taken the condition of the working-class family as the measure of the well-being of the general population. Whatever the defects, the measure possessed the virtue of an in-built life cycle perspective. Family fortunes, it was understood, depended upon the size and composition of the family and the movement of its members in and out of the labour market; these were age-related.

Booth, like others, was preoccupied with the reproduction of the labour force, with changes in its size and composition and with possible variations in its quality. His approach, however, pointed beyond contemporary concerns with urban degeneration. Comparing the ages of occupied males in each trade section with the age distribution of all occupied males in London, he was able to show the manner in which opportunities of employment necessarily shift from trades in decay with a surplus of old men; trades demanding great physical exertion with an excess of men in their prime; and less muscular pursuits in which juveniles had been substituted for more expensive adults. Booth's work connecting demography with the division of labour also raised generational and gender questions. The latter are now reasonably familiar; the former less so. Aves, summarising the results of the

[30] Webb, *Industrial Democracy*, pp. 539-45, 749-66; Webb, *History of Trade Unionism*, pp. 441-42. On the peculiarities of London as an industrial centre, see Gareth Stedman Jones, *Outcast London: A Study in the Relationship between Classes in Victorian Society* (Oxford, 1971), pp. 20-32.

[31] José Harris, *Beatrice Webb: The Ambivalent Feminist* (London School of Economics Lecture, 1984), p. 16.

investigation, drew attention to the impact of age differences in the formation of opinion within the labour movement. Even where concern about
displacement by young and cheap labour was not uppermost, trade unionists were often wary of industrial training. 'In a certain number of cases', he
wrote, 'a genuine interest is doubtless felt; occasionally, on the other hand,
we detect rather a fear of the rising generation, which if it uses to the full the
new opportunities not infrequently offered to acquiring thorough craft-
knowledge, may be able it is thought to oust the older generation before its
time.'[32] Booth, in short, gives us a working class that was as much divided by
age as by skill, income, occupation or gender.

Income, too, was age-and gender-related. Both dimensions were readily
understood. The institutional focus of the Webb trade union inquiry
created something of a blind spot in relation to problems of wage determination and regulation. As critics have noted, neither the *History of Trade
Unionism* nor its companion volume supply an adequate account of the
influence of collective bargaining upon wages and earnings.[33] Booth,
though mindful of these matters, was less impressed by the existence of an
approved standard rate of wages and more by the proportion of workers
who failed to obtain them. Inquiry in consequence focused upon actual
earnings on the principle that it was the average weekly earnings throughout the year rather than the nominal rate paid for a single week that
determined the standard of life. The knowledge base was formidable. In all,
particulars of the weekly earnings of 92,000 men, women, and juveniles
were obtained for wages paid in busy and slack weeks and for continuous
periods from which estimates of average annual income were made.[34]
Individual case histories, with exact earnings over several years, supplied a
further point of reference as did the job advertisements in the newspapers.[35] In addition to the information yielded by its own inquiries, Booth
was allowed access to the unpublished returns for the London trades
collected by the Board of Trade for the wage census of 1886. The Board of
Trade figures, though they made no allowance for overtime or short-time
working, enlarged the base on which his conclusions rested. Although the
data did not lend itself to easy generalities, the earnings survey provides a
very detailed portrait of pay for late-Victorian London on which there is
scope for further numerical work.[36]

The need for information on family income and patterns of expenditure

[32] *Industry*, 5, p. 163.
[33] See J.W.F. Rowe, *Wages in Practice and Theory* (London, 1928), p. 121.
[34] *Industry*, 5, pp. 272, 280.
[35] *Industry*, 1, pp. 126-27; *Industry*, 4, pp. 221-24.
[36] See M.J. Cullen, 'The 1887 Survey of the London Working Class,' *International Review of
Social History*, xx (1975), pp. 48-60.

was also recognised.[37] It is sometimes suggested that Booth was ignorant of Le Play's methods and procedures. 'I do not remember any mention of Le Play in his works', wrote S.H. Swinny, a Positivist acquaintance, 'Yet if Booth was not influenced by the author of the *Tableau des ouvriers Européens*, the coincidence of their methods is one of the most extraordinary in the history of science'. Paul Lazarsfeld, writing many years later, also found the unacknowledged similarity of method puzzling. 'Strangely enough', he remarked, '. . . I have in all the writings on Booth not been able to find any evidence that he was even aware of Le Play.'[38] This is not so. Booth, as noted earlier, was aware of the Frenchman and the possible application of his work.

Le Play's ideas were barely known in Britain before the 1890s. Although he was a pronounced Anglophile and an occasional visitor to meetings of the Social Science Association, his influence was negligible. A bowdlerised version, published by William Lucas Sargant in 1857, had introduced *Les Ouvriers Européens* to an English-speaking audience without any appreciable impact on methods of social inquiry.[39] His 'discovery' in the 1890s was in large part the work of Henry Higgs and other members of Booth's circle. Higgs, a civil servant by profession, was a former student of Foxwell and a specialist in French economic literature who found Le Play's family-centred approach both fascinating and relevant. By the beginning of 1890 he was already at work on one of the several publications which were soon to make family budget studies an important part of social investigation. Others too were captivated. Some, indeed, contemplated the formation of a British branch of La Réforme Sociale.[40] 'What puzzles me at present', Higgs wrote to his mentor, 'is that, except yourself, the people who know anything of Le Play seem to lose their heads over him.' James Bonar was a case in point. Notwithstanding 'a general racial contempt for modern Frenchmen', Dr Bonar, Higgs reported, 'spoke extravagantly of Le Play', describing him as 'the sociological superior in every respect of Comte and Spencer'.[41] Booth and Aves too were sufficiently impressed to co-organise a pilot study of workers' budgets and incorporate some of the findings into the *Life and Labour* inquiry.

[37] See Leone Levi's contribution to the discussion on Booth's pilot study, 'The Inhabitants of Tower Hamlets (School Board Division), their Condition and Occupations', *Journal of the Royal Statistical Society*, 1 (1887), p. 394.

[38] S.H. Swinny, 'Charles Booth', *Positivist Review*, xxvii (1919), pp. 63-66; Paul F. Lazarsfeld, Notes on the History of Quantification in Sociology: Trends, Sources and Problems, *Isis*, lii (1961), p. 322.

[39] W.L. Sargant, *Economy of the Labouring Classes* (London, 1857). See too Collet MS, 29/3/13/ 5/8. Henry Higgs to H.S. Foxwell, 18 July 1890: M.Z. Brook, *Le Play: Engineer and Social Scientist* (London, 1970), pp. 134-35.

[40] Collet MS, 29/3/13/5/4. Higgs to Foxwell, 26 February 1890; H. Higgs, 'Frédéric Le Play', *Quarterly Journal of Economics*, iv (1890-91), pp. 408-33.

[41] Collet MS, 29/3/13/5/11. Higgs to Foxwell, 13 August 1890.

By 1893 Higgs considered Le Play's *méthode d'observation* the alpha and omega of survey research.[42] Booth's was a more qualified response. Useful as it was, particularly in identifying connections between consumption, poverty and the poverty cycle, Le Play's intensive method did not go far enough. Booth, like Marshall, felt that it was too narrowly based to yield statistically reliable conclusions. As Booth put it:

> only when we know the manner of life of the people employed in any particular trade, and the scale of earnings which in any selected district is usually connected with such a style of life, can we enjoy the full benefit of such work as that of Mons. Le Play and his followers. Without such general knowledge we cannot tell whether the example given is truly typical or in what respects it diverges from a true type.[43]

The relationship between family and work, which so interested the Booth Inquiry, was rather marginal to the Webbs. The latter, though they lavished their modest income on costly researches, were not primarily interested in work or the workers. Their priorities lay with administration rather than production, with the structure of union bureaucracies, the supply and selection of union officers, their pay and conditions of work, and with their education, training and influence. Beatrice Webb, moreover, enjoyed the company of trade unionists, their gossip, politics and personalities. She was never happier than when maintaining a fly-on-the-wall presence at branch or delegate meetings and never more weary than when being shown over a factory by some misguided respondent who thought that work was important.[44] Workers associations were their true love. Rule-books and handbills, trade circulars and journals, pamphlets and price lists – such were their passion. 'Trade Unions and details of administration', wrote Sidney, 'are more to me than art or literature and I am keenly and absorbingly interested in the work.'[45] Beatrice was equally committed but less besotted. Booth had a larger purse and a more liberal vision.[46]

The nature of trade unionism, though important, was not the focus of the

---

[42] On his enthusiasm for family budget studies, see Henry Higgs, 'Workmen's Budgets', *Journal of the Royal Statistical Society*, lvi (1893), pp. 255-85; *Report of the British Association for the Advancement of Science* (1899), p. 818-19; *Bulletin of the International Statistical Institute*, v (1890), pp. 45-89.

[43] Charles Booth, 'Life and Labour of the People in London: First Results of an Inquiry Based on the 1891 Census', *Journal of the Royal Statistical Society*, lvi (1893), p. 591; Alfred Marshall, *Principles of Economics*, 8th edn (London, 1930), pp. 115-16.

[44] For the Webbs as participant observers, see Webb Trade Union Collection, EA XXIV, fos. 348-52; *Methods of Social Study*, pp. 138-39.

[45] Sidney Webb to Beatrice Potter, 9 December 1891, *Letters*, i, p. 347.

[46] Like Marx's *Capital*, the Booth and Webb Inquiries were funded from the profits of industry. The Booth survey cost and estimated £33,000; the Webb Inquiry upwards of £2,000: Simey, *Charles Booth*, p. 157; Sidney Webb to Edward Pease, 14 November 1897, *Letters*, ii, p. 56.

Life and Labour inquiry. It was the place of work in people's lives which supplied its point of departure. Booth's survey population embraced the whole of the labouring classes and not just the minority of organised workers. Servants, the largest occupational group, omitted by the Webbs, were of primary importance. Soldiers and even those, like the inmates of the workhouse, who were unfit to work but too poor to quit, were also noticed. What workers did for their income and what they did with it were of equal concern. The Webbs, by contrast, treated such issues as incidental to their main interests as social scientists. It wasn't that they were unaware or considered these things unimportant; rather that their theoretical frame-work precluded any deeper consideration of these dimensions. Their much criticised elitism and authoritarianism were no doubt serious defects, but their work did display a new sensitivity to the problems of trade union leadership and a new awareness of its position in a socialist state. The Webbs, as historians, though doubtless too schematic, did develop a distinct historical perspective which was a significant advance in its own terms and a major contribution to social and historical inquiry.[47]

The Booth and Webb inquiries also adopted different reporting styles. Reliance upon comparable research methods and sources yielded seminal but dissimilar studies. The Webbs were more successful in the presentation of their findings. Their lucid prose, originality and exemplary scholarship won instant recognition.[48] The Industry Series, though less conventional in format, was also less disciplined in composition and less coherent in struc-ture. The published results were in both cases so much less than they might have been. The impersonal social science that was so congenial to Sidney Webb, represented a form of self-denial to Beatrice and Booth, a source of repression which ensured that neither inquiry did justice to the wealth of interview material they had assembled.

Both wrote from rather different political perspectives. Booth appeared to the Webbs to be as much an individualist as they were collectivists. Sidney, having talked of socialism at their first meeting, observed that Booth was 'very much wedded to the City notion that competitive pricing was the *ne plus ultra* of social nexus'.[49] The report is accurate; the conclusion false. Conscious of his position as a captain of industry Booth's conversation was

   [47] Varying estimates of their work are presented by V.L. Allen, A.E. Musson and H. Clegg in a symposium on 'The Webbs as Historians of Trade Unionism', *Bulletin of the Society for the Study of Labour History*, iv (1962), pp. 4-9. Royden Harrison supplies a brief but rounded assessment with a paper of the same title in R. Samuel, ed., *People's History and Socialist Theory* (London, 1981), pp. 322-26. See, too, V.L. Allen, *The Sociology of Industrial Relations* (London, 1971), pp. 25-36.
   [48] Booth himself, it might be noted, thought well of the *History of Trade Unions* and took a friendly interest in the reception of *Industrial Democracy:* see BLPES, F.W. Galton Correspon-dence, Coll. Misc., 658/6, Charles Booth to Beatrice Webb, 9 January 1898.
   [49] Sidney Webb to Beatrice Potter, 15 October 1890, *Letters,* i, p. 218.

more conventional than his ideas. That he was no socialist is certain, but
neither was he an uncritical admirer of economic liberalism. His views are,
in fact, difficult to characterise. Those closest to him were no more successful than subsequent scholars have been in presenting a coherent statement
of his ideas. His widow, for example, readily identified those programmes
and positions from which he dissented – his distance from Positivism, drift
from Liberalism, difference with Conservatism and detestation of Collectivism – but found the substance of his social thought resisted summary.[50]
William Ritchie, a close son-in-law, thought that Booth was 'an unique
personality, as baffling in his inner thoughts as in his personal appearance'.[51] There was, he wrote, a spectrum which included Socialistic Individuals and Individualistic Socialists but as to Booth's location, he could not
say.[52] Belinda Norman-Butler, Ritchie's daughter, who presents Charles
and Mary Booth as an intellectual partnership comparable with that of the
Sidgwicks, the Webbs or the Bosanquets, found her grandfather's ideas just
as perplexing.[53] So have Booth's biographers. Concerned to rescue him
from the condescension of 'American positivism and German abstractio-
nism', and 'to demonstrate that *Life and Labour* can be used as a foundation
for the building up of a typically British type of empirical British sociology',
the Simeys tended to detach the man and his ideas from their context.[54]
These ideas, though influenced by the findings of the great Inquiry and the
events of the 1880s, grew out of an earlier exposure to Positivism.

Comtean Positivism was to the 1860s what Marxism was to the 1960s. No
intelligent person could pass through the two decades without some kind of
engagement. Comte offered the young, the intellectually curious and those
of unsettled faith a humanist religion and a new ethic of personal social
obligation. Booth was one of them. Positivism was central to his intellectual
formation. Booth was born into the aristocracy of intellect, that cousinhood
of businessmen and bankers, mandarins and merchants, scholars and
scientists, who were so important to the public life of the period. His wife, a
Macaulay, was a niece of the great historian and granddaughter of 'Radical
Dick' Potter of *Manchester Guardian* fame. Her husband's family were no less
radical. The Crompton brothers, Henry and Albert, the celebrated Positivists, were Booth's cousins, as was E.S. Beesly, Professor of History at
University College, London, who was equally well-known as a Positivist

[50] See Mary Booth, *Charles Booth: A Memoir* (London, 1918).
[51] Booth was a tall thin man who picked at his food and looked like a well-clothed scarecrow:
Beatrice Webb, *My Apprenticeship* (Harmondsworth, 1971), p. 228.
[52] Booth Correspondence, MS 797 II/86/13, memorandum of W.T.D. Ritchie, n.d. 1959.
[53] See *Victorian Aspirations: The Life and Labour of Charles and Mary Booth* (London, 1972).
[54] Booth Correspondence, MS 797 I/6031/(ii), T.S. Simey to G.M. Booth, 29 May 1959.

adviser to the labour movement. W. S. Jevons, the economist, who first discovered the marginal utility concept, was yet another cousin.[55]

Positivism provided a secular substitute for the evangelical faith which members of the intelligentsia had in many cases lost. Booth was 'fairly captivated' by the new moral order unfolded by the Cromptons and their friends. 'Whenever the cousins met', his widow wrote, 'the three talked over continually, both with one another and with Dr Congreve, the system of Positive Philosophy in all its various aspects.'[56] The record, though thin, shows Booth at the opening of the 1870s, searching for a personal identity and social purpose, and struggling to overcome the moral confusion and doubts created by the separation of science and belief. Positivists found themselves at war with orthodox Christianity on one front and Darwinian science on another. And it was the scientists who were the more damaging. The role of chance in the evolution process undermined the predictable social laws on which Positivism was premised and raised awkward questions about the development of social morality. The latter Booth tried to answer.[57] He also explored problems of scientific explanation, worked over concepts of right and wrong and grappled with some epistemological difficulties arising from the emotions and the intellect.[58] It was not a solo effort. Mary Booth, in old age, recalled the flow of discussion and remembered how 'the Benthaminites, Mill, Comte and the abounding Unitarians, Positivists and other faiths came to be as much part of breakfast as marmalade'.[59]

The crisis of authority had a material as well as a spiritual dimension and Positivists were as much preoccupied with the 'social question' as any other. None more so than Henry Compton, an able lawyer with an engaging personality to whom Booth was close. Crompton was one of several Positivists who enjoyed a special relationship with the trade union movement during the 1860s and 70s.[60] As a legal authority and expert draftsman, he made a significant contribution to the campaign for the reform of the

[55] Not all the Booths were of advanced outlook. Booth's uncle James, a civil servant of distinction, was a member of the Royal Commission on Trades Unions of 1867-69 and the author of its majority report. On Comtean influences, see T.R. Wright, *The Religion of Humanity: The Impact of Comtean Positivism on Victorian Britain* (Cambridge, 1986); on the significance of family connection, see Noel Annan, 'The Intellectual Aristocracy', in J.H. Plumb, ed., *Studies in Social History* (London, 1955), pp. 241-87; Obituary, 'James Booth', *Annual Register* (London, 1880) pp. 166-67.

[56] Mary Booth, *Memoir*, p. 8.

[57] See Booth Correspondence, MS 797 II/26/2/(i-iv), Darwin on Social Instincts, June 1871.

[58] There are some fragmentary notes in Booth Correspondence, MS 797 II/26/5/i-xxiv.

[59] Booth Correspondence, MS 797 I/3115, Margaret Ritchie to George Booth, 3 and 9 January 1961.

[60] The classic study of this special relationship is 'The Positivists: A Study of Labour's Intellectuals', in Royden Harrison, *Before the Socialists: Studies in Labour and Politics, 1861-1881* (London, 1965).

labour laws. He also wrote widely on labour questions. His book *Industrial Conciliation* (1876), described by the Webbs as 'the classic work' on the subject, was translated into French.[61]

Crompton was very much the complete Positivist. His brother, Albert, was the founder of the Positivist church at Liverpool; his wife, the youngest daughter of Lord Romilly, became a Positivist. He himself assumed the master's mantle when Congreve died in 1899. Crompton, though, was no mystic. His numerous contributions to the *Bee-Hive*, the *Labour Standard* and other journals consistently applied Positivist principles to contemporary affairs. His exposition centred on problems of property, its social nature and the functions and duties arising therefrom. Social reconstruction, from the Positivist perspective, relied not upon dispossession but upon the development of a sense of social responsibility among workers and their employers. Trade unions were the moral training grounds of the masses. Powerful workmen's combinations, Crompton argued, were indispensable in transforming producers into independent and socially aware citizens capable of bearing the burdens laid upon them by Humanity. Political economy, with its abstract-deductive reasoning, self-regarding character and hopeless finality, was repellant on grounds of method and morals. Positivism offered a decidedly more optimistic social prognosis, one in which the possibilities of working-class improvement were rather less confined.[62]

Booth encountered Political Economy just as the ground beneath it shifted. The 1870s, the decade which saw the death of Mill, also saw the abandonment of the labour and cost of production theories; and a growing unrest among historical economists who felt that Political Economy lacked reality and social economists who felt that it lacked morality. Positivists, who were sceptical of the self-sufficiency of the Ricardian system and conscious of the need to relate economics to ethics, were vociferous critics. But it was the manifest inadequacies of classical economics in relation to the social question that made reconstruction urgent. Jevons tried and failed, and his failure gave the lead to an institutional and historical approach which seemed altogether more capable of producing answers to pressing social problems. As Toynbee put it, 'It was the labour question, unsolved by that

---

[61] On Crompton and his brother, see J.E. McGee, *A Crusade for Humanity: The History of Organized Positivism in England* (London, 1931), pp. 80- 81, 130-38, 188-91; S. and B. Webb, *History of Trade Unionism*, p. 338.

[62] Crompton's views are conveniently collected in his *Letters on Social and Political Subjects Reprinted from the Sheffield Independent* (London, 1870), especially pp. 8-12, 15-19, 23-26.

removal of restrictions which was all deductive political economy had to offer, that revived the method of observation. Political Economy was transformed by the working classes'.[63]

Unlike Sidney Webb, who had also been touched by Positivism, Booth felt no urge to reconstruct economic theory. Beatrice in due course persuaded Sidney that his gifts lay elsewhere. Booth knew his own limitations and required no such prompting. 'I am . . . out of my depth here', he remarked in 1886, having tried to elucidate Jevons for her benefit. The qualities of mind which made a man a competent social investigator, he later wrote, 'are the least of all likely to give him that elevation of soul, sympathetic insight, and sublime confidence which must go into the making of a great regenerating teacher'.[64] The more modest role which he reserved for himself did not, however, entail any disengagement from the advancement of social theory or the debates and arguments attendant upon it.[65]

Booth was critical but not dismissive of Political Economy. In particular his rejection of the Utilitarian psychology on which it rested was partial. He remained a firm believer in private property and in the merits of a market economy. Like Comte he could not imagine a society which had advanced beyond the necessity of wage labour or in which the captains of industry would not perform an economically essential and socially useful role. What he required was an economic theory which was less abstract, less deductive and rather more serviceable than that of the classical school. F.A. Walker supplied it. The son of a successful businessman and economist, and a man of remarkable talents, Walker achieved distinction as a soldier, civil servant and teacher. He was the first President of the American Economic Association and the only U.S economist of his generation to enjoy an international reputation. He was a capable and prolific author who wrote for a specialist and popular audience with equal facility. His work was respected by

[63] On Jevons and the renovation of political economy, see Reba N. Soffer, *Ethics and Society in England: The Revolution in the Social Sciences, 1870-1914* (Berkeley, 1978), pp. 60-68. Quotation from Charles Gide and Charles Rist, *A History of Economic Doctrines: From the Time of the Physiocrats to the Present Day*, (2 ed., London, 1948), p. 390.

[64] Passfield II i (iII), Charles Booth to Beatrice Potter, 31 July 1886. See too, Charles Booth to Beatrice Potter 15 July 1891 in unpublished diaries of Beatrice Webb xiv, fo 1243. Quotation from Booth, *Final Volume*, p. 216. On the influence of Positivism upon Sidney Webb, see Willard Wolfe, *From Radicalism to Socialism: Men and Ideas in the Formation of Fabian Socialist Doctrines, 1881-1889* (New Haven and London, 1975), pp. 183-214.

[65] Included in an inventory of personal papers submitted to Booth's biographers is an envelope containing notes on political economy from about 1871 to 1915. See Booth Correspondence, MS 797 II/86/5, List of Documents sent to Professor and Mrs Simey, 18 February 1955.

Marshall and widely admired by contemporaries. He was, said Schumpeter, 'the kind of man who cannot touch anything without improving it'.[66]

Walker, it is well known, was the chief source for the Fabian theory of rent. His extension of the Ricardian theory to other factors of production was picked up by Sidney Webb, who claimed thereby to have supplied a common centre to the laws of distribution.[67] But it was by no means only members of the *nouvelle couche sociale* who found Walker's work congenial. Booth was equally impressed. 'I have been reading Walker's book which seems to contain almost all my ideas as well as many more', he wrote to Beatrice Potter in 1886. 'It touches closely on many points which affect us', he remarked, and pronounced it 'the ablest book I have read'.[68] The reasons are not far to seek.

'Ricardian Political Economy', wrote the American, '. . . should constitute the skeleton of all economical reasoning; but upon this ghastly framework should be imposed the flesh and blood of an actual vital Political Economy which takes account of men and societies as they are, with all their sympathies, apathies, and antipathies; with every organ developed, as in life; every nerve of motion or sensibility in full play.'[69] His realism coupled with a predisposition towards laissez-faire created an attraction which Booth found wanting in orthodox exponents of political economy. Walker, notwithstanding the isolation of the United States, was au fait with the writings of Roscher, Knies and the German Historical School. The critical works of Cliffe Leslie and Thorold Rogers were equally familiar as was that of Jevons, whose concept of final utility was incorporated into his own value theory. Walker may well have provided Booth with his first introduction to the work of Alfred Marshall.

Political Economy, published in 1883, included a rent theory of profits, a residual theory of wages and a 'highest cost of production final utility' theory of value. With the first of these Booth was particularly taken. Walker's text also served as a checklist of items for further inquiry. His analysis of the influence of food, shelter and industrial morale upon the varying efficiency of labour identified some of the heads under which information should be collected. Equally suggestive was the presentation of industrial organisation in terms of the division of labour, the differentiation

[66] On Walker's career and reception, see J.P. Munroe, *A Life of Francis Amasa Walker* (New York, 1923), pp. 251-52, 273, 348; and for a commentary on his work see Bernard Newton, *The Economics of Francis Amasa Walker: American Economics in Transition* (New York, 1968). Quotation from Joseph Schumpeter, *A History of Economic Analysis* (London, 1954), p. 867.

[67] A.M. McBriar, *Fabian Socialism and English Politics, 1884-1918* (Cambridge, 1966), pp. 35-41; 'The Fabians Reconsidered' in E.J. Hobsbawm, *Labouring Men* (London, 1964), pp. 251-71; D.M. Ricci, 'Fabian Socialism: The Theory of Rent as Exploitation', *Journal of British Studies*, ix (1969), pp. 105-21.

[68] Passfield II i (II), Charles Booth to Beatrice Potter, 10 September 1886.

[69] F.A. Walker, *Political Economy* (London, 1883), pp. 17-18.

of productive processes, specialisation of trades and the organisation of productive forces. Walker's work on real and nominal wages, family income, – 'the true unit in the comparison of wages is the family' – payment systems, irregular employment and trade unions, if it did not indicate new areas for investigation, confirmed that Booth was on the right track.

The importance which Walker assigned to consumption served a similar function. Walker thought it regrettable that 'the fascinations of the mathematical treatment of economical questions, and the ambition to make political economy an exact science should have led to the practical excision of the whole department of consumption from so many recent works'. The absence of such a theory, he added, left 'the most important chapter of political economy . . . almost a blank'.[70] Booth, conscious of the beneficial and harmful effects of certain forms of working-class expenditure, might reasonably have hoped to collect some of the empirical data from which such theory might be constructed.

It was *The Wages Question*, published in 1876, that brought Walker to the fore. W.T. Thornton's *On Labour* (1869) had shaken the foundations of the wages fund theory, but it was Walker who completed the work of demolition. Having done so, Walker tried to demonstrate that wages were partly determined by the productivity of the undertaking and that profit was not the outcome of exploitation but the special remuneration due to the entrepreneur. High profits and high wages were, he argued, mutually supportive. The free enterprise economy, though productive of good, was not without serious flaws. Some, like the booms and slumps of the trade cycle, were said to be a necessary defect in a system of every growing complexity. Others seemed remediable.

Walker believed in competition but recognised its imperfections:

> The political economist who undertakes the explanation of the actual phenomena of the industrial world is bound to note, not only that the assumption of full and free competition, which underlines this theory of the self-protecting power of labour, is wholly gratuitous . . . The tendency of purely economical forces . . . is to widen the differences existing in the constitution of industrial society, and to subject every person or class, who may, from any cause, be put to disadvantage, to a constantly increasing burden.[71]

Trade unions, he argued, had an important role in resisting the 'destructive pressure' of unequal competition and in enabling the worker to act as the maximising man beloved of the economists. Walker maintained that trade unionism, by promoting the efficiency with which the labouring class sought its own interest in the distribution of the product of industry, served

---

[70] Ibid., pp. 298-323.
[71] Ibid., pp. 274-76.

to reward efficient employers and eliminate incompetents and so contribute to economic and social betterment.[72]

It was the structure of the argument, its accessible prose and unambiguous conclusions, which made the work compelling. The recognition of entrepreneurial gains as rents of ability struck Booth as it struck Sidney Webb, though with rather different outcomes. Booth, with an assured position in the social hierarchy, found Walker's explanation sufficient. The status anxieties of the salaried middle classes, which gave Fabian Socialism a certain creative bite, found no expression in Booth's thinking. Walker's conception of the entrepreneur, as functionally distinct from the capitalist and the central figure in the production process, fitted well with Booth's ideas and self-image. In relation to Walker's work, further theoretical innovation appeared to be superfluous or dangerous.

In his conclusion to the Industry Series Booth identified the increased responsibility of management as the 'essential characteristic' of modern industry. The altered character of markets had, he believed, placed a premium upon the skills and capacities of the entrepreneur. 'Without his aid it is with difficulty that anyone cane produce anything to advantage for sale, or offer acceptable service of any kind.' 'In the making of a market', he wrote, 'the mere producer is helpless.'[73] The standard of life, he continued, depended upon the application of brains to capital and of both to business management.[74]

Moving from observation to analysis, he dismissed as primitive the division of the agents of production into land, capital and labour. 'The further analysis, showing management as a distinct and most important form of industrial effort with profit as its characteristic mode of remuneration, has', he observed, 'only had full recognition in more recent years.' Booth also followed Walker in viewing profit not as a morally reprehensible or socially damaging pursuit but as the best available measure of business efficiency.

Walker's disproportionate production theory was equally important in framing Booth's conclusions. In seeking the connection between industry and poverty Booth, like the American, argued that it was the interdependence of modern industry which made for its greater vulnerability to cyclical movements in the economy. Progress, though it had made subsistence crises a thing of the past, had not removed fluctuations of prosperity and depression. As Booth put it: 'We escape from the grip of dearth only to suffer the strange and monstrous strangulation of over-production.' Walker located the cycle within the framework of an economy characterised by a

---

[72] Ibid., pp. 285-86, 368-74.

[73] *Industry*, 5, p. 71.

[74] Ibid.; for an elaboration, see Charles Booth, *Industrial Unrest and Trade Union Policy* (London, 1913). pp. 8-9.

high degree of specialisation, with a large amount of fixed capital, in which the scope for business error was enlarged because the entrepreneur must anticipate changing consumer demand. Booth likewise hit upon the fundamental shift in the relation of supply and demand with the gradual removal of the productive impulse from the immediate requirements of the actual consumer and the increased space occupied by speculation and the manipulation of markets.[75] Booth also followed Walker's characterisation of the depression process as a cumulative downward movement that accelerates across the economy and is arrested by the irreducible demand for basic necessities and the return of confidence.[76]

Whereas Walker saw these periodic crises almost wholly in negative terms – 'a cause of waste and mischief' injurious to capital and labour alike – Booth saw them as the economic equivalent of natural selection, an inescapable audit from which in the long run the best and most efficient elements would emerge invigorated and with strengthened characters. In the short run, though, his attention fastened on the paradox whereby 'modern industry, with all its advantages yet evolves an ill-regulated life of its own, with the periodical recurrence of glutted markets and workless workers'.[77]

Booth, though wary of ill-advised interventions, was certain that some form of social action was both necessary and desirable. By the conclusion of the *Life and Labour* inquiry he was sceptical as to the possible contribution of trades unionism. 'Combination', he declared, 'while usually able to cope successfully with many questions affecting the *conditions* of employment, is powerless to increase the *volume* of work – happy indeed if it does not diminish it.'[78] Useful as character-forming agents, important in improving working conditions and living standards, and forceful in expressing the aspirations of the wage-earner, trade unions yet fell short of the high ideals which formally gave them priority in his social thought.

It is sometimes suggested that Booth as a social theorist was primarily interested in those who were incapable of independent existence and that the rest of the community could be left to look after itself.[79] This is not so. Booth was as much concerned with the condition and conduct of the self-supporting working class as with the restructuring of the labour market and repression of the residuum. The latter indeed required special action to

---

[75] *Industry*, 5, pp. 73-75.
[76] Walker, *Political Economy*, pp. 184-96.
[77] *Industry*, 5, p. 75.
[78] *Industry*, 5, pp. 80, 305.
[79] Maurice Bruce, *The Coming of the Welfare State* (London, 1961), p. 145.

safeguard the former. The segregation of the inefficients, he explained, 'is not for their sake but for the sake of those who are left'. The object of social policy was to secure the future progress of the working class.[80]

Booth believed that trade unions had a critical role to perform in the social integration of the working classes, in their moral training and material comfort. Combination, necessary to redress the inequality between employer and employed, was also conducive to social betterment and ethical improvement. State action in the industrial sphere, permissible when private initiative was unavailing, deprived workers of the educative side of voluntary effort. Society men, by contrast, received instruction in habits of business, developed a larger acquaintance with the circumstances of the trade, learned to work together, to respect public opinion and to appreciate self-control, patience, resolution and leadership. The strike weapon, though inseparable from free collective bargaining, diminished in importance as both sides mastered the art of industrial diplomacy. On the structure and organisation of trade unions he had comparatively little say. The adjustments demanded by the Webbs and other socialist theorists meant little to someone who thought of trade unionism as an aid to assist the operation of a moralised capitalism. In this respect, he advanced no further than the Positivism of his earlier years. The source of his disenchantment indeed, lay in the contrast between promise and performance, between the hopeful expectations of the 1870s and the strife-torn realities of the Edwardian era. 'How does it happen', he wrote in 1913, 'that the bright outlook of earlier days seems to have faded; to be succeeded by doubt, disappointment, heartburning and disunion?' His pamphlet *Industrial Unrest and Trade Union Policy* gave the answer in no uncertain terms.

This under-noticed text, published ten years after the *Life and Labour* survey, was in fact a late outgrowth of the earlier inquiry. It included material which had been omitted from the final edition, because of its overly prescriptive nature, and some fresh thoughts on industrial participation, formulated in the context of the 'labour unrest' – again with the assistance of Aves. The tone was critical. The failure of trade unionism, Booth argued, was primarily economic and arose from the pursuit of an industrial policy that worked against the grain of the market economy and so obtained less than was either feasible or desirable. Trade unionism, in his view, had pursued a narrowly conceived and self-defeating strategy that did nothing

---

[80] *Select Committee on Distress from Want of Employment*, [363] PP. 1895 (ix), qq. 10,569-73, 10,597-98.

to increase the efficiency of labour, ignored the interests of employers, did little for wealth creation and even less for its wider distribution:

> Even as regards wages, the effect genuinely produced by Trade Unionism is questionable. They have, it is true, often opportunely pushed a rise or have successfully maintained the rate secured; but amongst the economic bases of wages collective bargaining has played but a small part. The wide range existing in rates of remuneration is surely due to other causes, as are also the general cyclic movements up or down; and it would seem that unionism itself, and the kind of organisation found practicable, depend upon the scale of remuneration rather than the amount of remuneration on unionism. Undoubtedly stronger organisation accompanies higher pay, but in each separate sphere of wage earning, from the highest to the lowest scale of remuneration, I can find no permanent and assured advantage for organised over unorganised labour, either in earnings or in the security and continuity of employment. The unorganised have indeed been helped by the action of the organised, but what is more marked is that the conditions of employment in both have responded to influences common to the whole field of industry.[81]

The difficulties of trade unionism were more than simply strategic. Booth did not share Walker's belief in the inevitability of industrial concentration. The Fabian vision of large-scale industry run by propertyless managers, which drew substance from Walker's work, seemed inconsistent with the versatility and ready adaptability of London's small producers. 'It would be as reasonable to suppose that the day of small businesses is over as to look for an end to gnats, because of the strong flight and open beak of the swallow, or of small fishes because of the whale's great mouth', he wrote.[82] It was the persistent vitality of small-scale production which also set limits upon trade union growth. 'Only certain trades seem capable of effective combination', he wrote, 'and their number does not appear to grow larger. It is, I know, commonly supposed that under modern development trade becomes more and more suitable for elaborate organization, but I can find no sure ground for this belief.'[83]

The proliferation of localised trade societies – fourteen for the painters, twenty-three for wood-workers, and sixteen a piece in the leather, print and metal (excluding iron and steel) trades – made for stultifying parochialism and 'half developed sense of responsibility'. 'On the whole', Aves concluded, 'in spite of certain opposing tendencies trade unionism is to be regarded

---

[81] Booth, *Industrial Unrest and Trade Union Policy*, pp. 5-6.
[82] *Industry*, 5, p. 69.
[83] *Industry*, 5, p. 79.

rather as representing an expanding form of individualism than any thorough collectivism.'[84] Fragmented and self-regarding, stagnant and exclusive, London's trade societies seemed suspicious of change, indifferent to training, restrictionist in outlook and ever keen to arrogate essential managerial functions to themselves. There was little here to support Walker's conception of trade unionism as an equalising agent making for more perfect competition. Booth, though not denying that an employer might become more efficient in consequence of a powerful trade union presence, often found it difficult to think of industrial action except in dysfunctional terms, and was in fact closer to Marshall than to Walker in his concern about the deadening effects of the work fund theory upon the productivity of labour. Aves, the future chairman of the Trade Boards, warned that the application of a fixed minimum might jeopardise efficiency and diminish employment.[85]

The maintenance of wages was not dependent upon protective action alone. Provident action to eliminate the competition of the aged and the unfit was equally important and indeed accounted for the greater part of trade union expenditure. Apart from the provision of out-of-work benefit, sick pay and superannuation allowance, trade unions performed an important role as an information service for members in search of alternate employment. These efforts were praiseworthy but incomplete; it was this incompleteness which was a principle limitation on the efficacy of trade unions as remedial agencies. The partial nature of trade unionism created instability in the workplace and insecurity in the boardroom; it also gave collective bargaining a sectional, exclusive and anti-social character.

Booth's concern for industrial stability led him into 'tariff reform' and trade union policy.[86] Booth believed that any solution had to connect wages with efficiency and create arrangements that gave employees a practical interest in advancing productivity. What he required was a scheme which raised real wages and reduced insecurity but yet created stronger unions and larger profits. The growth of industrial militancy in the years before the First World War made the search for some such solution urgent. Like his contemporaries, Booth found the theorists of workers' control difficult to ignore. Indeed, it was the Webbs' pamphlet *What Syndicalism Means* that prompted his own intervention. Characteristically Booth drew conclusions

---

[84] *Industry,* 5, p. 150.

[85] *Industry,* 5, p. 165-72.

[86] Booth's ideas on protectionism are developed in his article 'Fiscal Reform', *National Review*, xliii (January 1904), pp. 686-701.

opposite to those of the authors. Fabian Socialism, which allowed little space for trade union participation in the management of industry, was at first hostile to Guild Socialism, but later became more accommodating. Booth, by contrast, sought a solution that was designed to strengthen capitalism rather than supersede it.

Booth's conception of associated industry which, he said, 'might even be regarded as timid approaches to the dreams of Guild Socialism', took the form of a preferential scheme whereby employers who chose to meet trade union standards in terms of pay and conditions would be free to manage their business without further intervention while those outside the scheme would be exposed to the full pressure of collective bargaining. 'The object', he explained, 'is progressive improvement upon the best existing conditions at the time in the trade to which the system is applied, to be secured and maintained by force of competition.' To this end trade unions were to make careful classification of employers and to select the best in terms of business performance, remuneration and conditions of service for special treatment. No formal consultation or bargain was necessary: an open policy, once announced would create its own momentum. Booth explained:

> The best advantage that could be offered would be non-interference; securing freedom of action to the accepted employers; and, incidentally, some measure of stability calculated to increase their efficiency, and so strengthen their position as industrial leaders, a position of which good uses could be made. Non-interference might well be complete; employers and employed being left to settle freely hours of work and terms of pay, as these practically could not fall behind, and would presumably tend to improve on, the standard fixed by the outside market for labour, the market of the unaccepted . . . The advantage given would create competition in the uses to be made of it amongst those that have it, and competition to qualify for it by those who would wish for it, but have it not . . . The character and trade position of the non-accepted would also be gradually affected. There would be increased pressure upon the less efficient, as part of a general rise in the standard of business efficiency; and in any contest they may have with the Trade Unions their position would be weakened.

From such an initiative there would follow an automatic general improvement in conditions of employment and a levelling upwards towards the accepted standard; trade unionism would be strengthened, the balance of power shifted and the basis of a new industrial partnership created. By such means trade unions might be shifted from their defensive restrictionist strategy towards a more constructive co-operation with management, Henry Crompton had been dead for nearly ten years, but his spirit still lived on.

4. Conclusion

'None of the writers . . . including Mr Booth himself, seems to be aware of the value of detail in describing a place or scene. For lack of it they hardly ever succeed in calling up a definite picture before the mind, and that is rather a pity.'[1] To a Victorian audience accustomed to the sensational low-life studies of Manby Smith, Sims or Sala, Booth's matter-of-fact prose may well have seemed remote, impersonal and drab. The *Saturday Review's* criticisms of the *Life and Labour* inquiry have nevertheless retained their currency. Modern scholars in search of an authentic working class find it equally deficient. Mayhew's work, we are told, is more lively and more 'scientific'.[2] There is indeed undeniably a disjuncture between the buttoned-up Booth of the printed survey – very grave and very eminent – and the more approachable Booth of the unpublished notebooks. Booth's rejections of the structures and strategies employed in *London Labour and the London Poor* served to differentiate his from Mayhew's survey and to impress the reader with its scientific detachment, system and rigour.[3] The curiosity and commitment, enthusiasm and energy, sympathy and humanity, so evident in the notebooks and manuscripts, were all concealed within a set of literary devices that distanced the author and acted as a barrier against reader involvement with the subject of the text.

Booth, like Mayhew, applied a camera technique to the presentation of his findings. The effect, though, was not entirely to his liking. Whereas Mayhew sought to convey his impressions through a narrowing focus, Booth could manage no more than a static image that faded quickly. In the industrial sphere, he confessed, developments had been so rapid 'as to have, perhaps, rather blurred the picture of some of the trades we have studied; disturbing the "instantaneous" character of the "photograph" which we have tried to produce . . .'[4] Booth produced a set of snaps which conveyed size, scale and variety but not individuality. Direct quotation and the reproduction of idiomatic expression or the use of dialect – stratagems which might so easily have relieved the oppressive weight of detail and humanised his findings –

[1] 'Life and Labour in London', *Saturday Review* (6 October 1894), pp. 386-87.

[2] Anne Humphreys, *Travels into the Poor Man's Country: The Work of Henry Mayhew* (Athens, 1977), pp. 135-44. The 'scientific' status of Mayhew's work has, however, been vigorously contested: see Gertrude Himmelfarb, *The Idea of Poverty, England in the Early Industrial Age* (London, 1985), pp. 312-62.

[3] See, for example, Booth Collection, A5B, fo. 79, press-cutting from *Pall Mall Gazette,* 31 July 1891.

[4] *Industry,* 5, p. 78. See, too, H. Llewellyn Smith, 'The New Survey of London Life and Labour', *Journal of Royal Statistical Society,* xcii (1929), p. 531.

were applied sparingly. It was as though Mayhew operated a zoom facility and Booth a box camera.

Impressions deceive. The Booth of the notebooks, the unknown Booth, presents a less aloof form of inquiry. Unconstrained by the reporting conventions of Victorian social science, the notebooks show us a privileged collective trying to overcome the burdens of birth, rank and property. Not that their prejudices were conquered; rather they were contained so as to enable them to record faithfully the work situation of labouring London, its rewards and satisfactions, and its hopes and fears. The notebooks, in fact, are far more engaging than the published text. Generalisation rendered in a passive voice gives way to contemporary profiles in specific settings, generally reported in the first person, which are full of interesting detail and display a sensitivity to the language and sentiments of working people. Booth's associates, though neither shy nor retiring, were by no means predictable in their interventions. We find them evaluating both the data and substance of the survey and also responding to individuals in ways that reinforce our involvement with them. For all the attempts to attain uniformity and comparability, the notebooks remain highly personal documents. Variations in hand-writing and syntax, and other idiosyncracies, all serve to enliven the text and assist identification with interviewers and respondents. The notebooks are also a forceful reminder that, notwithstanding assertions to the contrary, Booth did not rely on a door-to-door poverty census, but acquired information in a manner not dissimilar from Mayhew. As Anne Humphreys so rightly observes, 'Booth's . . . notebooks have much of Mayhew's quality of vividness, immediacy, and preciseness'.[5]

Booth will also stand comparison with Mayhew in terms of ideas. In some respect they were remarkably similar. Both were sceptics in regard to Political Economy. Both felt that it was in need of revision and each hoped to supply some of the necessary empirical data for that purpose. Both became protectionists. Neither was a socialist. Each was convinced that theoretical and social requirements could be satisfied without the wholesale transformation of property relations. The sources of their radicalism were, however, different. Booth, though he had a dishevelled bohemian appearance, never moved in the disreputable literary circles in which Mayhew's ideas were formed. Booth's thought, moreover, was the more systematic. Although he eschewed the subcultural Positivism of certain relatives and contemporaries, he remained deeply impressed with much of the teaching of Comte.

Mayhew's best work was completed before political and economic changes and the erosion in orthodox economics had begun to influence social theory. Booth's work, by contrast, is best viewed as part of the reconstruction process that followed the displacement of classical economics. Positivism, along with Liberalism and Idealism, brought a new optimism to the possibi-

---

[5] *Travels into the Poor Man's Country*, p. 221.

lities of working-class advance. An industrial system of unlimited potential, and a working population capable of being made rational moral beings, presented possibilities for progress which had earlier seemed unimaginable. The dock strike, demonstrating the existence of a reserve power of corporate action among the unorganised, served, if anything, to confirm this prognosis. Yet, by the close of the *Life and Labour* survey, Booth was markedly less hopeful. Careful inquiry led him to the conclusion that trade unionism was not in its current form an engine for the moral regeneration of the masses and that, without a change of heart, the working class would remain stunted in its material as in its moral development. That such a change was a possibility he did not deny; that it was probable seemed unlikely.[6]

The contrast between the conclusions of the Booth Inquiry and those of the Webb trade union inquiry was striking. Interview-based, following broadly similar methods, and sometimes asking the same questions, the Booths and the Webbs yet formed radically differing estimates of the possibilities of industrial democracy. These differences betray contrasting social visions which were at bottom political and ideological. The bridge from Positivism to Socialism, crossed by so many during the 1880s, was by-passed by Booth, who was older and socially more secure than Sidney Webb or the generality of converts to Fabian Collectivism. The Booths, though they often read the same books, – Charles read Walker, Mary read Marx – were not tempted to deviate from their own path. On the contrary. Walker struck a chord because he supplied, among other things, a rationale for the privileged position which Comte prescribed for industrial management. Booth, though conscious of its defects, particularly in relation to distribution, never abandoned belief in competition as productive of social good. The role of trade unionism in state and society also served to differentiate the Booths from the Webbs. Whereas Sidney Webb led the way in confronting the future socialist state with a strong trade union movement, Booth hankered after a Comtean capitalism moralised and made noble by a reformed trade unionism. He died disappointed.

---

[6] BLPES, Cannan Correspondence, 1022, Charles Booth to Edwin Cannan, 18 November 1913.

III

The Religious Influences Series

The 'New Booth'

The Religious Influences Series

> I was staying last Sunday at Kennington and found them out upon the
> drawing room table and each member of the Talbot family referring to
> them. The bishop rather sad about some passages on which he had opened
> but avowing that he meant to go steadily through all that concerned South
> London and volume seven besides – Lord Robert Cecil was also there: he had
> bought and meant to read the whole set. The ferment is only just about to
> begin. I saw the *Times Literary* editor in the Tube this evening and he began at
> once by saying that he had suppressed his first article in the Friday sup-
> plement to make room for a special review of the 'New Booth'.
>
> (G. H. Duckworth to Charles Booth, 1 April 1903).[1]

The 'New Booth'? The books to which the *TLS* editor referred were not the
Poverty Series of great renown, nor yet the Industry Series but the seven-
volume survey of Religious Influences.

The Religious Influences Series which forms the third and final part of
Charles Booth's *Life and Labour of the People in London* has come in for a bad
press from modern scholars – that is, when it has been noticed at all.[2] A
number of commentators have completely ignored the part which the series
played, and was intended to play, in Booth's total inquiry. It was no accident
that Booth republished a revised version of the first two series on Poverty
and Industry to accompany the new Religious Influences Series in 1902/3.
The three were to be seen as integrated parts of the whole. In 1929,
introducing his *New Survey of London Life and Labour* to the Royal Statistical

---

[1] Booth Correspondence, MS 797 1/4846, (iii); see *Times Literary Supplement*, 3 April 1903 for
a laudatory if bland review on the front page.
[2] See Hugh McLeod, *Class and Religion in the Late Victorian City*, (London, 1974). for
appreciation of and expert use of Booth data. Owen Chadwick barely uses Booth and
mistakenly asserts that the work was 'impressionistic' see *The Victorian Church*, 2 (London, 1970)
p. 234; D.B. McIlhiney, 'A Gentleman in Every Slum: Church of England Missions in East
London, 1837-1914' (Princeton University Ph.D. thesis, 1977) did not use the archive. K.D.
Brown, *A Social History of the Nonconformist Ministry in England and Wales, 1800-1930* (Oxford,
1988) made no use of either printed volumes or the archive.

Society, Hubert Llewellyn Smith said that the survey concluded 'with a remarkable series of volumes whose title, *Religious Influences*, scarcely gives an idea of the breadth and variety of the influences and agencies brought under review, which included all forms of social organisation as well as the institutions of organised religious life'.[3] For Booth and his helpmeet, Mary Macaulay Booth, this new series was a work from the heart. Contemporaries either received it rapturously or slated it as unfair and inaccurate. All took it seriously.

Why is there such a mismatch between the views of modern scholars and those of Booth and his contemporaries? The main explanation would seem to lie in the approach which Booth adopted in this part of the survey. 'The New Booth' which late-Victorian London so celebrated used a non-statistical approach to its subject matter – the influence of religion upon the people of London. Modern proponents of the scientific history and the social sciences find Booth's rejection of quantification unpalatable and the fruits of his labours "useless". W.S.F. Pickering's attack in *Archives de sociologie des religions* of 1972 is characteristic. Whereas Robertson Nicoll's survey of church attendance on 24 October 1886 and R. Mudie-Smith's *Daily News* survey of 1902-03 come in for praise, Booth is dismissed as follows:

> The work of Charles Booth which was also published about this time proved to be disappointing in the matter of religion. Although seven volumes in his great report *Life and Labour of the People in London* (1902) were the results of tireless investigations about the London churches, the sum total of what was presented was a host of personal observations about individual churches. Unlike other surveyors, Booth made no attempt to use statistics and the conclusions about what he and his fellow observed were of a subjective kind.[4]

More recently, Ross McKibbin has stated unequivocally, 'The Religious Influences' section of Booth's *Life and Labour* is extraordinarily ill-conceived for its purpose, and its information is redundant to most questions the historian might wish to ask'.[5]

No modern scholar has been able to reconcile the printed Religious Influences Series with the 'old Booth' of the Poverty and Industry Series, which saw their beginnings in the Mansion House statistical inquiries and papers for the Royal Statistical Society. Moreover, it was perfectly possible to approach the question of religious activity and religious participation in a statistical way and Booth's contemporaries were busy doing this. Witness R. Mudie-Smith, Robertson Nicoll and Seebohm Rowntree. Rowntree was

[3] H. Llewellyn Smith, 'The New Survey of London Life and Labour', *Journal of the Royal Statistical Society*, xcii (1929), p. 531.

[4] W.S.F. Pickering, 'Abraham Hume (1814-1884): A Forgotten Pioneer in Religious Sociology', *Archives de sociologie des religions*, xxxiii, (1972), pp. 33-34.

[5] R.I. McKibbin, 'Social Class and Social Observation in Edwardian England', *Transactions of the Royal Historical Society*, 5th series, xxviii (1978), p. 176.

still at it in the 1940s. What was Booth up to? Why did Booth make such an extensive inquiry into religious influences and why did he adopt the approach and methodology he did?

From the start the contrast between the 'New' and the 'Old' Booth worried the Simeys. So stunned were they by the absence of statistics in the series and the form of the inquiry that they sought at first a personal explanation. The subject matter itself seemed improbable. 'We also want to know why the early Survey was followed up by "*Religious* Influences" – Was he turning from Positivism to more orthodox views? Why the "Hope of the World"[6] episode? did he sense that Science alone was not enough?'[7] In October 1957 they were still groping for an answer. 'We have the impression that in this third series the scientific approach was overwhelmed by the personal interest Mr Booth took in the various teachings of the churches. The story is told in the first person – there are no statistics – it reads as a personal quest rather than a scientific inquiry etc. Any comments or reminiscences on this subject, however trivial, would be a help.'[8]

This interpretation rang no bells with the Booth descendants. They struggled with the evidence and with their family memories to convey the truth to the Simeys. Meg wrote to her brother George on 25 April 1958:

> I agree with you the words 'profoundly disturbed' do *not* describe father – again that his inquiry into religious influences was a personal quest for spiritual truth was not so. He probably was disturbed early in life when he described himself as a Positivist – but at the time of his inquiry I am convinced he was *not*. He was deeply interested in an impersonal way. He was not thinking of himself at all – religious influences, I think he was disturbed, because his observation told him, immense efforts were being made to give people uplift and were not succeeding.[9]

She believed that her mother was in sympathy with Booth's conclusions and recited an anecdote to indicate her mother's religious position:

> When Mrs Saunders came to work in Thringstone Mother told her she was not an orthodox believer. Miss Saunders said she did not think work among the poor did good unaccompanied by the imparting of religious faith and hope. Mother told me of this conversation. I quote from memory. Mother inserted into her Women's Trust Endowment for Thringstone the wish that the children should be taught the Christian religion. I believe Father was in agreement. He looked forward to a better way of giving uplift than those he observed.[10]

---

[6] Sic.

[7] Booth Correspondence, MS 797 I/5985, Margaret Simey to George Booth, 14 May 1955.

[8] Booth Correspondence, MS 797 I/5997, Margaret Simey to George Booth, 13 October 1957.

[9] Booth Correspondence, MS 797 I/3071, Margaret [Booth] Ritchie to George Booth, 25 April 1958.

[10] Ibid., fo. 3.

The children of Charles Booth were quick to assure the Simeys that their view of Charles Booth as a man searching for personal religious assurance was far from the truth. Charles Booth was 'a reverent unbeliever', his wife, of a more spiritual bent, held unorthodox beliefs but conformed outwardly. As a result the offending sentences implying that the survey was a personal search for a religious creed were removed from early drafts of the Simeys' book.[11]

One further piece of evidence finally lays to rest the theory of Booths Religious Influence inquiry was a personal quest. This time it takes the form of a draft section, which Booth apparently intended for the printed volumes, entitled 'The Attitude of the Writer in Dealing with this Subject'. This was not included in the published work.[12]

This statement is important for a number of reasons. Firstly, it makes clear that Booth was not concerned either to discuss or establish religious truth. He was not involved in a religious quest through his inquiry. Secondly, it makes plain that he had definite views about religion of which he was well aware. He knew that he had to guard against bias in his writing. Scholars studying Booth's Religious Influences survey have been led astray by taking the printed volumes as their starting point. The Religious Influences series was the ending point not the starting point of the inquiry. T.S. Simey assumed that Booth had started out with the intention of studying social influences. Simey wrote to George Booth in 1959: 'The problem is to explain why Booth started out to survey *social* influences and ended up with one almost wholly devoted to *religious* influences . . .' This is predicated on the assumption that Booth separated in his mind religious from social influences. It is clear from Volume I of the Religious Influences Series that he never did any such thing: 'So there are other social influences which form part of the very structure of life, and some account of them is necessary to complete the picture of things as they are. Among these influences Religion claims the chief part . . .'[13] He continues to say that the investigation of religious effort has 'taken the first and largest part in the additional inquiry of which I now give the results . . .' And from the very start of the survey this had been the case. Interviewees from the various religious groups outnumbered other interviewees by about 3:1. The questionnaires distributed to ministers of religion were heavily concerned with religious matters, assigning very few questions to such issues as prostitution, crime and health. There is some evidence that some of his associates and his wife wished him to accord greater attention to secular social influences but this does not undermine the argument that for Booth it was always an inquiry first and foremost into religious influences.

---

[11] Booth Correspondence, MS 797 I/6031 (ii), T.S. Simey to George Booth, 29 May 1959.
[12] Booth Correspondence, MS 797 II/1-27. Appendix V.
[13] *Religious Influences*, 1, p. 4.

The point is worth reiteration. Booth saw religious influences as a social influence. Booth had long been aware of the need for a consideration of moral questions. This had been drawn to his attention at the discussion of his paper on Tower Hamlets at the Royal Statistical Society in June 1887.[14] There is no need to see the Religious Influences series as an aberration. It was rather a natural extension of his earlier work.

The precise shape of that Religious Influences inquiry may well have changed over the years. There is a distinct possibility that Booth (when he embarked on the Religious Influences inquiry in 1897) had in mind a rather different project than that which saw the light of day in 1903 and which he described in the first pages of the published work.[15] For about five years he and his team of assistants methodically and systematically collected interview data which would have allowed them to evaluate the work and attitudes of the Christian ministry in London.[16] Neither Booth nor his associates were fools and it is unwise to start from the assumption that they simply used inappropriate sources and methods to glean the information to support a study of religious influences as described in the published work.

It is much more fruitful to assume that Booth's ideas about what he wanted to write about evolved as he worked. Like all researchers, he interacted with his data and with current scholarly preoccupations – framing new questions as he went, seeing matters in a new light, rejecting old premises and old approaches. On top of this, he became aware of problems associated with boldly assessing the work of the ministry which had not seemed terribly important in 1897.

As the key to the shape and structure of the Religious Influences Inquiry lies neither in personal religious disturbance nor in accident, it is possible that it lies in the very process of making the survey and writing up the results. Is the historian able to trace this process of evolution? We think so. This is not to deny that there will always be gaps in our knowledge. Nevertheless, we can glean from the archive sufficient clues to piece together a convincing picture of the making of the Religious Influences inquiry from start to finish.

The Simeys alleged that the Booth archive was silent concerning the production of the Religious Influence Series. This is far from the case, although it is true that Booth wrote little specifically to explain what he did and what he was attempting to do. What there are are, casual references to the making of the series. The scholar must piece together, painstakingly, tiny fragments of evidence to puzzle out how the inquiry itself was staged

---

[14] *Journal of the Royal Statistical Society*, 1 (1887), p. 401.

[15] R. O'Day, 'Interviews and Investigations: Charles Booth and the Making of the Religious Influences Survey', *History*, lxxiv (1989), pp. 361-77 and particularly pp. 364, 366 and 376.

[16] It is intriguing to note that Anthony Russell, *The Clerical Profession*, (London, 1980) makes no use of the huge Booth archive. See R. O'Day, 'The Men from the Ministry' in G. Parsons (ed.), *Religion in Victorian Britain* (Manchester, 1988), pp. 258-79, for a corrective.

and how the volumes arising out of the inquiry were written. For the first (the process of investigation) the papers now held at the London School of Economics are invaluable; for the second (the writing) these papers must be supplemented by the correspondence now held at the Senate House Library, University of London; by Mary Booth's diaries; and by draft chapters held at the University of Liverpool.

Charles Booth began preparations for his inquiry into religious influences upon the people in London a month after the publication of his Industry Series in March 1897. The old age pensions problem no longer preoccupied him. His interest in the Religious Influences Inquiry was lively from the start and remained so until 1903. He decided who he was going to employ as his associates. A.L. Baxter, unable to join in the Industries survey, now joined the select team (the others were Ernest Aves, George Arkell, Jesse Argyle and George Duckworth).[17] Booth solicited the help of church leaders such as the Anglican bishops of London, Rochester and Southwark and the Catholic Archbishop of Westminster. They responded by issuing letters to the clergy instructing them to co-operate in the inquiry. Preparatory work in the Adelphi Terrace office included production of lists of churches and clergy to be approached (probably using lists provided by the Archdeacons of London and Richmond amongst others) and eventually visited and the production of interviewing schedules. Members of the clergy were themselves consulted about the best way to proceed. Booth was always eager to use existing expertise. Ernest Aves, for example, interviewed F.W. Kingsford in his capacity as the Rural Dean of Hackney. While Kingsford assured Aves that it was not 'within his province to know *how* the parishes were worked', he did advise and inform about the character of each parish and each incumbent and on 'the advisability of sending the full or shortened Schedule A'.[18] Aves came away from the interview with a detailed listing of this information which provided the basis for action in the months that followed. When interviewing began, Charles Booth and his associates operated from local offices. These lists and schedules were not, as the Simeys seem to imply, the result of long months of inquiry but rather the starting point of the regional inquiry.[19] The form of the schedules (and the content of the interview reports) demonstrates that at *this* stage Booth was very concerned to collect quantitative and comparable data about Christian activities and popular participation in church life. He had not abandoned statistics.

From each 'camp' Booth and his associates went out to interview the

[17] Esmé Howard was not involved. The Simeys list him in their biography of Booth on p. 141 and not Baxter.

[18] Booth Collection, B191, Preliminary Interview of F.W. Kingsford, Rural Dean of Hackney and Rector of St Thomas, Stamford Hill, by Ernest Aves, *c.* August or September 1897, fo. 3.

[19] T.S. and M.B. Simey, *Charles Booth: Social Scientist* (Oxford, 1960) p. 141.

Christian ministers and missionaries of the metropolis. The 1800 interviews were eventually written up by the interviewer and entered into notebooks.[20] One of the most innovative features of Booth's developing survey methodology was his appreciation of the importance of a structured interviewing technique and his refinement of the method over the years 1886 to 1903. It is in the inquiry into religious influences, not the early Poverty Series, that this technique was finally perfected. Much attention was accorded the form of the interviews which were to provide the basis of the Religious Influences survey. With the original letter of invitation was enclosed a printed schedule of questions which was to act as a checklist for the interview. Although interviewees were not requested to complete the pro forma, in practice many did so and some survive in the notebooks, replete with information.[21] A minister would be sent Schedule A if he belonged to the Church of England, Schedule B if he were a nonconformist minister. There were additional schedules for those with special knowledge of local government, for example, and these were used as supplementaries.

Booth sought information of a statistical nature: How many clubs are there? How many people attend them? How many people attend morning and evening service? How many celebrations of the communion are there? What are the average figures of communicants? How many paid workers are there in the parish? How many people are visited? How many children attend Sunday School? How many people are touched by the work of church or chapel?

The questions relate to the formal activities of the church and the extent to which the population at large participates in them or is impinged upon by them. There are no questions relating to the effectiveness of these activities in terms of the spiritual life either of participants or non-participants. When Booth designed the survey he undoubtedly intended the information collected to be comparable. The questions which were posed and the replies collected cried out for statistical expression.

Booth sought also to impose some uniformity of approach upon the interview itself. About two and a half hours were devoted to each interview (although some took much longer).[22] The interviews appear to have followed the schedule reasonably closely although interviewers felt free to range more widely and to take advantage of an interviewee's particular interests and expertise. During the meeting, the interviewer was expected to observe the interviewee very closely and make an assessment of character, reliability and so on, as well as to make detailed notes of his or her comments. After the event, the interviewer wrote a report of the interview.

---

[20] These are contained in Booth Collection, B169-B315.
[21] E.g. Booth Collection, A54. See, too, below Appendix VI.
[22] Booth Collection, B169, interview of Revd A, Chandler of All Saints, Poplar, fos. 1-4.

These reports follow a broadly similar pattern; a record of the name and status of the subject and the date and location of the interview; a brief description of the interviewee, including age, length of service, previous experience, and thumbnail sketch which often uses the physical characteristics of the subject as a clue to his or her character and abilities; mediated responses to the schedule questions with some direct quotation and a variety of statistical material in addition to the assessments made by the interviewer.[23] Sometimes, encouraged by the responsiveness of the subject, an interviewer would depart radically from the schedule to pursue an interesting line of inquiry and then return again to the schedule. Carroll of St Frideswide's comments about Scott Holland were thought worthy of detailed note.[24] Mr Mason of St Stephen's, North Bow was asked what the fundamental aim of his ministry was and his reply was carefully noted.[25] Often copies of annual reports, parish magazines, portraits and other ephemera were included in the note books.

Such interviews did not provide objective data and neither did they supply simple evidence of the attitudes of the men and women involved. When they wrote up their reports interviewers selected the material they considered most valuable to Booth's purposes but the reader is not made privy to the criteria for selection. Booth showed himself aware in other contexts of the issue of bias but no discussion of the nature of the interaction between interviewer and interviewed and its effects has so far been discovered.[26]

The secretaries also collected materials to produce descriptions of the work of various institutions. For instance, Ernest Aves was responsible for an informative description of the Bethnal Green Museum, which Booth toned down and reworded slightly for use.[27] Such accounts were based upon official information, observation and opinion: 'On three days in the week it is open till 10 p.m. and on the other days, including Sundays, till dusk'; 'Outside, the building is unattractive, and inside it has all the symmetry of a Charing Cross railway terminus, but [it] is full of interesting and instructive exhibits . . .'[28]

---

[23] Booth Collection, B175, fos. 19-48; B301, fo. 1; B304, fo. 83; B306, fos. 11, 39, 99; B307, fos. 117-24; for a more detailed analysis see O'Day, 'Interviews and Investigations', pp. 367-75.

[24] Booth Collection, B175, fos. 113-15.

[25] Booth Collection, B175, fos. 19-48.

[26] See O'Day, 'Interviews and Investigations', passim. McLeod, *Class and Religion*, pp. 250-54 represents an early attempt to assess such material.

[27] *Religious Influences*, 2, pp. 100-1.

[28] Booth Collection, A39, 7, fos 19-21.

Booth and his secretaries visited many places of worship during these years and recorded the information and impressions they gleaned.

Last Sunday I went to Hare Court Chapel, and heard Campbell Morgan preach his last two sermons there, as pastor . . . In the morning, I got a seat, but that was all. The chapel was packed, and people were asked 'to sit close'. Even at the Communion, for which, with a few others I stayed in the gallery, the body of the Chapel was quite full, and camp-stools were put up one aisle . . .[29]

The papers relevant to the Religious Influences Inquiry also contain many of Booth's own working papers. He produced ledgers full of digests of the interview and other material.[30] A typical ledger would contain a list of all of the places of worship and their ministers in a given area. Booth then appears to have read through all the interviews for the area and summarised the major points established under the various headings of the schedule – e.g. prostitution; visiting; nursing. Then a detailed breakdown of the staffing of each place of worship and of the services, societies and so on organised under its auspices was provided, divided into Church of England material and nonconformist material. Local Government, Police and Miscellaneous notes were also assembled. Sometimes he had missionaries' diaries to work from, which recorded the views of men and women in their districts. For example a Poplar missionary reported, amongst other conversations with 'locals', a meeting with a Mrs Marlow. 'Invited her to church; says that her husband does not attend and does not like her to be out when he is at home.' He also reported a conversation 'with man at Hairdressers in Greenman Street. He is a careless and drinking man, yet he said he was quite prepared to die and feared nothing. Spoke to him of the foundations upon which we must build our hopes.'[31] Finally, Booth requested the associates chiefly responsible for work within an area to prepare "reports" or essays on its organised religious life and he produced a 'General Review' of the results of the inquiry for their criticism.[32]

Booth probably worked almost exclusively from these ledger abstracts of the inquiry papers. They made manageable the unwieldy mass of raw data. Some of the material was incorporated, more or less unchanged, in the book. In addition a map (Argyle's responsibility) was coloured showing places of worship, public houses and Board Schools.

---

[29] Booth Correspondence, MS 797 1/21/(i), Ernest Aves to Charles Booth, 3 April 1901. See also Booth Collection, A39, 7, fos 1-7, 22; and B385 for visits in Districts 10-13.

[30] E.g., Booth Collection, A32.

[31] Booth Collection, A37, 11, fo. 81.

[32] E.g., Booth Collection, A32, 1, 31 fos.

1. Evaluate not Enumerate

When Booth came to writing he seems to have already decided that statistics as such would play a relatively small part in his work. He was fully aware of the religious censuses being undertaken by others. In fact Booth had provided R. Mudie-Smith with lists of churches and chapels at the outset of his work.[1] Although there is no indication that he disapproved of counting attendances at religious services, there was no incentive to simply repeat Robertson Nicoll's or Mudie-Smith's work. Moreover, he came more and more to doubt whether counting religious attendances went far towards answering the questions which intrigued him most. His aim was not to calculate how many people went to church but to describe religious influences and the extent to which and the manner in which the people responded to them. It was not the 'spiritual impact' of religious effort which engrossed him but its social impact. This was a more ambitious aim by far.

When he decided that he did not want to count but to observe and evaluate, he could have used the raw data to write a blow-by-blow account of the work of each church or chapel in London to influence the people, giving his opinion as to its success. This would have been unutterably boring. It would also have involved him in precise identification of each and every of his informants. This was something which Booth hesitated to do. It would have introduced a new practice: interviews are not attributed in the two earlier series. Some ministers co-operated only on the understanding that they would remain anonymous. 'Mr Short', reported Duckworth, 'hopes that his name will not be mentioned.'[2] Interviewed by both Duckworth and Aves, Father Lawless, a Catholic priest in Poplar, was 'very nervous at my taking notes, so much so that in the end I desisted. Wanted no statement to be made that could possibly be traced to him; wanted even to see the result of this interview but did not insist'.[3] They had their careers and their relations with their congregations to think about. A format which permitted Booth to specify certain facts and generalise others was imperative. Even so, such a method would not afford Booth complete protection. His anticipation of a hostile response acted as a brake upon the free use of his critical powers. In March 1903 Mary Booth remembered her husband's earlier fears about the reactions of the ministers to his evaluation of their work

---

[1] E.g., Booth Collection, A31, fo. 89, J. Argyle to Mary Booth, 10 June 1903.

[2] Booth Collection, B304, interview of Pastor A.G. Short of the Herne Hill Tabernacle, by George Duckworth, 8 November 1900, fo. 43.

[3] Booth Collection, B180, interview of Father Lawless at the Presbytery, Corner of Upper North Street & Canton Street, Poplar East, by Ernest Aves and George Duckworth, 19 May 1897, fo. 69.

when Mr Herbert Stead wrote heatedly to him about Booth's assessment of his work at Browning Hall. Stead (an associate of Booth's in the fight to establish pensions) had been most co-operative to start with but now he objected. It had been, said Mary, the flattery of the fulsome. Was this the first note of the chorus of blame which they had all along feared? Charlie must resist challenging the declared motives of the ministers and missionaries – must take their motives at their word.[4] Contemporaries were extraordinary sensitive to any hint of criticism. Booth's qualified enthusiasm for the Browning Hall Settlement, Walworth, clearly cut Stead to the core. 'The success attained is considerable, but somewhat spasmodic and strained. It seems to lack the full flow of Wesleyan enthusiasm and not to possess the solid character of Baptist work.'[5] The Miller libel case (which grew out of a critical point made in the Poverty Series) must have reinforced the moral: accurate and specific reporting of contemporary events had its dangers. A covering letter to Mary of 15 March 1903, accompanying a copy of Booth's letter in reply to Stead, made it clear that Charles did not think Stead's would be the last letter of outraged complaint, even if Stead were more than usually sensitive. 'It is an excellent object lesson. Few, if any, have the same personal feelings to be roused. They will simply curse me and pass on. I am very glad to be going away and hope you will be thick-skinned enough not to mind whatever is said.'[6] Sure enough, Spurgeon's ruffled feathers had to be soothed in April (this time by Ernest Aves) and reviews in the press indicated that the entire Methodist ministry was being goaded into retaliatory action, on the basis of unfair assessment, by Robertson Nicoll of the *British Weekly*.[7] And all this happened after Charles Booth had taken great care not to aggravate. Goodness knows what the reaction would have been had Charles Booth not excised from his account the more acerbic judgements of the character and work of contemporary ministers made by his associates.

> In view of the staffing of the church, the idea that it can have any important local influence becomes either pathetic or absurd. Both the vicar and the senior curate ought to be superannuated, and the other curate is a converted Jew, whose work seems ineffective except with a poor class that can be bribed. And effectiveness of that kind ought to be described as failure.[8]

On the books' publication, Booth, concerned to avoid trouble, rather oddly decided to give each interviewee a volume other than that in which he

---

[4] Booth Correspondence, MS 797 I/3900; 3903; 3905, Mary Booth to Charles Booth, 2, 13, 14 March 1903.

[5] *Religious Influences*, 4, pp. 85-87.

[6] Norman-Butler, *Victorian Aspirations*, p. 133.

[7] Booth Correspondence, MS 797 I/3918 (i) and (ii), Mary Booth to Charles Booth, 20 April 1903. Nicoll's review appeared in *British Weekly*, 2 April 1903.

[8] Booth Collection, A39, report on District 7, fo. 34.

himself was directly involved. The attempt backfired: Booth received requests to exchange the volumes. Jesse Argyle felt unable to satisfy the requests: 'Perhaps it is a little cowardly to put the onus on Mr Booth's shoulders.' Booth might comply in the end but 'we all agree it would be a mistake to do so now, but on the whole a strictly non-committal attitude may be best'.[9]

The book, then, might describe, assess and criticise the work of organised religion in the metropolis but it must do so in a way calculated not to ruffle the feathers of the people involved, some of them senior ecclesiastics with high political connections. Yet it must do so in an interesting manner, bringing out the many points which Booth and his associates thought worthy of consideration within a given number of pages without undue repetition. There are hints that Booth and his associates were well aware of the potential difficulties involved in presenting the results of the inquiry to the public. George Duckworth gave the following advice to Charles in September 1900:

> As much must in any case be omitted I think you will have to say in the Preface that the Districts have, as far as possible, been taken as typical of some particular phase of religious effort. This leads to the neglect of some important men in districts where their work is not typical of the locality. But that can't be helped: their opinions are not lost but used elsewhere.

Comparability between districts was, however, of great importance. Duckworth recommended:

> As to the plan of the Chapters: I think that in each case you ought to start with a general description, social and physical, of the whole area covering the whole ground, even at the risk of repetition of things that have been stated in the earlier volumes. After that you can pick and choose and give particular attention to special areas or typical efforts.[10]

To some extent Booth appears to have followed this advice. Each volume does contain a general description. He did not, however, adopt the recommendation that a clear statement be included regarding the basis of selection. Perhaps further readers would have found the books more comprehensible had he done so.

---

[9] Booth Collection, A31, fos. 60 a and b; Mary had to soothe ruffled feathers with a form letter, Booth Collection, A31, fo. 61. Somewhere between 1,100 and 1,200 presentation copies were sent out. Booth Correspondence, MS 797 I/10, Jesse Argyle to Charles Booth, 18 April 1903.

[10] Booth Correspondence, MS 797 I/4839 (i) and (ii), G.H. Duckworth to Charles Booth, 30 September 1900.

2. Summing up the Survey

It is worthwhile to trace, briefly, the chronology of the writing-up period. In part, because this is interesting for itself; in part, because it allows us some insight into why the final series took the form that it did. This series was written by Booth himself. While the contribution of the associates to the inquiry is acknowledged on the title pages, it was Booth who produced a continuous text and who was responsible for the selection of materials, the opinions expressed, the language used. The series was, therefore, different in kind from the earlier Poverty and Industry Series which consisted of essays by various members of the team. We shall probably never know for sure why Booth decided to produce the books himself. The decision perhaps arose as much out of his appreciation of the intractability of the materials and the delicacy of the political implications as out of his personal interest in religious institutions. After all, he had been as interested in the material conditions surrounding poverty. Once he abandoned statistics as a method of organising the books about religious influences, it would have been difficult to have controlled adequately the disparate perspectives of himself and his five associates – writing the books himself he stood more chance of preserving comparability of approach between areas. As the reports by his associates show, the team did not always have quite the same view of the purpose of the survey or its conditions as he did. Moreover, Booth had been partially distracted from the Industry Series by his concern to win old age pensions. Now he was well and truly involved again in the inquiry.

This said, we must not fall into the trap of believing that because Booth was the author of the religious influences volumes, he therefore had no substantive assistance in the writing thereof. This is far from the truth. As the correspondence demonstrates, Booth had frequent and important discussions with his wife and his associates – especially Ernest Aves and George Duckworth – both about what the evidence meant and about what he should or should not include in the volumes. To picture Booth working in isolation and rejecting assistance with his monumental task is misleading in the extreme. To see his secretaries as mere dogsbodies is equally mistaken. It is because Charles Booth spent so much time apart from both his family and his associates that so many clues survive about his method of working. He wrote to his wife and to members of the team; they wrote to him and to each other.[1]

---

[1] Most of the surviving correspondence appears to be in the Booth Correspondence, MS 797, although a small number of letters are at the BLPES in the Booth Collection in A31.

The business of writing seems to have begun in earnest in early 1900. This was before the inquiry itself was completed. (Booth did not leave writing, as the Simeys appear to have thought, until after October 1900.)[2] At a time when the 'team' were still conducting interviews and writing reports, Booth's wife, Mary, was continuing to read through the materials already collected (this time for North East London) and was making her own notes. Initially her plan was to acquaint herself with the material via Booth's own abstracts but she found this unsatisfactory. Like the present authors she found the interview reports much more congenial reading:

> I have been able to read a good deal of Hoxton. I have reverted to the old plan of reading the interviews through; having come to the conclusion that the extremely concentrated form of nourishment of your notes is too much for my weak mental digestion. I make my own notes now on bits of paper here and there, and if they are often only the same as some of yours, it doesn't matter and I certainly get a more vivid and definite impression, I think mainly from the mere length of time given to reading about each man.[3]

In that same month of March 1900 Booth was hoping to devote Easter to writing the book. We know that by late summer he had some parts of the text in a readable draft. On 30 August 1900 Mary reported that she had been 'tearing away' at South London,

> and really I don't think your account of the Bermondsey, Lambeth and Rother-hithe districts could be much improved, nor much amplified with any great addition to the effect. You paint a wonderfully vivid picture and it makes a deep impression.[4]

On another occasion she had 'had an interesting morning over Clapham and Wandsworth and Putney'. At about this time, if not before, the associates were being sent the drafts for comment. On 30 September George Duckworth wrote to the 'Chief': 'I have just finished reading "Hampstead".[5] At this stage, Booth and Argyle were assembling material for Volume One (London North of the Thames).[6] This took many weeks. The volumes were not, therefore, written in the published order.

As part of the basis of these drafts he used the digests of interviews provided by his team and the essay reports about religious influences (district by district) which they had compiled for his use. From the start,

---

[2] Simey, *Charles Booth*, p. 145.

[3] Booth Correspondence, MS 797 I/3722, Mary Booth to Charles Booth, 7 March 1900.

[4] Booth Correspondence, MS 797 I/3791, Mary Booth to Charles Booth, 30 August 1900.

[5] Booth Correspondence, MS 797 I/4839 (i) and (ii), G.H. Duckworth to Charles Booth, 30 September 1900.

[6] Booth Collection, A32, vii, fo. i.

therefore, the impact of the team's views was extremely important in the making of the finished volumes. George Duckworth used his reports to suggest and experiment with various approaches to the material. For instance his lengthy essay on Hackney and South Hackney began with a seven- page description of the character of Hackney in which he sought to compare its present to its past. 'At this point I stuck, finding that I was not bringing out what I wanted to', he remarked, adding, 'I leave this opening for what it is worth as giving some indication of what I think wants doing.'[7] He strove also to assess the evidence, making shrewd comments and criticisms and showing himself by no means afraid to reach conclusions which differed from ideas held by Charles Booth.

> I have placed religion last because though it takes the first place in our evidence I believe that on the whole it plays a less important part in the lives of the people than either education or government activity, whether central or local.[8]

In the event much of this material was incorporated in Booth's printed text and signs of Duckworth's style are evident, although his report is much condensed.[9] Booth sometimes disagreed with Duckworth's analysis and certainly did not accept his conclusions about the relative unimportance of religion as an influence upon the people at large. While to some extent Ernest Aves' contribution to Booth's Inquiry has been acknowledged that of George Duckworth has been unaccountably overlooked. His dilettante life style has been emphasised, his morals impugned on the basis of little evidence, but his weighty contribution to Booth's work has gone unnoticed.[10]

Immediately he had written chapters, Booth sent out these drafts for a first reading by the associates and his wife. They brought to their reading an intimate knowledge of the evidence he had written from. Their detailed opinions amounted to suggested revisions of the draft. In August Charles wrote to Aves to this effect:

> My wife is at work upon Box 1 but, like the rest, is working independently – thus I shall have no less than six critical versions to help me when I pick up the threads again.[11]

---

[7] Booth Collection, A35 report on Hackney and South Hackney by G.H. Duckworth, 8, fos. 7-8.

[8] Booth Collection, A37, report on District 14 & 16 by G.H. Duckworth, 8, fo. 64.

[9] *Religious Influences*, 1, pp. 73-113.

[10] See for example Alan and Veronica Palmer, *Who's Who in Bloomsbury* (Brighton, 1987), pp. 44-45.

[11] Mary Booth, *Charles Booth: A Memoir* (London, 1918), p. 136, Charles Booth to Ernest Aves, 6 August 1900. This letter is not in the Booth Correspondence.

Relatively few of these comments exist in the archive. Those which do, suggest the independence of mind of all the secretaries, including the intrepid Jesse Argyle, who expressed his reservations about the short chapter treating North London.

> The district by this chapter includes 4,000,000 people. I think it is hardly ample enough and lays so much stress on one class as to give a possibly misleading idea of the district. I would suggest . . .[12]

Ernest Aves made a special visit to validate the description of one church and found Booth's account wanting. 'I think that there is no reason to describe the congregation as "almost entirely middle class" or any special reason to say that any come 'from a distance.'[13] Not only did the secretaries offer constructive criticism, they sometimes proved unwilling to let matters go when their initial misgivings, spoken or written, were rejected by Charles Booth. Sometimes the documentation suggests vigorous discussions about the material, lending credence to Mary Booth's memories of long conversations between Booth and Aves.

> I have always, and the point has been much discussed at Adelphi Terrace, opposed this interpretation of purple. Our colours show a condition of life, not a transition.[14]

What we have here is the tip of the iceberg. Most of the volumes, if not all, seem to have existed in first draft by August 1902. At this time Booth was editing and revising the drafts – allowing two days per volume. The task was time consuming and Booth's business commitments led him so share it with Aves and with Mary. Aves, however, was in Tenby and his absence from London occasioned a detailed correspondence because there was still a good deal of work to be done on Volume Seven. Aves was given a minute breakdown of Booth's method of working.

> Arkell is here helping to put all the material in to final order before it is packed up to go to Tenby. I will explain the system on which I have been working and on which I think you will find it convenient to work.
>   The boxes as I am using them have been cleared of everything except the interview books and the original draft reports. This leaves the books easy of access for reference. The boxes are ranged in order each containing the books that belong to it, which is the best order to keep for ready reference. The abstracts etc are ranged on sundry window ledges and shelves in the same order and finally the

---

[12] Booth Collection, A37, 13, memorandum on *Religious Influences*, 1, Chapter 3 part 1, fo. 2.
[13] Booth Collection, A39, 7, fo. 10, a letter from Ernest Aves to Charles Booth re *Religious Influences*, 2, chapter 2.
[14] Booth Collection. A37, 13, fo. 3; see *Religious Influences*, 1, Chapter 3 pp. 149-50.

bundles of materials are spread out on tables. I believe you will find it quite essential to observe and maintain some such order but it takes up a lot of room.

Arkell is now going through the material bundle by bundle putting letters A.B.C. etc on documents which have been added since my numbering was done. He at the same time withdraws any part of the material which applies to Volume Seven in any special way – such as Salvation Army or sisterhoods etc, – or to the Final Volume on Social Influences, and will add them to the existing bundle for these subjects – but at the same time he will leave a slip in the original place for reference.

The bundles that refer to the districts and to Volume Seven will also be sent to you – but those concerning the Social Influences can remain here till we come to that part.

Aves was to work on Volume Seven. Most of the chapters in this volume were to include extracts 'arranged in some kind of luminous order and helped where needed by short remarks'. Booth had already copied out extracts 'partly from the boxes and partly from the bundles'. 'I hope you will interest yourself in these extract sections as I think a great deal can be made of them. They are to Volume Seven what the illustrations are to the other volumes; and I suggest, should be printed in the smaller type. I have chosen a great mass of them but there are still many fish in the sea and better selections may be made. Please note that the new (lettered material) has not yet been ransacked. I went through all the rest when I numbered it. If you make use of this or any of the material which I have not used please put references in margin.'[15] Booth then went through each chapter in turn, reporting the stage that the work was at and drawing Aves' attention to where he could most help. For example:

Chapter IV (Missions) The extracts in this case are very voluminous and not very luminous. I think better can be done. On the other hand they contain some amazing specimens. Query how much editing, by way of remarks to point a moral, will they stand? I have been anxious to leave these extracts to tell their own story as much as possible. Section (5) called 'Summary' is unwritten. I thought something would be needed.

Chapter VI (prostitution etc) is very imperfect. I have had some idea of writing a section dealing with its developments district by district – working from Baxter's notes.[16] In some way we need to emphasise the wide spread character of the evil. There are also many opinions worth quoting as well as extracts from printed matter. Chapter VII.

The extracts need to be found and when found will complete the whole very well.

Booth retained in his hands the important decisions about the form of the

---

[15] Booth Correspondence, MS 797 I/1522 (iv), Charles Booth to Ernest Aves, 1902.
[16] We have been unable to identify these notes.

series. For example, he rejected Aves' suggestions about reorganising the order of the chapters in Volume Seven – 'I think they will be best kept where they are' – and the weight which Aves seemed to want to attach to the Social Influences volume. 'I incline more and more to make less of and depend less upon the Social Influences volume. I do not think it will be wise to pin much upon it – we won't print any contents in advance, but merely refer to it as a winding up volume – a thin volume I hope.'[17] In the event, sometimes his intentions were subverted. (see below, pp. 180-81, 186-87)

Nevertheless, he was conscious of how much he relied upon Aves for support and stimulation. 'I cannot tell you how grateful I am for your patient thorough work over the revision and it will be the same in bringing everything to a focus in this last volume. I have been put to it to keep any thing like a clear mind – business and other things have been so very disturbing – so I lean on you very much.' By February 1903 Aves had completed many of the revisions to Volume Seven and Booth enthused about his patient endeavours: 'I do indeed not know how to find words that will sufficiently recognise the value that your revisions have been through-out – so thorough in things large or small, so endlessly patient and so necessary. How much the book owes to you no one can ever know.'[18] Booth would never accept any alteration with which he did not entirely agree but he was grateful for the critical perspective which Aves brought to bear upon the work. A man of real scholarly humility, he was willing to consider every suggestion. Like many great men, Booth was practised in using his associates' skills to considerable advantage while retaining the reins in his own capable hands. Nobody doubted whose survey it was – it 'Mr Booth's Inquiry' – yet, equally, each associate felt involved and appreciated.

There was a continuing dialogue by post between Aves and Booth regarding Volume Seven. Many small changes were made. Aves submitted to Booth his own selections of extracts. Booth sent Aves the final chapters. The chapters were returned to Booth as Aves finished with them. Thus on 13 January Aves wrote that he was sending chapters 1-3 by post and had now 'done up to chapter 7, so I will send more very soon'. By 30 January all but chapter 11 had been returned to Booth.[19] When he returned them Aves made some recommendations:

In going through the Extracts of the Church of England and the nonconformists I have had no inclination to cut down, unless, possibly one or two of the Congregationalist programmes or Societies. There are rather many of these, but the mass has the merit of giving a vivid impression of internal activity and vigour. This was doubtless the object, but if room is wanted, I feel that a page or two

[17] Booth Correspondence, MS 797 I/1522 (vi), Charles Booth to Ernest Aves, 26 August 1902.
[18] Booth Correspondence, MS 797 I/1532, Charles Booth to Ernest Aves, February 1903.
[19] Booth Correspondence, MS 797 I/24 (ii) Ernest Aves to Charles Booth, 30 January 1903.

might be saved here. I suppose that my suggested extracts of the poor Positivists, Ethical Culturists etc are doomed to exclusion? It is perhaps better so, but I can't help being sorry.

Often it is impossible to know how seriously Booth took Aves' advice. In the same letter Aves 'suggested that the Chapters or Sections of Extracts be called "Appendices" and have mentioned reasons as being so largely quotations from printed matter, I think they ought to be marked off in some definite way from the text proper'.[20] Booth did not accept this precise recommendation in the published version but he did label the chapters distinctly as 'Illustrations' and made it clear that these were 'selections from printed documents'. Booth lost no time in submitting the chapters from Aves to the press. By late January 1903 the book was within sight of final proof. Booth and his office tried to keep Aves' tinkering tendencies in check. Aves, however, was indefatigable. 'I will keep it a very little time, and will remember what you say about the decision not to alter the paging to any great extent. I don't think that this should be necessary, but a read right through, critically in general, rather than in detail, is sure to suggest something . . .'[21] Booth seems to have complied with his wish for in March 1903 we read that Aves suggests an amendment to page 393 of Volume Seven. This change appears to have been incorporated in the completed book. Aves wrote:

> Ought Shuttleworth's name to have been included among the great dead (at end of section on polytechnics)? I think perhaps not, but it might be well to insert something, e.g. the words 'at least' before the numeral ('five' or 'six') of the sheets have not been struck off. There have been several other deaths: Brooke Lambert; Reaney; etc.

On page 393 we read: 'Mr Hogg is at least the sixth great man whose influence upon the social conditions and religious life of London has been cut short by death while I have been trying to record it . . .'[22] To the end there were detailed comments on Booth's text – most notably a highly critical response to Booth's assertion that the proportion of serious readers in the population had decreased markedly.[23] This criticism appears to have been taken to heart: neither the offending statement nor Aves' reasoned modification seems to occur in the text of Volume Seven or the Star Volume.

While Aves was still preoccupied with Volume Seven, the final volume of the Religious Influences Series, Booth had moved on to work almost

---

[20] Booth Collection, A31, fo. 51 Ernest Aves to Charles Booth, 13 January 1903.
[21] Booth Correspondence, MS 797 1/24, Ernest Aves to Charles Booth, 30 January 1903.
[22] *Religious Influences*, 7, p. 393.
[23] Booth Collection A31, fo. 66.

exclusively on the so-called Star Volume. He felt that with Volume Seven he had 'reached; the "as good as I can point".[24] In February 1903 he was writing 'Housing' and 'Expansion'.[25] In August 1902 Booth had expressed the opinion that too much weight should not be attached to this volume on Social Influences. He wanted it to be relatively short and was unprepared to state in advance what it should contain. He certainly found it an intractable volume to write. On 2 March he wrote jokingly to Mary of his desperation:

> My work stuck fast on Sunday I made ever so many false starts and laughed as I went to bed at my absolute incapacity to finish my own book – but today has gone better I think I started all right. Egad I hope so for the time gets short.[26]

The occasion for hurry was Booth's planned business trip to Manaos. Aves had heard it rumoured that Booth wanted the Star Volume to be in final proof before he went abroad. It was at this juncture that his wife's help proved most invaluable to him. At this time Mary was very unwell but even this did not prevent her commenting in detail on Booth's drafts not Booth assuming that everything (including his wife's health) would be sacrificed to the success of the inquiry: 'but everything and everybody must be sacrificed to what I have to do, every time . . .'[27]

Mary's comments were honest and not always laudatory by any means. While it would be incorrect to suggest that she wrote the Star Volume, she certainly helped to shape it and had a far great impact upon its final form that any have allowed to date. Mary Booth was an avid reader of serious works. Charles confessed that a rigorous programme of reading was beyond him;[28] the Booth children agreed that his rooms were almost devoid of books and that he did not work from them.[29] Effectively Mary often did this work for him. They discussed his work in the light of her reading and opinions both in person and by letter. They read J.S. Mill and Barnet together. She read Marx and James, among others. Sufficient traces of this interchange of ideas remain to make it clear how important Mary's support was to Charles Booth and his inquiry into religious influences. On 28 February she criticised the inclusion of a section on Dives and Lazarus and

[24] Booth Correspondence, MS 797 I/1543, Charles Booth to Mary Booth, 3 March 1903.
[25] Booth Correspondence, MS 797 I/1532, Charles Booth to Ernest Aves, 13 February 1903; Booth Correspondence, MS 797 I/1537, Charles Booth to Mary Booth, 18 February 1903; and Booth Correspondence, MS 797 I/1538, Charles to Mary Booth, 20 February 1903.
[26] Booth Correspondence, MS 797 I/1542, Charles Booth to Mary Booth, 2 March 1903.
[27] Booth Correspondence, MS 797 I/1541, Charles Booth to Mary Booth, 1 March 1903.
[28] See above pp. 11, 34.
[29] Booth Correspondence, MS 797 I/3033, Meg Booth Ritchie to George Booth, 13 April 1956.

recommended several excisions.[30] Booth responded positively – the changes 'certainly made it less objectionable', 'the Lazarus piece is certainly better out'.[31] On 2 March she was pleased that he agreed with her about the Lazarus section. She forwarded, along with Mr Stead's irate comments, a critique of his locomotion proposal. She felt that the Star Volume was characterised by muddle – science and statesmanship were confused.[32] What historians and social scientists have often observed and even oftener criticised – that Booth made few detailed practical policy recommendations in his printed series – may owe more to Mary Booth's influence than has been recognised. She certainly wanted him to stick to observation and excise much of the material on practical remedies. This was not because she thought practical proposals inappropriate or outside his brief. Rather she wanted him to restrict the series to observation and publish his practical recommendations separately. She would also have liked Charles to have expanded the Star Volume considerably. While Charles valued her criticism and acted upon some of it, she did not have her way in major respects. He persisted in making some practical proposals and he refused to expand the Star Volume. On 3 March he replied to Mary about the communication from Herbert Stead and declared that he did not want to write again 'for years, if at all – or at least, not publish. No magazine articles for me!'[33]

When Charles left for a business trip in late March the seven volumes were ready for publication and the Star Volume was in a late draft, with some parts in proof.[34] It was left to Mary and the associates to see the new book through the proofing stage and into print. It should be understood that often extensive alterations were made to a book at the proofs stage – a process which would be unthinkable for reasons of cost today was unthinkingly undertaken in the early years of the century. The task before Mary Booth, Jesse Argyle, Arthur Baxter, Ernest Aves and George Duckworth was a much more responsible one than merely dotting i's and crossing t's. Moreover, some parts of the book were still in typed and often rough draft.

The surviving correspondence allows us to piece together the way in which Mary and Jesse Argyle set about preparing the typescript Star Volume for the printer. Mary was especially concerned about some aspects of the volume. On 15 April Mary wrote to Booth about the chapter on the 'Economic Conditions of Life'.[35] She thought that this was potentially difficult for the reader. Aves was requested to work upon it to effect improvements. On 20 April she repeated to Booth her concerns, asserting

[30] Booth Correspondence, MS 797 I/3899, Mary Booth to Charles Booth, 28 February 1903.
[31] Booth Correspondence, MS 797 I/1541, Charles Booth to Mary Booth, 1 March 1903.
[32] Booth Correspondence, MS 797 I/1541, Mary Booth to Charles Booth, 2 March 1903.
[33] Booth Correspondence, MS 797 I/1543, Charles Booth to Mary Booth, 3 March 1903.
[34] Booth Correspondence, MS 797 I/3906, Mary Booth to Charles Booth, 15 March 1903.
[35] *Religious Influences*, part II, section 7.

that the section was too concentrated.[36] Aves sent Mary his recommended
changes by 27 April 1903.[37] In this same letter of thanks Mary stated that
she would call in the other copies of the Economic Conditions section from
Argyle and, if necessary, choose between the recommended revisions.[38]
Mary seems to have anticipated that Charles might be more than a little
alarmed to hear of the work on this section. In the evening of 3 May Arthur
Baxter visited them. 'Arthur and I had a good bout of Star book. He has
taken away the Economic Conditions of Life to think over the alterations
which I proposed to Mr Aves, amended by those which Mr Aves made on
me, amended by those which I made on Mr Aves again!!! *Don't be frightened!*
Nothing has touched me more than to see the affectionate almost reverent
way in which the whole staff treats your text in your absence, fearing to lose
a shadow of a shade of your full meaning. They are *nice* people.'[39] On 4 May
Mary wrote to Aves of her discussions with Baxter.[40] She reported that she
and Baxter had gone along with many of his suggestions but that Baxter was
going to try to 'knock out some amendations which will prevent confusion as
to the two uses of the word 'spend''. Aves appears to have liked the final
version. Mary wrote, 'I am quite happy about the result of our joint labours
over it; all the staff!'[41]

Other parts of the work also needed attention. Late in April Aves was
returning Sections 1-5 of Part III and asking Mary whether she wanted
more material on nursing.[42] He also sent the interviews from which the
chapter had been written. He had reservations about the section on the
attitudes of the people to death – feeling this to be too superficial. Aves had
evidence to the contrary which he offered.[43] When Mary wrote to him on 4
May she agreed with this criticism, commenting: 'It is true only of certain
kinds of people and under certain conditions. I remember that a cousin of
mine, a clergyman's wife, told me that one of the saddest things she had to
see was the grief and anxiety of dying mothers of little children, who knew
that as a matter of course their husbands would marry again, as a working
man almost must; and looking forward with dread to the step mother's
treatment of their little children.' On the 30 April Mary received a letter
from George Duckworth accompanying the proofs of Volume Eight which

[36] Booth Correspondence, MS 797 I/3918, Mary Booth to Charles Booth, 20 April 1903.
[37] Booth Correspondence, MS 797 I/3920, Mary Booth to Ernest Aves, 27 April 1903.
[38] Ibid.
[39] Booth Correspondence, MS 797 I/3922, Mary Booth to Charles Booth, 3 May 1903.
[40] Booth Correspondence, MS 797 I/3923, Mary Booth to Ernest Aves, 4 May 1903.
[41] Booth Correspondence, MS 797 I/3929, Mary Booth to Ernest Aves, 21 May 1903.
[42] Public Houses; Prostitution; Police and Crime; The Organisation of Charity; Hospitals
and Nursing.
[43] Booth Collection, A31 fo. 63, Ernest Aves to Mary Booth, 29 April 1903.

had been sent to him for suggestions. He too requested more material on nurses.[44]

Occasionally Mary looked outside the circle of associates for assistance. On 3 May she 'had a glorious morning over the Star book'. Her son-in-law 'Kind Malcolm' Macnaughton 'brought me back the copy I had sent him for his remarks on the Licensing and the Police, and he spent a good hour with me over it going through it carefully. All his suggestions seem to me most helpful and I think you would agree to what he proposes'.[45] When she wrote to Aves on 4 May she again mentioned that Malcolm had read through 'Public Houses' and might have some suggestions. On the 8 of the month Malcolm wrote to her his approbation of Booth's interpretation of the laws on street betting.[46]

Meanwhile Charles had forwarded a new section from Madeira, regarding omitted questions. On 4 May Mary thanked Aves for his criticisms of this piece 'with which I agree'. 'I have read all your revise (except the piece I have received this morning) and collated it with GHD[uckworth]'s copy and my own and Charlie's and I think I have adopted almost all of your suggestions. A few I have put aside to be talked over with Mr Argyle, as being more in his province than mine.'[47] She informed Charles on 12 May of the reorganisation of the conclusion.[48] In a letter of 20 May Mary asked Aves for his opinion of the revised section of text.[49] Aves seems to have thought that the text would appear about half way through the book. Mary was full of apologies and expressed willingness to reconsider:

'I fully thought I had mentioned this in writing to you, and am sorry I did not. If you think otherwise, and would prefer to insert it on 91, please let me know. And we will send down this passage, which has been altered a good deal, to you at once to be looked over. I do think it comes best on 214, just after his mention of the other omitted questions. It seemed to me that to put it in on 91, could be to do twice what should be done only once. These are my reasons, which ought to have been given you long ago.'[50]

Mary got her way. She thanked Aves for his concurrence on 24 May and the text was relocated to pages 214 and 215.[51] Aves nevertheless appears to have quibbled over the wording of the passage. Mary had this to say:

'About the wording and general scope of the new bit, I felt very puzzled. I did not

[44] Booth Correspondence, MS 797 I/4847, George Duckworth to Mary Booth, 30 April 1903.
[45] Booth Correspondence, MS 797 I/3922, Mary Booth to Charles Booth, 3 May 1903.
[46] Booth Collection, A31, fo. 68.
[47] Booth Correspondence, MS 797 I/3923, Mary Booth to Ernest Aves, 4 May 1903.
[48] Booth Correspondence, MS 797 I/3929, Mary Booth to Charles Booth, 12 May 1903.
[49] Booth Correspondence, MS 797 I/3928, Mary Booth to Ernest Aves, 20 May 1903.
[50] Booth Correspondence, MS 797 I/3929, Mary Booth to Ernest Aves, 21 May 1903.
[51] Booth Correspondence, MS 797 I/3931, Mary Booth to Ernest Aves, 24 May 1903.

entirely like my husband's, wrote one of my own and did not like that; then wrote
two more unsuccessfully, and finally asked Mr Baxter to take my last and Charlie's
and try at them which he did; and then he and I and Mr Argyle did it together;
and put it into the shape in which it has been sent to you. It seemed hard not to say
too much; and finally you may think we have said too little; a mere summation,
except for the keeping intact of Charlie's last paragraph, which we all agreed in
liking and wanting to leave just as he wrote it.[52]

Irritation reigned in Adelphi Terrace when Ernest Aves persisted in
finding more and more items to correct or change. When Mary wrote to
Charles on 12 May it was to report that:

I had the morning there[53] today with Mr Argyle and Arthur, and we have come to
an end now of our criticisms. The final revise is to go now to Mr Aves – to be
returned by him to me; and that finishes swiftly. Arthur was today amusingly
insistent with Mr Argyle to be very stringent in not allowing Mr Aves too much
time for this final look over; as Arthur says Mr Aves can't help always wanting to
alter everything. Mr Argyle was very calm and delightful, said it was Mr Aves's
right, and that he must have the thing sent him; but that he would suggest the
desirability of speed.[54]

But Argyle himself expressed impatience with Aves' constant tinkering
with the proofs in a letter to Mary on 27 May.[55] Interestingly, when Mary
wrote to Aves on 13 May she emphasised the importance of expediting
publication, using a ploy which she hoped would influence Aves. 'I think we
ought not to be long about this last reading. I have Charlie's words ringing in
my ears: "Mind you publish before I come back".'[56] Aves sent back the
revised pages little by little and on 24 May she reinforced the message: 'we
shall have to do all we know to have the book out before he comes on the 22
June.'[57] The team were still working on the clarity of the book on 31 May:
'We are getting on splendidly with regard to page 197. I feel a little doubtful
myself as to Mr Booth's exact meaning and am writing to Mr Argyle to say
so, asking him and Mr Baxter to settle it; and saying that I am telling you so
that you and they could communicate directly if you thought well. I think he
means that the increase used by the site rating could be balanced by the
ground owner; by a reduction in existing central charge.' There seems to be
an echo of this debate in a letter which Argyle sent to Mary on 2 June 1903
discussing Aves and Booth on rents.[58]

[52] Booth Correspondence, MS 797 I/3931, Mary Booth to Ernest Aves, 24 May 1903.
[53] At Adelphi Terrace.
[54] Booth Correspondence, MS 797 I/3925, Mary Booth to Charles Booth, 12 May 1903.
[55] Booth Collection, A31, fo. 80, Jesse Argyle to Mary Booth, 27 May 1903.
[56] Booth Correspondence, MS 797 I/3926, Mary Booth to Ernest Aves, 13 May 1903.
[57] Booth Correspondence, MS 797 I/3931, Mary Booth to Ernest Aves, 24 May 1903.
[58] Booth Collection, A31, fo. 83, Jesse Argyle to Mary Booth, 2 June 1903.

Late April, May and June at Adelphi Terrace were devoted to tidying up the ends. If Mary Booth, Ernest Aves and, to some extent, George Duckworth and Theodore Llewellyn Davies were drawn in to settling the precise text which would go into print, it was left to Jesse Argyle and Arthur Baxter to check the tables, finalise the maps, collect together the revised typescript, prepare the abstract and the index and send the whole off to the printers. Argyle had checked the tabular material in Booth's text against Arkell's copy by late April.[59] On 12 May Mary was sent the revised map for approval by George Arkell.[60] Arthur Baxter seems to have been responsible for preparing an abstract to the entire seventeen volumes. On 8 May he wrote to Mary saying that he was glad she liked the summary.[61] And on the same date Argyle referred to Baxter's abstract in a letter to Mary.[62] This was reported to be ready for the proof stage on 18 May,[63] when Argyle urged Aves to hurry up with Volume Five of the Industry Series so that it could be referred to in the abstract. A proof existed by 27 May,[64] and an index by 29 May.[65] At this same time Argyle discussed with Mary the advisability of advertising. He was convinced that it was necessary to keep the 'pot boiling'.[66] Meanwhile Baxter and Argyle were concentrating on the final proof correction stage. In a letter to Mary Booth on 2 June Argyle reported that he and Baxter had gone through her corrected proofs together and asked Mary's approval for placing the index at the end of the volume.[67] Aves was holding them up. Argyle asked Mary to write to him asking him for the missing sections of manuscripts to be inserted on page 214.[68] Mary duly wrote asking for the material on 5 June.[69] Aves replied in alarm that Mary had not received the pages which he had returned a week earlier.[70] With this issues cleared up, things proceeded apace. Mary was sent a dummy binding and map on 4 June[71] and informed on 6 June that the Star Volume, which would be thick, was all ready for the printer. Arrangements would be made for advanced copies for the press.[72] At this juncture Argyle began to split his attentions between the publication of the Star Volume and the rebinding and reissue of

[59] Booth Collection, A31, fo. 61, Jesse Argyle to Mary Booth, 28 April 1903.
[60] Booth Collection, A31, fo. 75, a and b, George Arkell to Mary Booth, 12 May 1903.
[61] Booth Collection, A31, fo. 72, Arthur Baxter to Mary Booth, 8 May 1903.
[62] Booth Collection, A31, fo. 70, Jesse Argyle to Mary Booth, 8 May 1903.
[63] Booth Collection, A31, fo. 77, Jesse Argyle to Mary Booth, 18 May 1903.
[64] Booth Collection, A31, fo. 80, Jesse Argyle to Mary Booth, 27 May 1903.
[65] Booth Collection, A31, fo. 81, Jesse Argyle to Mary Booth, 29 May 1903.
[66] Booth Collection, A31, fo. 81, Jesse Argyle to Mary Booth, 27 May 1903.
[67] Booth Collection, A31, fo. 83, Jesse Argyle to Mary Booth, 2 June 1903.
[68] See above; Booth Collection, A31, fo. 84, Jesse Argyle to Mary Booth, 4 June 1903.
[69] Booth Correspondence, MS 797 I/3933, Mary Booth to Ernest Aves, 5 June 1903.
[70] Booth Collection, A31, fo. 86, Ernest Aves to Mary Booth, 8 June 1903.
[71] Booth Collection, A31, fo. 85, Jesse Argyle to Mary Booth, 4 June 1903.
[72] Booth Collection, A31, fo. 87, Jesse Argyle to Mary Booth, 6 June 1903.

the Industry Series.[73] A final proof of the Star Volume was sent to her and also to Aves for checking and last minute correction on 11 June.[74] On 13 June Mary was asked to select the preferred shade of purple for the top edging of the pages and to approve Argyle's suggestion of a better map pocket in a letter which reported that the publication date would be 23rd June.[75] Binding was ordered by 15 June.[76] In the event publication was delayed until 26 June and Macmillan promised to rush two copies to Adelphi Terrace by the night of 25 June. The publisher had forgotten to print the wrappers.[77] Ernest Aves had received his copy by 8 July when he wrote to tell Charles Booth, now back in Britain, how pleased he was to have participated.[78]

It may never be possible to assess precisely how much Charles Booth's Star Volume was modified by the team left in charge of the final stages of preparation and publication. Booth was responsible for its overall authorship. The 'final draft' which he left with the team was, like all works, the product of many influences (the research investigation, the views of his associates and Mary, the views of other authors and contemporaries) but even so it was Charles Booth's book. Nonetheless, the team were charged with improving his text for publication. By piecing together painstakingly the surviving fragments of evidence we can show that they took this task seriously and did make significant modifications. They concentrated on clarity and no doubt were sincere in their attempt to remain faithful to every shade or shadow of Booth's meaning. Yet we do know that some of the associates, notably Aves and Duckworth, had decided ideas of their own which did not necessarily coincide with Booth's and that Aves, at least, was tempted to debate with Booth's text about rates and rents in Booth's absence. We also know that Mary used her initiative when it came to relocating text or reformulating material. Moreover, Mary, who was after all a Macaulay and much influenced by histories written in a particular literary tradition, had and expressed strong views about the presentation of the religious influences findings. Her family maintained that she wrote many of the more literary passages.[79] She appears to have succeeded in persuading her husband of the advisability of steering away as far as possible from making proposals for remedy in this work. She influenced him to regard

[73] Booth Collection, A31, fo. 88, Jesse Argyle to Mary Booth, 8 June 1903 and Booth Collection, A31, fo. 89, Jesse Argyle to Mary Booth, 10 June 1903.

[74] Booth Collection, A31, fo. 90, Jesse Argyle to Mary Booth, 11 June 1903.

[75] Booth Collection, A31, fo. 91, Jesse Argyle to Mary Booth, 13 June 1903.

[76] Booth Collection, A31, fo. 92, Jesse Argyle to Mary Booth, 15 June 1903.

[77] Booth Collection, A31, fo. 94, Jesse Argyle to Mary Booth, 24 June 1903.

[78] Booth Correspondence, MS 797 I/27, Ernest to Mary Booth, 8 July 1903.

[79] Booth Correspondence, MS 797 I/3030, Meg Booth Ritchie, daughter of Charles Booth to George Booth, son of Charles Booth, 22 January 1956; MS 797 I/2402 (ii), George Booth to Margaret Simey, 23 January 1956.

verbatim quotation in a somewhat liberal light to improve the flow of the text and make it more acceptable.

> Also I am not sure whether the excessive colloquialism of some of the quotation might not be modified. After all, what passed the lips of your interviewed people is not a sacred text, verbally inspired.[80]

She modified some of his metaphors – Dives and Lazarus being one such example.

3. Charles Booth and Social Science

It has become customary to regard Booth's Inquiry as a stage in the development of British social science – there is a line which runs through Mayhew, Booth, Rowntree and Llewellyn Smith. There is much to be said for such a perspective but it does have its dangers. Firstly, it assumes that Booth's inquiry was primarily concerned with poverty. This was not the case and was never intended to be the case. Out of seventeen volumes, nine were concerned with the *material* conditions of life of the people in London – people who included the middle and working classes as well as the residuum. In the words which Booth used at the close of the Star Volume: 'the object of the sixteen volumes has been to describe London as it appeared in the last decade of the nineteenth century.' Secondly, it might lead us to compare Booth's survey with a late twentieth-century social survey – this would inevitably be different in its intention, execution and presentation. Charles Booth was not an academic social scientist in the late twentieth-century mode. He was a private person, a prosperous business man with a social conscience and a keen intellect. 'For the treatment of disease, it is first necessary to establish the facts as to its character, extent and symptoms.' This was the motivation behind his entire inquiry – to describe things as they are. To this end Booth paid a small fortune and devoted seventeen years of his life. He had no training (there was no one to train him) and he pioneered techniques of social investigation and of organisation which others were to develop further: mass interviewing; complicated correlations of social and economic statistics; social and economic cartography. Often he came unstuck. He had bitten off more than any man could hope to chew – even one with five or more paid assistants, an extremely able and devoted wife and an apparently bottomless pocket. But it was he who had this splendid vision and who sought to realise it. To state, as did one recent scholar, that

---

[80] Booth Correspondence, MS 797 I/3894a, Mary Booth to Charles Booth, 17 February 1903.

Booth's principal contribution to scholarship was $3,000,000 of his own money is an unduly negative remark which tells us more about modern sociology than Booth's contribution.

4. The Religious Influences Series: The Printed Books

The view of Booth's printed work as a faltering step on the path to a perfected social science has done him a disservice – it has been like a cataract obscuring our vision. Only by reading the printed work (in the light of what we now know about the investigations upon which it was based and the manner of its production) can we assess what Booth was attempting to do, what he did and how successful he was in achieving his own ends.

To suggest that Booth's aims were less ambitious and worthwhile than those who attempted to measure the religious response in terms of statistics of church attendance is indefensible. Booth was no number cruncher. He thought that bald statistics of church attendance said relatively little about the response of the populace to the religious effort of ministers and their helpers. What did high levels of Roman Catholic attendance at Mass signify if drunkenness, gambling and borrowing money were rife among this congregation?[1] High attendance at a given church did not in itself tell much of that church's local impact unless one could identify the geographical as well as the social origins of those present at service. Booth wanted to go much further and describe the role of religion as a civilising agent in the metropolis. This involved describing the effort itself in great detail (hence the description of what the churches were attempting) and the response.

Let us reiterate. The survey was not about the creeds of people. Booth was not concerned to evaluate religious response in terms of its spiritual worth. He was not attempting to assess what was genuine religiosity and what was not, although he might well comment on the reasons which his informants identified for the social composition of their congregations, the absence of great numbers at services and so forth:

> My concern in the matter of religion is solely with the extent to which people accept the doctrines, conform to the disciplines and share in the work of the religious bodies, and with the effect produced, or apparently produced, on their lives. In a similar way an attempt is made to show in what manner the action of Local Authorities and County Councils . . . affect the condition of the people.[2]

Booth was fully aware that there was no reliable and detailed account of the

---

[1] *Religious Influences*, 4, p. 13.
[2] *Religious Influences*, 1, p. 5.

religious effort in the metropolis. Yet any reasoned assessment of the effects of religious action upon the people demanded such an account. He set out to supply it. And where must historians turn if they need to know about religious organisation in London in the 1890s? To Booth.

To suggest that this account was undocumented and based upon mere personal observation, as Pickering claimed, is ill-informed. Pickering never bothered to examine the archive and seems to have read little of the printed work. To suggest that it was ill-conceived for its purpose and redundant for the historian, as McKibbin urged, displays a total misunderstanding of Booth's purpose or the relevance of his work for the study of Victorian society and, once again, a sad ignorance of the survey materials.

Scholars have had difficulty assessing Booth's printed work because he did not observe modern scholarly conventions of footnoting and reference. (To criticise him for not following a practice which was not commonly adopted by British scholars until the later 1960s seems a trifle unfair). There is some evidence that Booth intended initially to reference his description of religious action (the work of the ministry) very precisely but that experience of libel cases, irate responses from informants and the confidential nature of some of the information given persuaded him to tread a much more cautious path. This view is further supported by a tell-tale paragraph in the printed work:

> If in the use of this material I appear at times to be vague when I ought to be explicit, or personal when it might seem that I ought to stop at generalities, I hope the great difficulties of my task will be remembered. I have veiled identity where it seemed desirable so to do, or where individual action appeared merged in a mass of similar effort. But in cases in which the work is too large or too peculiar to be so treated or when it is definitely associated with a particular man's name, it would have been useless and even absurd to suppress the name.[3]

When information given in confidence was cited it was quoted only when all clues to identification had been removed. Single quotation marks signified a conversation which had been reported in the notes of the inquiry. Double quotation marks were reserved for precise quotation from printed or written sources.

It is certainly true that the absence of precise referencing limits the value of the printed work for the historian or social scientist. It is far from the truth, however, that Booth fabricated the evidence or that it was based upon a 'host of personal observations about individual churches'. A comparison of the printed text with the inquiry archive suggests that Booth kept closely to the information supplied by his 1,450 ministerial informants to the interviewing team. Standards of accuracy were enviably high. He was an inveter-

---

[3] *Religious Influences*, 1, p. 8.

ate abstractor; the volumes rely heavily upon a mixture of direct quotation, paraphrased comment and Booth's reflections. (The summary volume contains large numbers of extracts from printed materials submitted to Booth during the course of the investigation. His penchant for including such material had to be held in check by Mary and his associates.) There are occasional slight errors of transcription of a trivial nature, which found their way into the printed volumes. For example, the report of an interview with Miss Smith of the training school for nurses reads: 'People indifferent. They have had too much of religion. "You can hardly find a person who has not heard of the Gospel but who at the same time have not accepted the way of salvation".'[4] In Booth's abstract this became 'Miss Smith of training school for nurses.' "Have had too much religion. You can hardly find a person who has not heard of the Gospel – but at the same time they do not accept the way of salvation."'[5] This found its way into print as 'They have had too much of religion. There are none who have not heard of the Gospel, but at the same time they do not accept the way of salvation.'[6] This is attributed to 'an Evangelical deaconess, in charge of a nurse's institute', as a reported comment, despite the changes which Booth made to it. Booth may have been influenced by Mary's view that precise accuracy in quotation was inessential and sometimes he did, as a result of minor inaccuracy, alter the exact meaning of what was said.[7] But it must be stressed that this does not seem to have happened more than a dozen times in seven long volumes. Booth's technique involved weaving brief quotations and the views of expert witnesses into a seamless descriptive account of religious activity and response. It is possible to trace the opinions expressed and the examples quoted in the archive. For example, 'An old man who knows his people well, vicar of a large parish which contains few but the best of the working class . . .'[8] is Hobbins of Stepney:[9] 'Mr H. convinced from his own observation of comfort of his people – has twice taken census going personally into almost every house.' 'Clean, bright happy homes' larger margin to play with than most clergy.'[10] Certainly Booth supplemented this interview material with observation of what was going on in London's churches, missions and clubs. The evidence is that this observation was carefully done and followed a pattern as did the interviews. It was no less 'scientific' than interviewing. It was used to verify the data provided by the interviews. The Revd Charles Neil, vicar of St Matthias, Poplar in a full interview, 'warned me against exaggerated statements . . .', yet when Baxter visited St Matthias' at

[4] Booth Collection, B173, fo. 215.

[5] Booth Collection, A32. District 12, fo. 4; see, *Religious Influences*, 5, p. 211.

[6] *Religious Influences*, 1, p. 26.

[7] Booth Correspondence. MS 797 I/3894a, Mary Booth to Charles Booth, 17 February 1903.

[8] *Religious Influences*, 1, p. 23.

[9] Booth Collection, A327, 3, fo. 14.

[10] Compare also *Religious Influences*, 7, p. 37 and Booth Collection, B173, fo. 31.

the morning service he discovered not the congregation of 120 excluding children that Neil had described but rather a congregation of 60 including youngsters.[11] Such visits were rarely if ever used as the basis of the printed text, however. Despite singling out St Mary's, Spital Square for special attention,[12] Booth does not seem to have used material from Duckworth's detailed description of the congregation and sermon in that church on 12 December 1897.[13]

A far more convincing criticism of Booth's work is that he relied much too heavily on the evidence of ministers for an account of religious activity in London.[14] Elsewhere it has been suggested that he may well have intended at the outset to focus more closely on an assessment of the attitudes and morale of the ministry. Whatever the truth of this, he had certainly rejected such an approach by 1902 and yet was left heavily reliant upon interviews which revealed only one side of he picture – the official side. It was perhaps understandable that Booth would expect the 'experts' to provide the most reliable information about what was really being done. The tradition of questioning 'expert' witnesses was well-established through the parliamentary enquiry procedure. Yet Booth was not naive.

Initially he attempted to interview the 'people' about their response to religious activity. He failed miserably in any attempt to question 'workers' and their families although he did interview a substantial number of school-teachers, employers and councillors. For the rest he was forced back upon his personal observations and the opinions of interviewees. On occasion, these included diaries of their work which recorded the views of local people.[15] He was aware that the informants were giving their version of affairs and sought to solve this problem by balancing:

the tendency of informants to magnify their office [by] insight gained by a long series of such interviews [and] by what we have seen when we have ourselves visited the churches and institutions in question [and] we have also been able in most cases to compare what men say of themselves with what others say of them.[16]

In other words he employed the common-sense techniques which most human beings use when assessing the validity of information – they test it against other sources of knowledge, experiential and acquired, using their judgement. He claimed that long experience of the interviewing method and long acquaintance with the practice of precise observation (after all, a

[11] Booth Collection, B169, fo. 45; A32, 8, 3, District 11 fo. 11b.
[12] *Religious Influences*, 2, p. 13.
[13] Booth Collection, A39,. 7, fos. 1-7.
[14] This was one of the chief criticisms of the work offered by R. Mudie Smith in a review of the Religious Influences Series in *The Bookman* (June 1903), pp. 97-100.
[15] See above p. 169.
[16] *Religious Influences*, 1, p. 8.

much acclaimed scientific skill) more than equipped the team to assess their evidence, retain the wheat and discard the chaff. When there was doubt, all the evidence would be displayed. Moreover, if the ministers and missioners condemned their efforts out of their own mouths (or, at most, blessed them with faint praise), surely this could be relied upon as indicative of the failure of religious influence.

In one of Booth's most laudable aims lay the seeds of one of the principal problems in his approach to his evidence. Booth seems to have determined not to stand between the 'voices' of his archive and his audience. The materials would speak for themselves and describe religious activity in London and its impact upon the people. He rejected an openly critical approach to the data. Yet, inevitably, Booth did process the archive, selecting material using unknown criteria to support particular lines of argument. Sometimes he was even led to comment upon the deficiency of the data. But there is lacking in this series the distinct authorial voice to be found for instance in the secretaries' reports. Let us compare the passage on p.27 of *Religious Influences*, Volume One: 'At the same time there is little or no active hostility, no public scoffing, and many of the aims of the Church meet with general sympathy', with this extract from a secretary's report:

> The only point on which the evidence suggests any new thoughts is the often repeated remark that there is no hostility to religion: in a broad sense this is probably true, but it may be well to remark that nearly all our testimony on this point comes from ministers of religion, and the growing politeness and urbanity produced by education would make such hostility less patent to them even if it existed; but even from the clergy (e.g. Mr Dalton) one hears that the general opinion of the working man is that the clergy are either knaves or fools, while Mr Bray, a schoolmaster of unusual culture emphasises this point and seems rather to approve the verdict which he quotes that ministers of religion are 'rather a poor lot', worse rather than better than their fellow men. There is no doubt that this feeling is widespread, and if it does not constitute hostility to religion it does at least show a very considerable prejudice against the churches, a prejudice which even men of the undeniable goodness and strength of Dalton or Howard have the greatest difficulty in breaking down.[17]

Booth's desire to step back from the fray led him to follow the archive uncritically, rejecting the eminently sensible comments of his associates.[18] Some of the real deficiencies of his printed work only become apparent after comparison with the data and comment at his disposal.

This said, he provided the only comprehensive description of religious

---

[17] Booth Collection, A33, 9, District 10, Report on Mile End Old Town by GHD[uckworth], fos. 34-35.

[18] Booth Collection, A37, 8, Districts 14 and 16, fo. 64. Duckworth's diminishing of importance of religion was rejected.

activity in late Victorian London available to us or to contemporaries. His vision lay in his detailed knowledge of the social, occupational and physical geography of the metropolis and his appreciation of the interaction between this geography and the nature of religious activity and its influence. One might sum up the import of the series in the following way – the religious response of the people was not commensurate to the amount of religious effort put in; but in so doing one would miss the essential greatness of what he achieved. The 'New Booth' was not the master of generalisation; but he offered insights into the localisation of religion which historians and others would do well to explore further.[19]

The obsession with locality is well illustrated by the manner in which the team continued to 'walk the beat' during this last inquiry. When George Duckworth emerged at 7.30 of an evening 'in full Sunday toggery, i.e. Top hat, frock coat, patent leather shoes, silver handled stick', he can scarcely have hoped to fade into the shadows of Bow but he did hope to discover just what Sunday evening yielded up. He found much to comment on, not least the closed up appearance of one of the Catholic churches – 'lights out, iron gate padlocked, no sign of a recent service'; the well- dressed congregations of the Anglican and Catholic churches (duly counted) returning home after 'vespers'; and the bustling trade of the Barratt sweetshop.[20]

Jesse Argyle prepared 'the material for our church and public houses map – classifying every place of worship and testing each by the "Sunday adult service" standard'. In other words this was a map showing churches, chapels and missions in use, rather than merely religious architecture. Reports such as Duckworth's provided much of the data. As Argyle wrote in 1899 'the map will be quite a revelation to most people'.[21]

In the Religious Influences Series Booth retained his demographic framework for study. While he moved away from a survey based on the family he nonetheless carried his appreciation of the importance of demographic factors into the study of religious influences. It was not, for Booth, a simple matter of describing the type and extent of religious effort on the one hand and the degree of success in terms of church attendance on the other. He was far too sophisticated for that, much more sophisticated than his critics (Mudie-Smith and Robertson Nicoll). It was a matter of *explaining* why the great religious effort was having relatively little direct effect. Booth

[19] R. Mudie-Smith's review in *The Bookman* (June 1903), pp. 97-100 appears mean-spirited in its criticisms of the series. He narrowly fixed upon Booth's treatment of religious attendance and minor inaccuracies, ignoring totally Booth's contextualisation of the religious life of each district. Jesse Argyle was exasperated, 'because we went to some pains in supplying him with advanced proofs of our lists to work upon. He is not correct in what he says either'. Booth Collection, A31, fo. 89 Jesse Argyle to Mary Catherine Booth, 10 June 1903.

[20] Booth Collection, B180, fos. 71-79. George Duckworth's Sunday evening in Bow, 24 May 1897.

[21] Booth Correspondence, MS 797 I/6. Jesse Argyle to Charles Booth, 30 November 1899.

can be criticised fairly for not taking this further – for not observing directly
the religious life of individual families, for relying too much upon second-
hand opinion and explanations based on his knowledge of particular
localities and their demographic structure. He cannot fairly be criticised for
lack of sophistication and simple-mindedness as some recent scholars have
thought.

The religious life of London varied according to locality, according to
class composition, according to residence patterns, according to personnel
and so on. London was alive for Booth. To understand the civilising
influence of religion one had to understand the living London. Statistics of
church attendance told one something but they didn't really tell you much
about the process of influencing people for the better. To discover *that* one
had to be aware of the characteristics of the area and its population, the
appropriateness of the religious effort, the personnel available to make it,
the attitudes of the populace. This is what Booth set out to provide. In the
process he told us much about formal religious behaviour in that society
which is now commonplace but to contemporaries was novel and thought
provoking. The prefatory chapters to each volume, which described the
various areas in some detail, were not a frill; they were seen as crucial to any
understanding of religious influence in the area concerned. In describing
Inner South London in Volume Four, Booth was at pains to explain the
worsening of the area between the Borough and Blackfriars Road and its
relationship to the problems of making religion felt in that area. This begins
with a general statement: 'There is in this part a great concentration of evil
living and low conditions of life that strikes the imagination and leads almost
irresistibly to sensational statement' but it is the specific content which makes
it useful. 'The palm for degradation was, at the time of our inquiry, still to be
given to the group of old courts laying between Red Cross Street and the
Borough High Street'; 'waterside labourers and market porters and others
of the lowest casual and loafing class, including thieves and the bullies who
live on the earnings of prostitutes';[22] 'The character of these places varies
somewhat in detail, but in general it is lowness and wickedness that impress
here rather than poverty'; 'These streets contain some of the worst blocks of
so-called "model" dwellings to be found anywhere in London; designed, it
would almost seem, to concentrate every horror of low and vicious life';[23] 'as
we pass South and West the industrial element, which is never absent,
increases and becomes dominant'; 'Many are costers'; 'The bulk of the
inhabitants work as well as sleep in or near the district, and form one vast
group of families whose lives are well known to one another. There is more
street life here even than in the East End, more women gossiping at the
doors; more children playing in the gutters. In some places there is almost

[22] *Religious Influences*, 4, p. 8.
[23] *Religious Influences*, 4, p. 9.

village life';[24] 'In Southwark the rich have gone, the fairly comfortable are leaving, while the poor remain, and will remain till evicted';[25] 'Here it is not easy to trace the improvement which should follow when the poorest, whose houses are destroyed, move into the quarters abandoned by the better off.'[26] Then Booth proceeds to analyse the work of the religious bodies in relation to this particular social situation. The church of St Saviour's 'hardly pretends to grapple seriously with local needs'; its stately interior seems best suited to satisfy the religious needs of non-parishoners. 'The population of the parish is decreasing, and some rearrangement will probably be made so that its remaining inhabitants may be attached to one or other of the adjacent parish churches. Nearly all are poor, and many are very poor.'[27] 'Their faith, so far as it goes, is childlike' describes the position of women and pensioners, who look to the church for rites of passage and solace in time of trouble.[28] Because there are many humble and rough Irish Catholics in the area a church has been built. But the nature of development there dooms this congregation to a short life: 'the courts, where the bulk of his people live, are among those scheduled for destruction. The ground on which he works is undermined, and it is doubtful if many, or even any, of his flock will occupy the new model dwellings'. 'More likely they will drift further East, clinging to the river side, and thus this church may be left high and dry.'[29] The priests have an intimate knowledge of the way of life of the people and the people attend Mass. But drink, gambling and borrowing money are prevalent and lead the people into poverty. 'What role can religion play in the cure of these evil conditions?'[30] 'The people we are told are "too poor for Dissent" but mission work goes on' and seems to have had some civilising effect – bad language in the market is much less evident as is drunkenness in public.[31] Booth not only identified the nature of religious effort; he made it possible for the informed reader to measure this effort against the nature and extent of local social, moral and economical problems.

The class limitations of the religious effort of the churches was a subject to which Booth constantly returned. So when he wrote about Hackney, for example, he provided a vivid general overview before proceeding to discuss the response to religion and wrote:

The changes in progress, and the varieties of class to which we have referred,

[24] *Religious Influences*, 4, p. 10.
[25] *Religious Influences*, 4, p. 11.
[26] *Religious Influences*, 4, p. 12.
[27] *Religious Influences*, 4, p. 12.
[28] *Religious Influences*, 4, p. 13.
[29] *Religious Influences*, 4, p. 13.
[30] *Religious Influences*, 4, p. 14.
[31] Ibid.

render seemingly inconsistent evidence quite compatible with truth: as when we are told on the one hand, that 'the people of Hackney require no urging to go to church', and on the other that Sunday is 'merely a holiday'.

Those who need 'no urging' are mainly the middle class, and it is they who make up the bulk of the good congregation usually obtained. The great mass of artisans and mechanics, and the working class generally, hold aloof here . . . for them Sunday is merely a holiday; while the quite poor, if they attend any religious service, are confessedly more or less bribed, and become, as one of the clergy quaintly describes them, 'the camp-followers of the church'.[32]

There were individuals from among the poor who 'once attached to Church, or Chapel or Mission, became its staunchest supporters' but 'with these exceptions the Churches do not reach either the working classes or the poor'. The attitude of the people concerned was described: the churches could influence these people only if their clubs and other organisations had no overt religious content.[33]

As with every point, Booth was determined to go beyond generalising and look at detailed cases. The goal was to provide the empirical evidence which would enable the professionals to answer the important questions: To what extent was religion a civilising influence? Why did people respond to religion in the way that he described? There were many reasons why the poor and the working classes in general avoided organised religion and resisted its influence. Booth tried to explain the situation in detail. He employed a broad vocabulary of class with the gradations of which we are scarcely familiar. 'Lowness and wickedness' as much as 'poverty' were class descriptions. To use his work successfully we have to make ourselves conversant with this language of class. His intimate knowledge of London built up over seventeen years of laborious investigation helped him further to identify specific local conditions and problems. The maps, which had already undergone revision in the first half of the decade, were hawked around the respondents to check their accuracy. Booth tried not to be judgemental. This often makes the printed work difficult to read and handle. He is as likely to give a range of suggested explanations for behaviour, with supporting or contradictory opinion and evidence, as to put forward one categorical explanation.

We could do worse than read the printed volumes with Duckworth's advice to Booth in mind: each chapter will have a general social and physical description and overview of the whole area, followed by a treatment of special areas and typical efforts. Careful reading of the series will give us a detailed appreciation of the variety of religious activity and response in the metropolis – which will counter and lend depth to the overly pessimistic

[33] *Religious Influences*, 1, p. 80.
[33] Ibid.

general impression which historians and social scientists have derived from the work.

When the Religious Influence Series appeared in print it caused a stir. The Bishop of Rochester alluded to it at the London Diocesan Conference and the Bishop of Stepney who viewed it as 'an epoch in the history of the Clergy of the Church of England' announced his intention to take each of his clergy in turn through the account of religious effort in their parishes.[34] Leading nonconformists were struck to the quick by what they regarded as unfair assessments in the volumes. Clearly all regarded the series as in some sense an account of the work of the ministry and, in the case of Robertson Nicoll, as an unfair indictment thereof. But the usefulness of the series for the bishops and the ministers lay above all in the vivid evocation of the various localities and their populations and the way in which existing religious effort related to these. While Booth made no recommendations for practical change, he did provide those in pastoral positions in the churches with the materials they needed if they were to make religion important in the *Life and Labour of the People in London.* Canon C.E. Escreet, the left-wing, reforming clergyman from Woolwich, was widely known to regard 'Mr Booth's books as the next most important thing for a clergyman after the Bible.'[35] In the years to come clergymen of the Church of England were advised to read in addition to the Scriptures not the Fathers or the Reformation Divines but Charles Booth on London Life.[36]

This was the value of the 'New Booth' to the contemporary audience for whom it was intended – an audience of the informed, concerned and involved middle class, of ministers and philanthropists. Yet historians and sociologists find it difficult and irritating to draw their own conclusions from this evidence. They look for meaningful generalisations about religious behaviour and find instead particularlisation and localisation. They look for either a doctoral thesis or a policy statement and, finding neither, despair of finding anything worthwhile. If, however, we turn to the 'New Booth' as the work of a tireless investigator who described religious effort and response in London's myriad districts and offered insights born of studying the socio-economic composition of these geographical areas, we cannot fail to be impressed by his work or to gain immeasurably in historical insight from it. The teleological bias of sociologists means that the 'New Booth' dismays and disappoints; for historians, however, the method and substance of the work

---

[34] Booth Correspondence, MS 797 I/4847, G.H. Duckworth to Mary Booth, 30 April 1903. The Booths were avid readers of the reviews, not all of which were laudatory or even sympathetic. See, for example, Hastings Rashdall, 'Some Notes on Mr Booth's Account of Church Work in London,' *Economic Review*, xiii (1903), pp. 429-35 for a sympathetic but critical account.

[35] Booth Collection, B305, Browne interview, fo. 69.

[36] J.M. Wilson, *Cambridge Lectures on Pastoral Theology* (London, 1903), cited in Owen Chadwick, *The Victorian Church,* (2nd ed., London, 1972), ii, p. 174.

should be much more congenial. Whatever the defects and limitations of Booth's Religious Influence Survey, scholars, concurring with the view of a Yorkshire paper at the time that neither Mr Booth's 'figures nor his conclusions have been seriously challenged', and with the treasure trove of the survey materials beside them to add depth and clarify to the account, should confidently use it as a detailed, almost photographic, record of religious activity in late Victorian London. If his photography failed to keep pace with urban change it is nonetheless valuable for the moment it recorded. Like all photographers, Booth composed his shots. Historians would not consider discarding photographs as historical evidence, neither should they discard the 'New Booth'.

Appendix I

Tabulation of Booth's Special Street Survey

This is printed in the Poverty Series, vol. 2, pp. 40-235; Booth gave the streets fake names in the printed text and did not identify his sources.

Poverty, 2, pp. 226-28

(1) Details from A2, fos. 14-16. (True) / (Fake)	(2) Location	(3) Map ref.	(4) Source	(5) Volume 2 page ref.	(6) Wording in vol. 2	(7) Comment
DARK BLUE WITH BLACK LINE						
Devonshire Place *(Little Tarlton Street)*	Marylebone [A2, p. 167]	D4-D5	A2, p. 55. From Mr Dodge. 25 July 1889. Skinner's interview with curate	84-85	Comment is based on Skinner; remainder doubtful origin	See also Chelsea B66, p. 26.
Cleveland Terrace *(Portland Cottages)*	South Lambeth [B72, p. 249]		B72, pp. 249-51. Visitor of All Saints S. Lambeth	92-93	Slightly modified from notes given by D.V. of All Saints Lambeth, B72	
Burdock Road *(Orville Street (Road))*	West Lambeth	?B11	B72, pp. 199-205 Nov. 4 1890. From Mrs Gilmore Head of Rochester Dioc. Deaconess's Instn B72, p. 199	86-87	Modified from Mrs Gilmore in B72 The introductory comment to the street is also taken from her. Detail more limited than B72. Letters given	See Balfour's books for SBV notes ref. [B72, p. 199]

Key

(1) In Booth Collection, A2 fos 14-16, occurs a list of fake and true names
(2) The location of the street identified from various sources
(3) The map reference on Booth's map
(4) The sources of the material he used; this gives the reference in the collection
(5) The page references in volume 2
(6) What the wording in volume 2 is based upon
(7) General comments

(Fake)	(1) Details from A2, fos. 14-16. (True)	(2) Location	(3) Map ref.	(4) Source	(5) Volume 2. page ref.	(6) Wording in vol. 2	(7) Comment
Rydal Street	Felstone Street		?		90-91		
Flint Street	Hollington Street	East Lambeth [A2, p. 16]	G10		88-89		
DARK BLUE							
Moreton Place	Pond Terrace	Chelsea [A2, p. 15]	C9	A2, pp. 40-45. Detailed but no attribution	122-23		See also Chelsea B66, p. 97
Short's Place	Collins Place	Bethnal Green	Not on map		132-33		
Henley Street	Townley Street	E Lambeth [A2, p. 16]	H9		116-17		
Sunnyside Terrace	Lansdowne Place	Southwark [A2, p. 16]	H8	B74. Mr Simpson, Missionary in St Stephen's Parish Bermondsey pp. 261-75	112-13	Edited version of B74	
Golden Place	Bond Court	Waterloo Rd Area [B72, p. 222]	H6	B74, p. 222-28. Mr Wheeler a visitor at St John's, Waterloo Rd, 10 Nov. 1890, used notes to aid memory	108-09	Good detail for whole street in B72 – covers only six houses in book; abbreviated version of B72. Mr Wheeler. Letter class given	Previously stables; now converted
Stocking Yard	Star and Garter Yard	St George's in the East	K6		138		
Assembly Court	Parliament Court ?		K4		135-36		
Bear Alley	Seven Star Alley	St George's in the East	K6		137		

Fake name	True name	Location	Map ref	Sources	Page refs	Comments	Wording
Assembly Street	Parliament Street		K4		134-35		
Manor Gardens	Pascal Street	Battersea	E10	B72, pp. 252-53	130-31	Closely follows B72 including introductory comment; slightly larger specimen in B72 (also 33, 41, 43, 45, 47, 49). No letters	[Pascal St. B72, p. 252]
Summer Gardens	Half Nichol Street	Shoreditch [A2, pp. 1-10]	J4	A2, pp. 1-10. Journal of Rupert St Leger, Curate, Holy Trinity, Shoreditch	96-101	Notes of Rupert St Leger	
Marshall Street	Eagle Street	Finsbury [A2, p. 16] [B68]	F5	B68, pp. 203-5. From Revd N. Coney	128-29		
Latin Place, South	Hope Place, West	Finsbury [A2, p. 16] [B68]	F1	B68, pp. 214-15. From visitor (?)	123		
Greek Row	Milton Place	Finsbury [A2, p. 16] [B65]	F1	B68. Information by Mr Walkerdene St James's Holloway (Pl)	124-25		
Sun and Moon Courts	Adam's Place Eve's Gardens	Southwark [A2, p. 16]	?K8	B74, pp. 216-19. From Mr Boddington, St Mary Rotherhithe	120-21	Edited versions of B74	
Tabernacle Yard	Playhouse Yard?	Finsbury [A2, p. ??] [B68]	H4-H5	B68, pp. 193-96. From Revd C. W. Sparkes	126-27		

Key

(1) In Booth Collection, A2 fos 14-16, occurs a list of fake and true names
(2) The location of the street identified from various sources
(3) The map reference on Booth's map
(4) The sources of the material he used: this gives the reference in the collection
(5) The page references in volume 2
(6) What the wording in volume 2 is based upon
(7) General comments

(Fake)	(1) Details from A2, fos. 14-16. (True)	(2) Location	(3) Map ref.	(4) Source	(5) Volume 2. page ref.	(6) Wording in vol. 2	(7) Comment
Island Street	Salisbury Street	Southwark [A2, p. 16]	H3	B74. From Mr Wilson LCM, pp. 196-213	110-11		Light blue on map
Minton Place	King Street	Kennington Rd [B72]	F9	B72, pp. 270-76, 172-77. From Revd C.R. Lilley of Vicarage, Kennington Road	118-19	Abbreviated comment from Lilley 17 houses only, although details of 46 known. Introductory comment incorporated Lilley too	See also B72, p. 177, for interview with Mr Ibbott of 130 Stanford Street re King St
Rupert Place	Surrey Row	Southwark [A2, p. 16]	G7	A2, p. 59. From Mr Dodge, 25 July 1889. B74. All Hallows Mission, pp. 170-90	102-07		
Lady Street	Verney Road	E Lambeth	K10		114-15		
LIGHT BLUE							
Ginger Street	Gun Street	Southwark [A2, p. 14]	J5	A2, p. 56. From Revd Mr Dodge, 25 July 1889. B74, pp. 136-48. From Sister Louise Mary, St Alphege Home	139-41	Edited version of B74 with personal names changed	
Durham and Lincoln Gardens	Balls Pond Place and Prospect Place	Finsbury [A2, p. 14] [B68]	H1 (2 poss refs Prospect Place)	B68, p. 216. From Mission Visitor, St Paul's Balls Pond	162-63	Edited version of B68	In *Poverty*, 2, p. 22 is listed as Stoke Newington, H1
Palmers Place	Tarver Road	E. Lambeth [A2, p. 14]	G9		148-49		

(1)		(2)	(3)	(4)	(5)	(7)
Havelock Street	Graham Street	Finsbury [A2, p. 14] [B68]	G3	B68, pp. 142-51. From Mrs Perry, Visitor, wife of Revd Perry of St Matthews, City Rd	150-51	Edited version of B68
Headley Street	Crown Street	E. Lambeth [A2, p. 14]	G10		146-47	
Orchard Lane	Cardigan Street	Princes Rd? [B72, p. 264]	F9	B72. Interview with Miss Severn and Revd H.W. Bromfield at Vicarage, Princes Rd	152-53	Does just over half street; abbreviated version of Severn and Lilley material for nos. 1-49, odd nos. only although had evens too
Tangley Street	Benfield Street	Battersea [B72, p. 254]	B12	B72, pp. 254-59. Rochester Diocesan Deaconess gave details of to Arkell	158-59	Does odd nos on one side of street and does not have many of rest based on Revd Joseph Milner and Roch. Deac. See Balfour's books ref. B72. p. 254
Hart Street (Place)	Fox's Buildings	Southwark [A2, p. 14]	?	A2, p. 57 Dodge, 25 July 1889 B74, pp. 118-31. From Revd P.N. Waggett, Charterhouse Mission	142-43	Edited version of B74. Waggett's account
Calliostro Street	Carpenter Street	Battersea Pk [B72, p. 212]	C12-D11	B72, pp. 212-13. Mr Pugh, Visitor of St Saviour's, Battersea Park, 17 Nov 1890	144	In fact only had information on ten houses, justified 'it is a long street'; based on Mr Pugh's account, slightly abbreviated
Cardinal Street	Ada Street	Hackney	K2		164-65	Given as road on map, not street
Ding Dong Lane	Broadwall	Southwark [A2, p. 14]		B74, pp. 106-17. Mr Meek, Scripture Reader	160-61	

Key

(1) In Booth Collection, A2 fos 14-16, occurs a list of fake and true names
(2) The location of the street identified from various sources
(3) The map reference on Booth's map
(4) The sources of the material he used; this gives the reference in the collection
(5) The page references in volume 2
(6) What the wording in volume 2 is based upon
(7) General comments

(1) Details from A2, fos. 14-16. (True) (Fake)	(2) Location	(3) Map ref.	(4) Source	(5) Volume 2. page ref.	(6) Wording in vol. 2	(7) Comment
Violet Place Gatward's or Gatsward Buildings	Finsbury [A2, p. 14]		Information in B68, pp. 183-87, given by female visitor of Revd G. Smith, St Pauls, Bunhill Row	157	Closely follows B68 accounts	
Bradley Street etc Hockley Street and Ribstone Street				166-67		Bradford, p. 166, *Poverty*, 2
Little Merton Street Little Tufton Street	Westminster [A2, p. 14]	E8	A2, pp. 46-47. St John's Mission House, Smith Square, Westminster	156		
Field Walk Long Hedge Street	Battersea Pk [B72, p. 212]	D11	B72, pp. 212, 215-18. From notes of Visitor Miss A. Mitchell of St Savior's Battersea Park and Mr Connelly	145	Used 6, 22, 32, 34, 38, 92, 96, 106 from Mitchell and Connelly but not 1-5, 7-21, etc which they also had. Based on abbreviated version	
Ancoats Street Pott Street	Bethnal Green	K4				
Braden Place Harris Terrace	St George's in the East	K6		?		
Bradford Street Ashwell Road	Bethnal Green	L3		170-71		Bradley and Grimthorne Lane, *Poverty*, 2
Clarence Square St Leonard's Square	Marylebone [A2, p. 14]	D1		154-55		
Marsh Row ?	?	?		?	?	
PURPLE						
Peel Street Hermans Street	S. Lambeth [B72, p. 247]	E10	B72, p. 247. Mrs Wood D.V. of All Saints S. Lambeth	188-89	Abbreviated version of Wood's material. Comment summarises part of Visitor's comment [B72, p. 249]	

Back Park Row	Little Albany Street	Marylebone [A2, p. 15] [B68]	D4	B68, pp. 206-10. From Revd E. Ponsonby's Visitor Revd A. Holland	186-87		
Bank Street	Hill Street	Finsbury [A2, p. 15] [B68]	?	B68. Information from female Visitor of Revd G. Smith, St Paul's Bunhill Row	206-7		
Gordon Road	Speke Street	Battersea [B72, p. 259]	B12	Battersea, p. 205. From Rochester Diocesan Deaconess, pp. 259-63	182-83	Abbreviated version of B72, pp. 259-63, only two thirds used of houses 22-66. Only did even nos. in B72, 22-92	Given as Speke Road in B72; See Balfour ref B72, p. 259
Norman Passage	Red Lion Passage	Finsbury [A2, p. 15] [B68]	F5	B68, pp. 197-202. From Revd Foster curate of Clergy House, Red Lion Square assisted by Lady Visitor	184-85	Edited version of B68	See B68, p. 152 for COS corrections
Roussillon Road	Alma Road	Hackney	L3		208-9		
Marshall Passage	Anchor and Hope Alley		? off map		210-11		
Tramp Road	Well (?) Road [St]	Poplar ?	off map		180-81		
Patriot Street	Union Street	Southwark [A2, p. 15]	G7-H7	B72, p. 190. Vauxhall COS report it as 'poorer than East St', 21 March 1890, and B68 interview with Sisters, All Hallows House, Union St, Southwark	204-5	Edited version of B68	

Key

(1) In Booth Collection, A2 fos 14-16, occurs a list of fake and true names
(2) The location of the street identified from various sources
(3) The map reference on Booth's map
(4) The sources of the material he used; this gives the reference in the collection
(5) The page references in volume 2
(6) What the wording in volume 2 is based upon
(7) General comments

(Fake)	(1) Details from A2. fos. 14-16. (True)	(2) Location	(3) Map ref.	(4) Source	(5) Volume 2. page ref.	(6) Wording in vol. 2	(7) Comment
Ross Street	Danson Street	E. Lambeth [A2, p. 15]	G9-10		200-1		Road on map
Upwell Road	Nealdon Street	Stockwell [B72, p. 239]	F12	B72, pp. 239-46. In detail from Revd Chas E. Escreet, St Andrew's, Stockwell: Assigned letters	194-95	Abbreviated version of 239-46: only uses part of Street although he has all	B72, p. 198. Police say Nealdon Street is Light Blue
Avon Road	Lorrimore Street	E. Lambeth [A2, p. 15]	G10		198-99		
Carver Street	Doon Street	St John's Waterloo Rd [B72, p. 229] Nr station	F7	B72, pp. 229-39. In detail from Mr Wheeler, D.V. of St John's Waterloo Rd: see also A2, p. 58 from Dodge material July 1889	176-79	Dealt with in detail and closely replicates B72 from Wheeler but omitted much of the street eg.s nos. 9-29 on which information was obtained	B72, p. 188: COS thought this was light blue
Mutimer Street	Hotspur Street	Kennington Rd [B72]	F9	B72, pp. 173-77. Hotspur Street in detail from Revd C.K. Lilley. Letters assigned	192-93	Closely based on B72 was downgraded to purple from pink as result of Lilley's views. Missed out some houses he had information for; changed letter class in some cases	Revised from pink, B72, p. 172
Major Road	Rowell Road	Southwark [A2, p. 15]		B74, pp. 254-56. From Mr Ackerman, St James's Bermondsey	190-91		
Turner Road	Delaford Road	E. Lambeth [A2, p. 15]	K9		196-97		
Cutters' Row	Boundary Street	Shoreditch [A2, pp. 1-2]	J4	A2. Journal of Rupert St Leger, Curate of Holy Trinity, Shoreditch	173-75		
Meldrum Street	Lyons Gardens	If Bldgs Shoreditch/Finsbury	H4		?		Is this Lyons Buildings?

Shakespear Place	Adams Gardens	Southwark [A2, p. 15]	off map	B74, pp. 220-27. From Mr Boddington of St Mary Rotherhithe (Visitor for Revd E.J. Beck), 28.10.1890	202-3	Edited version of B74. Mr Boddington
Flatter Street	Lamb Lane	Hackney	K2		212-13	
PINK						
Chesterfield Street	New Church Street	Southwark [A2, p. 15]	J4	A2, p. 55. Mr Dodge gives detailed information 25 July 1889 B74. From Mr Simpson, St Stephens	214-19	
Martin Street	Henry Street	Kennington [B72, p. 206]	F9-F10	B72, p. 206 5 Nov. 90. Revd Fergus Wood Curate of St Mark's – detailed pp. 206-11	220-21	Had some parts to no. 62 but left these out presumably because scanty. Otherwise account based on Wood. B72, p. 190 Vauxhall Committee of COS say 'should be purple'
Weaver Street	Sutton Street	Waterloo Road are anr Station [B72, p. 219]	?	B72, p. 219-22. Mr Moore a visitor of St John's Waterloo Rd, 10 Nov 1890 from memory; gives letters	222-23	Does 1-38 (has 1-43): based closely on Mr Moore's account. Ommitted by SBV [see B72, p. 219 for this]
Cherry Street	?	?	?	?	224-25	
Thanksgiving Place	Jubilee Place	Chelsea [B66, p. 97]			131	

Key

(1) In Booth Collection, A2 fos 14-16, occurs a list of fake and true names
(2) The location of the street identified from various sources
(3) The map reference on Booth's map
(4) The sources of the material he used; this gives the reference in the collection
(5) The page references in volume 2
(6) What the wording in volume 2 is based upon
(7) General comments

Appendix II

*Trade Interviews Questionnaire, Poverty Series (1888)**

Name

Address

Branch of trade

Way of learning the trade

No. of workers employed

Are workers usually paid by the 'time' or by 'piece'

If piece work, please give the prices paid for some articles, and times required for the work

Do you consider that wages have risen or fallen since you entered the trade?

If so, give instances showing the difference.

What are the causes of change in wages?

How has the use of machinery affected the trade?

Do you work for 'order' or 'stock'?

For what market do you make?

Have the rates paid for your goods risen or fallen since you entered the trade?

Give examples with date, prices and net profits.

What are the busy and slack seasons in your trade?

Other remarks on the general condition of the trade, changes in the condition, changes of style, the Factory Act, foreign competition, etc.

* Source: Booth Collection, A6, fos. 49-50.

Appendix III

Trade Union Questionnaire
*Information from Trade Union for Mr Charles Booth**

Trade Organisation

(1) What organisation exists and how long has it existed?
(2) What proportion of unionists to non-unionists?
(3) Do unionists and non-unionists work together?
(4) Of what character are the present relations of employer and employed?
(5) Are there any recognized boards of arbitration or conciliation?

Wages

(1) What number of working hours and rates of wages (including overtime) are recognized by the union?
(2) At what age is capacity lost, or does employment become most difficult to obtain?

Regularity of Work

(1) What are the busy and slack seasons, and are they applicable to all branches of the trade?
(2) Is overtime usual; if so, to what extent?
(3) In slack time are some men fully employed and others not at all, or is the work shared?
(4) Do unemployed in slack time find other employment, and if so, what?
(5) Do men shift from one branch of the trade to another, according as work offers?
(6) Do men shift frequently from one employer to another in the same branch of the trade?

* Source: Booth Collection, A9, fo. 16.

Methods of Training

(1) What methods are recognized by the Union?
(2) What are the conditions (as to skill) of admission to the Society?

Copies of Rules, Reports, Circulars, Agreements, or any other printed matter relating to the trade, will be very acceptable.

Appendix IV

Employers' Questionnaire
Information for Mr Charles Booth
to be used for statistical purposes only[*]

Trade

Rates of Wages
(in various branches of the work)

Regularity & c

(1) Busy and slack season and their causes.
(2) What proportion of those employed have regular work?
(3) How much work do the rest get?
(4) Do men shift from one employment to another? Or in what branches do they do so?
(5) What was condition of trade in Spring 1891 compared to before and since.

Methods of Training
(in various branches of the work)

(1) Extent of skill required.
(2) How is the business taught?
    How long does it take to learn?
(3) At what age is capacity lost?

Appendix V

*Booth on Religion, c. 1902**

It has been my object to consider whether, or in what way or in what proportion the people in London are touched by religious influences of whatever kind. It is hardly necessary for me to disclaim any judgment as to the truth of the doctrines taught. I am concerned only with the apparent effect on adherents or on those whom it is sought to impress. I may be permitted to regard all forms of religion as resting on one broad spiritual basis in as much as they have all sprung from, respond to and react upon spiritual experiences; and as being each one true for the souls that are attuned to it. Thus so far as I study religion at all it is in the varying light of human nature, and abstract truth sinks below my horizon.

In this way I have striven to attain the impartiality necessary for a just comparative appreciation of the religious influences at work in London, but so subtle are the hidden springs and secret workings of the mind that the best intentions and the soundest philosophical basis might not secure true impartiality. Thus I may perhaps be asked, not unreasonably, what my own creed is; or to put the question in another way, against what bias have I had to guard . . .

I am perhaps the more ready to respond as my own beliefs are in truth little more than the attitude in which I approach the beliefs of others. It is not so much a creed as a mental position that I hold.

I will try to make my meaning clear:

1. 'In the beginning' or at a period far beyond our ken 'God made man'. How or why we do not known, and so impenetrable are the methods of creation that the process of generation and growth, though happening around us and within us every moment of our existence, and shared by life in all its forms, are mysteries still. We, however, see that there is uniformity of plan and trace in it the thought of a Creator.

*Source: Booth correspondence, MS 797, II 32/3, Charles Booth, manuscript draft for Part II, Chapter III.

2. The mental and spiritual powers of man he also shares with other (or it may even be with all) forms of life in some measure. Amongst men these powers, while varying greatly in character and degree, between individuals and in different races, show hardly any change during the period of man's existence of which we have record. In all ages and with all races the spiritual phenomena which are the expression of these powers, have led men to the conception of a God or Gods, or personification of some Spiritual Beings or Powers, usually invisible, or only occasionally visible or incarnate.

3. It is said that 'God made man in His own image'. About this we do not know; and it is at least improbable. What we do know is that man, created and endowed with a spiritual nature, has usually endowed his conception of a God with human shape and human characteristics.

4. Of the creation of man by God we know nothing. Of the creation of God by man we know almost everything. Not only are the records on this subject by far the best of human records, but the process in all its forms goes on today; intelligibly under our eyes. There is comparatively little mystery about it. We can watch men of all races struggling to find their God, as plants turn towards the light, and achieving faith in the reality of their own conceptions.

5. In this way we are thrown back from the diverse and strange ideas that have resulted to the experiences and spiritual forces that underly them all. As these experiences vary we need no longer wonder that religions vary also . . .

6. To sum up, I believe that the religions of man spring from inborn, God given, spiritual perceptions. They seek to lay hold of the eternal, but the character and degree of these perceptions vary and the religions vary with them and with the habits and traditions that have given them their established shape. Their truth consists in their being true to the perceptions they reflect. No master key has yet been found.

7. Finally I will venture to represent my view of the spiritual history and present condition of the world by an allegory: I imagine a world like ours in every way except that in it the physical heavens are always veiled. The orbs of day and night are there, and shed their light, but are themselves unseen. Night follows day, the shining of the moon divides the months, the seasons take their course. Some by thought seek for and find an explanation in the rising and setting of a sun behind the veil; others with heightened sensitiveness of vision or self deceived by imagination, claim to have seen that this is so, and dwell upon the traditions of the past which tell how the heavens have veritably opened and the glorious orb itself been seen of men.

Appendix VI

The Church of England
Life and Labour of the People in London,
*Religious Influences. (Mr Charles Booth's Inquiry)**

1. What is the general character of the population?
2. What portion do the ministrations of the Church touch?
3. What persons are employed? (stating duties and whether paid or not)
4. What buildings are used? (including missions rooms, schools and clubs)
5. What services or other religious meetings are held and by whom and how many attended?
6. What social agencies are connected with the Church – institutes, societies, clubs, entertainments, meetings, etc.
7. What educational work is done?
8. To what extent are the people visited? (by Clergy or District Visitors)
9. What arrangements are there for nursing the sick?
10. To what extent is charitable relief given or administered by the Church?

General Questions

Under what other religious, charitable or philanthropic influences do the people come?
What co-operation is there between the Church and other bodies?
Remarks with reference to the district are wanted on –
Local Government (including Poor Law Administration)
Police
Drink
Prostitution
Crime
Marriage
Thrift
Health
Housing and Social Conditions generally

[signature]

[Where possible, a comparison should be made between Past and Present].
It is not intended that this Form should be filled up, but it may be found useful for making notes to an interview.

*Source: This Schedule is taken from Booth Collection, B222, fo. 81.

Select Bibliography

MANUSCRIPT SOURCES

BRITISH LIBRARY OF POLITICAL AND ECONOMIC SCIENCE,
LONDON SCHOOL OF ECONOMICS:

Beveridge Collection

Booth Collection

This is an enormous archive which we make no pretence to list here. Group A contains 57 volumes of material related to the *Life and Labour* Inquiry. Loosely speaking, A2 relates to the Poverty Series; A3-A30 pertain to the Industry Series; and A32-A57 contain material collected for the Religious Influences Series. The papers were found loose and have been grouped approximately according to the appropriate parts of the printed inquiry. There is, however, some considerable overlap and mingling of material. Volume 31 is a valuable collection of correspondence in two sections: A contains letters of a general nature from 1897 to 1902 and B contains letters relevant to the publication of the third series in 1902-3. Volume 58 of this group contains press cuttings relating to the printed inquiry.

Groups B contains 392 notebooks relating to the Poverty (notebooks 1-80: street notebooks and special streets investigations), Industry (81-168) and Religious Influences (169-392) Series.

Group C contains an inventory of the collection made in 1925.

Group D contains miscellaneous papers relating to the revision of the maps.

Cannan Correspondence

Courtney Paper: Kate Courtney's Diaries

Galton MSS: unpublished manuscript autobiography (1939-44); correspondence

214

Inhabitants of Katharine Buildings, 1885-90: Miscellaneous Collections

New Survey of London MSS

Schloss Collection: Miscellaneous Collections

Passfield Papers

Webb Trade Union Collection

UNIVERSITY OF LIVERPOOL LIBRARY

Booth Papers

A duplicate copy of the typescript of *Life and Labour of the People in London* with Ernest Aves' amendments and much omitted material.

UNIVERSITY OF LONDON LIBRARY

Booth Correspondence, MS 797

MS 797/I contains a substantial correspondence between Charles and Mary Booth. In addition there are many letters from other members of the family and their friends and acquaintances.

MS 797/II consists of large numbers of miscellaneous papers, including, for example, 7 volumes of *The Colony*.

UNIVERSITY OF WARWICK, MODERN RECORDS CENTRE

Collet MSS

PRINTED SOURCES

PRINCIPAL WORKS BY CHARLES BOOTH AND HIS TEAM

Charles Booth

'Occupations of the People of the United Kingdom, 1801-81', *Journal of the Royal Statistical Society*, xlix (1886)

England and Ireland: A Counter Proposal (London, 1886)

'The Inhabitants of Tower Hamlets (School Board Division), their Condition and Occupations', *Journal of the Royal Statistical Society*, 1 (1887)

'The Condition and Occupations of the People of East London and Hackney, 1887', *Journal of the Royal Statistical Society*, li (1888)

Life and Labour of the People, 2 vols (London, 1889) (Title of Vol 2 reads *Labour and Life of the People*)

Life and Labour of the People, 2 vols (London, 1889-93, 2nd edn)

'Enumeration and Classification of Paupers, and State Pensions for the Aged', *Journal of the Royal Statistical Society*, liv (1891)

Pauperism: A Picture. The Endowment of Old Age: an Argument (London, 1892)

Presidential Address 'Dock and Wharf Labour', *Journal of the Royal Statistical Society*, lv (1892)

Presidential Address: 'Life and Labour of the People in London: First Results of an Inquiry based on the 1891 Census'. *Journal of the Royal Statistical Society*, lvi (1893)

Life and Labour of the People in London, 10 vols (London, 1892-97). The last volume contains maps.

'Statistics of Pauperism in Old Age', *Journal of the Royal Statistical Society*, lvii (1894)

The Aged Poor in England and Wales: Condition (London, 1894)

Old Age Pensions and the Aged Poor: A Proposal (London, 1899)

Improved Means of Locomotion as a First Step Towards the Cure for the Housing Difficulties of London (London, 1901)

Life and Labour of the People in London, 17 vols, (London, 1902-03)

'Fiscal Reform', *National Review*, xliii (1904)

Fiscal Policy and British Shipping from the Free Trade Point of View (London, 1909)

Poor Law Reform (London, 1910)

Reform of the Poor Law by the Adaptation of the Existing Poor Law Areas, and their Administration (London, 1910)

Comments on Proposals for the Reform of the Poor Laws (London, 1911)

Industrial Unrest and Trade Union Policy (London, 1913)

(with Ernest Aves and Henry Higgs)

Family Budgets: Being the Income and Expenses of Twenty-Eight British Households, 1891-1894 (London, 1896)

Ernest Aves

'Some Recent Labour Disputes', *Economic Journal* (1897)
'Labour Notes', *Economic Journal* (1898-1906)
Co-operative Industry (London, 1907)

Mary Booth

Charles Booth: A Memoir (London, 1918)

Clara Collet

The Economic Position of Educated Working Women (London, 1902)
Women in Industry (London, 1911)
The History of the Collet Family (London, 1935)
'Some Recollections of Charles Booth', *Social Services Review*, i(1927)

G. H. Duckworth

'The Making, Prevention and Unmaking of a Slum', *Journal of the Institute of British Architects*, xxxiii (1926)
'The Work of the Select Committee of the House of Commons on Distress from Want of Employment', *Economic Journal*, vi(1896)

Stephen N. Fox

'The Factories and Workshops Bill', *Economic Journal*, x (1900)

Henry Higgs

'Workmen's Budgets', *Journal of the Royal Statistical Society*, lvi (1893)
'Frédéric Le Play', *Quarterly Journal of Economics*, iv (1890-91)

Esmé Howard

Theatre of Life, 2 vols (London, 1935)

Henry Woodd [sic] Nevinson

Neighbours of Ours (London, 1895)
Changes and Chances (London, 1925)
Last Changes, Last Chances (London, 1928)

David F. Schloss

Insurance Against Unemployment (London, 1909)
Methods of Industrial Remuneration (London, 1892)
'The Reorganisation of our Labour Department', *Journal of the Royal Statistical Society,* lvi (1893)
'Sweating System', *Encyclopaedia Britannica,* 11th edn

Hubert Llewellyn Smith

The Story of the Dockers' Strike [with Vaughan Nash] (London, 1890)
The Board of Trade (London, 1928)
History of East London (London, 1939)
New Survey of London Life and Labour (London, 1928-35)

Beatrice Webb (including work while she was Beatrice Potter)

My Apprenticeship (Harmondsworth, 1971 edn)
Our Partnership, B. Drake and M. Cole (eds.) (London, 1948)
'The Dock Life of East London', *Nineteenth Century,* xxii (1887)
'Pages from a Workgirl's Diary', *Nineteenth Century,* xxiv (1888)
The Co-operative Movement in Great Britain (London, 1891)

Sidney and Beatrice Webb

The History of Trade Unionism (London, 1894)
Industrial Democracy (London, 1902)
English Local Government (London, 1906-22)
English Poor Law History (London, 1927-1929)
Methods of Social Study (London, 1932)
Soviet Communism: A New Civilization? (London, 1935)

OFFICIAL PUBLICATIONS

Select Committee of the House of Lords on the Sweating System [361], PP 1888 (xx)
Royal Commission on Labour: Minutes of Evidence, Group 'C' [c.6708-vi], PP 1892 (xxxv); [c.7063-i], PP 1893-4 (xxxix)
Select Committee on Distress from Want of Employment [363], PP 1895 (ix)
Inter-Departmental Committee on Physical Deterioration: Minutes of Evidence [Cd. 2210], PP 1904 (xxxii); [Cd. 2175], PP 1904 (xxxvi)

PERIODICALS AND NEWSPAPERS CONSULTED

The Bookman
Charity Organization Review
Church Quarterly Review
Contemporary Review
Economic Journal
Gunton's Magazine
Journal of the Royal Statistical Society
Literary World
London Quarterly Review
National Review
Nineteenth Century
Pall Mall Gazette

Political Science Quarterly
Positivist Review
Saturday Review
School Board Chronicle
Social Services Review
The Colony (7 vols, 1866-71)
The Times Literary Supplement
Toynbee Record
Quarterly Journal of Economics
Quarterly Review
Yale Review

STANDARD WORKS OF REFERENCE

Dictionary of National Biography
Dictionary of Labour Biography

BOOKS THESES AND ARTICLES

Abel, Emily Klein, 'Canon Barnett and the First Thirty Years of Toynbee Hall' (Unpublished University of London Ph.D. Thesis, 1969)

Allen, V.L., 'Valuations and Historical Interpretations', in *The Sociology of Industrial Relations* (London, 1971)

Annan, Noel, 'The Intellectual Aristocracy', in J.H. Plumb (ed.), *Studies in Social History* (London, 1955)

Anon., 'East London', *Literary World,* xx (1889)

Anon., 'Life and Labour in East London', *London Quarterly Review,* lxxiv (1890)

Ashley, W.J., 'Booth's East London', *Political Science Quarterly,* v (1891)

Aves, Ernest, 'Obituary: Ernest Aves' by G.T.R., *Economic Journal,* xxvii (1917)

——, 'Obituary', *Toynbee Record,* xxix (1917)

Barnett, Henrietta, *Canon Barnett: His Life, Work and Friends* (London, 1921 3rd edn)

Bartlett, Alan, 'The Church in Bermondsey, 1880-1939' (Unpublished University of Birmingham Ph.D. Thesis, 1987)

Bell, Quentin, *Virginia Woolf: A Biography,* 2 vols (London, 1972)

Black, Clementina, 'Labour and Life in London', *Contemporary Review,* lx (1891)

Booth, Charles, 'Obituary: Charles Booth', by Ernest Aves, *Economic Journal,* xxi (1916)

Booth, James, 'Obituary of James Booth', *Annual Register* (London, 1880)

Bosanquet, Helen, *The Strength of the People: A Study in Social Economics* (London, 1903 2nd edition)

—, 'Physical Degeneration and the Poverty Line', *Contemporary Review*, lxxxv (1904)

Briggs, Asa and Anne Macartney, *Toynbee Hall: The First Hundred Years* (London, 1984)

Brown, K.D., *A Social History of the Nonconformist Ministry in England and Wales, 1800-1930* (Oxford, 1988)

Brown, John, 'Charles Booth and Labour Colonies', *Economic History Review*, 2nd ser. xxi (1968)

Bruce, Maurice, *The Coming of the Welfare State* (London, 1961)

Bulmer, M. (ed.), *Essays on the History of British Sociological Research* (Cambridge, 1985)

— et al., *The Social Survey in Historical Perspective, 1880-1940* (Cambridge, 1992)

Caine, Barbara, *Destined to be Wives: The Sisters of Beatrice Webb* (Oxford, 1986)

Carpenter, N. 'Social Surveys', in E.R.A. Seligman (ed.), *Encyclopaedia of the Social Sciences*, 15 vols (New York, 1930-35), xiv.

Clegg, H.A., Alan Fox and A.F. Thompson, *A History of British Trade Unions since 1889* (Oxford, 1964)

Cole, Margaret, *Beatrice Webb* (London, 1945)

—, (ed.) *The Webbs and their Work* (London, 1949)

—, and B. Drake (eds.), Beatrice Webb, *Our Partnership* (London,1945)

Collet, Clara, 'Two Obituaries of Clara Collet', *Journal of the Royal Statistical Society*, Series A, cxi (1948)

Collini, Stefan, *Liberalism and Sociology: L.T. Hobhouse and Political Argument in England, 1880-1919* (Cambridge, 1979)

Cox, Jeffrey, *The English Churches in a Secular Society* (Oxford, 1982)

Crompton, Henry, *Letters on Social and Political Subjects Reprinted from the Sheffield Independent* (London, 1870)

Cullen, M.J., 'The 1887 Survey of the London Working Class', *International Review of Social History*, xx (1975)

Dana, M. McG., 'Charles Booth and His Work', *Gunton's Magazine*, x (1896)

Davidson, Roger, *Whitehall and Labour Problem in Late Victorian and Edwardian Britain* (London, 1985)

—, 'Llewellyn Smith, the Labour Department and Government Growth, 1886-1909' in G. Sutherland (ed.), *Studies in the Growth of Nineteenth-Century Government* (London, 1972)

DeSalvo, Louise, *Virginia Woolf: The Impact of Childhood Sexual Abuse on her Life and Work* (London, 1989)

Dodd, George, *Days at the Factories* (London, 1843)

Duckworth, G.H., 'Obituary: Sir George Duckworth', *The Times*, 28 April 1934

—, 'Appreciation of Sir George Duckworth' by H.A.L. Fisher, *The Times*, 30 April 1934

Englander, David, 'Booth's Jews: The Presentation of Jews and Judaism in *Life and Labour of the People in London*', *Victorian Studies*, xxxii (1989)

Fried, A. and R. Elman (eds.), *Charles Booth's London: A Portrait of the Poor at the Turn of the Century. Drawn from his 'Life and Labour of the People in London'* (Harmondsworth, 1969)

Freeden, Michael, *The New Liberalism: An Ideology of Social Reform* (Oxford, 1978)

Galton, F., 'Investigating with the Webbs', in Margaret Cole (ed.), *The Webbs and their Work* (London, 1949)

Gardiner, A.G., *Pillars of Society* (London, 1916)

Gide, Charles and Charles Rist, *A History of Economic Doctrines: From the Time of the Physiocrats to the Present Day* (London, 1948, 2nd edn)

Gilbert, A.D., *Religion and Society in Industrial England: Church, Chapel and Social Change, 1740-1911* (London, 1976)

Goldmann, Lawrence, 'The Social Science Association and the Absence of Sociology in Nineteenth-Century Britain', *Past and Present*, cxiv (1987)

Green, David, 'The Poverty of an English Town', *Yale Review* (1903)

Harris, José, *Beatrice Webb: The Ambivalent Feminist*, London School of Economics Lecture (London, 1984)

Harrison, Brian, 'The Pub and the People', in H.G. Dyos & M. Wolff (eds), *The Victorian City: Images and Realities* (London, 1973)

Harrison, Royden, *Before the Socialists: Studies in Labour and Politics, 1861-1881* (London, 1965)

—, 'The Webbs as Historians of Trades Unionism', in Raphael Samuel (ed.), *People's History and Socialist Theory* (London, 1981)

—, and Jonathan Zeitlin, (eds)., *Divisions of Labour: Skilled Workers and Technological Change in Nineteenth-Century England* (Brighton, 1985)

Hennock, E.P., 'Poverty and Social Theory in England: The Experience of the Eighteen-Eighties', *Social History*, i (1976)

—, 'The Measurement of Urban Poverty: From the Metropolis to the Nation, 1880-1920', *Economic History Review*, 2nd ser. xi (1987)

—, 'Concepts of Poverty in the British Social Surveys from Charles Booth to Arthur Bowley', in M. Bulmer et al (eds.), *The Social Survey in Historical Perspective, 1880-1940* (Cambridge, 1992)

Higgs, Henry, 'Obituary of Henry Higgs', *Economic Journal*, l (1940)

Himmelfarb, Gertrude, *The Idea of Poverty: England in the Early Industrial Age* (London, 1985)

Hobsbawm, E.J., *Labouring Men* (London, 1964)

Humphreys, Anne, *Travels into the Poor Man's Country: The Work of Henry Mayhew* (Athens, Georgia, 1977)

Hunt, E.H., *British Labour History, 1815-1914* (London, 1981)

Huntington, F.C., 'East London', *Quarterly Journal of Economics*, iv (1887-88)

Hutchinson, T.W., *A Review of Economic Doctrines, 1870-1929* (Oxford, 1960)

Hyman, Herbert H., *Interviewing in Social Research* (Chicago, 1954)

Hyndman, H.M., *Record of an Adventurous Life* (London, 1911)

Jones, Gareth Stedman, *Outcast London: A Study in the Relationship between Classes in Victorian Society* (Oxford, 1971)

Kadish, Alon, *The Oxford Economists in the Late Nineteenth Century* (Oxford, 1982)

Kahn, Robert L. and Charles F. Cannel, 'Interviewing: Social Research', in David L. Sills (ed.), *International Encyclopaedia of Social Sciences*, 18 vols (New York, 1968-79)

Keating, P.J., *The Working Classes in Victorian Fiction* (London, 1971)

Kent, Raymond, *A History of Empirical Sociology* (Aldershot, 1981)

Lazarsfeld, Paul F., 'Notes on the History of Quantification in Sociology: Trends, Sources and Problems', *Isis*, lii (1961)

Lewis, Jane, 'Parents, Children, School Fees and the London School Board, 1870-1890', *History of Education*, xi (1982)

—, *Women and Social Action in Victorian and Edwardian England* (Aldershot, 1991)

Loewe, L.L., *Basil Henriques: A Portrait* (London, 1976)

Lovell, John, *Stevedores and Dockers* (London, 1969)

Lummis, Trevor, 'Charles Booth: Moralist or Social Scientist', *Economic History Review*, 2nd ser. xxiv (1971)

Macgregor, D.H., 'The Poverty Figures', *Economic Journal*, xx (1910)

Mackenzie, Norman (ed.), *The Letters of Sidney and Beatrice Webb*, 3 vols (London & Cambridge, 1978)

Mackenzie, Norman and Jeanne, *The Diary of Beatrice Webb*, 4 vols (London, 1982-86)

Madge, John, *The Origins of Scientific Sociology* (London, 1963)

Maloney, John, *Marshall, Orthodoxy and the Professionalisation of Economics* (Cambridge, 1985)

Marsden, W.E., 'Residential Segregation and the Hierarchy of Elementary Schooling from Charles Booth's London Surveys', *The London Journal*, xi (1985)

Marshall, Alfred, *Principles of Economics* (London, 1930)

Marshall, T.H., *The Right to Welfare and Other Essays* (London, 1981)

Masterman, C.F.G., 'The Social Abyss', *Contemporary Review*, lxxxi (1902)

Meacham, Standish, *Toynbee Hall and Social Reform, 1880-1914* (New Haven, 1987)

Miller, Jane, *Seductions* (London, 1990)

More, Charles, *Skill and the English Working Class, 1870-1914* (London, 1980)

Moser, C.A., *Survey Methods in Social Investigation* (London, 1958)

Munroe, J.P., *A Life of Francis Amasa Walker* (New York, 1923)

McBriar, A.M., *Fabian Socialism and English Politics, 1884-1918* (Cambridge, 1966)

—, *An Edwardian Mixed Doubles: The Bosanquets versus the Webbs. A Study in British Social Policy 1890-1929* (Oxford, 1987)

McGee, J.E., *A Crusade for Humanity: The History of Organized Positivism in England* (London, 1931)

McIlhinney, D.B., 'A Gentleman in Every Slum: Church of England Missions in East London, 1837-1914' (Unpublished Princeton University Ph.D. Thesis 1977)

McKibbin, R.I., 'Social Class and Social Observation in Edwardian England', *Transactions of the Royal Historical Society*, xxviii (1978)

McLeod, Hugh, *Class and Religion in the Late Victorian City* (London, 1974)

Nevinson, Margaret Wynne, *Life's Fitful Fever: A Volume of Memories* (London, 1926)

Newton, Bernard, *The Economics of Francis Amasa Walker: American Economics in Transition* (New York, 1968)

Nord, Deborah Epstein, *The Apprenticeship of Beatrice Webb* (London, 1985)

Norman-Butler, Belinda, *Victorian Aspirations: The Life and Labour of Charles and Mary Booth* (London, 1972)

O'Day, Rosemary, 'Interviews and Investigations: Charles Booth and the Making of the Religious Influences Series', *History*, lxxiv (1989)

—, 'The Men from the Ministry', in Gerald Parsons (ed.) *Religion in Victorian Britain*, 4 vols (Manchester, 1988), ii.

Okey, Thomas, *A Basketful of Memories* (London, 1930)

Pfautz, Harold W. (ed.), *Charles Booth and the City* (Chicago and London, 1967)

Phillips, Gordon and Noel Whiteside, *Casual Labour: The Unemployment Question in the Port Transport Industry, 1880-1970* (Oxford, 1985)

Pimlott, J.R., *Toynbee Hall* (London, 1935)

Price, L.L., 'Labour and Life of the People', *Economic Journal*, i (1891)

Ricci, D.M., 'Fabian Socialism: The Theory of Rent as Exploitation', *Journal of British Studies*, ix (1969)

Rogers, Frederick, *Labour Life and Literature: Some Memories of Sixty Years* (London, 1913)

Rowe, J.W.F., *Wages in Practice and Theory* (London, 1928)

Rowntree, B.S., *Poverty: A Study of Town Life* (London, 1901)

—, *The Poverty Line: A Reply* (London, 1904)

Royle, Edward, *Modern Britain: A Social History, 1750-1985* (London, 1986)

Rubinstein, David, 'Booth and Hyndman', *Bulletin of the Society for the Study of Labour History*, xvi (1968)

—, *School Attendance in London, 1870-1906: A Social History*, Occasional Papers in Economic and Social History, i (Hull, 1969)

Samuel, Raphael, 'Comers and Goers', in H.G. Dyos & M. Wolff (eds), *The Victorian City: Images and Realities*, 2 vols (London, 1973)

Sargant, W.L., *Economy of the Labouring Classes* (London, 1857)

Schloss, David, 'Obituary: David Frederick Schloss', *Economic Journal*, xxii (1912)

Schumpeter, Joseph, *A History of Economic Analysis* (London, 1954)

Selvin, H.C., 'Durkheim, Booth and Yule: The Non-Diffusion of an Intellectual Innovation', *European Journal of Sociology*, xvii (1976)

Simey, T.S., 'The Contribution of Sidney and Beatrice Webb to Sociology', *British Journal of Sociology*, xii (1960)

—, and M.B. Simey, *Charles Booth: Social Scientist* (Oxford, 1960)

Soffer, Reba N., *Ethics and Society in England: The Revolution in the Social Sciences, 1870-1914* (Berkeley, 1978)

Spotts, Frederic (ed.), *Letters of Leonard Woolf* (London, 1989)

Sprott, W.J., 'Sociology in Britain: Preoccupations', in Howard Becker and Alvon Boskoff (eds), *Modern Sociological Theory in Continuity and Change* (New York, 1957)

Swinny, S.H., 'Charles Booth', *Positivist Review*, xxvii (1919)

Topalov, Christian, 'La ville "terre inconnue": L'enquête de Charles Booth et le peuple de Londres, 1886-1891', *Geneses*, v (1991)

Thompson, E.P. and Eileen Yeo, *The Unknown Mayhew* (Harmondsworth, 1973)

Treble, J.H., *Urban Poverty in Britain* (London, 1979)

Veit-Wilson, J.H., 'Paradigms of Poverty: A Rehabilitation of B.S. Rowntree', *Journal of Social Policy*, xv (1986)

Walker, Francis Amasa, *Political Economy* (London, 1883)

—, *The Wages Question: A Treatise on Wages and the Wages Class* (London, 1876)

Wells, A.F., *The Local Social Survey in Great Britain* (London, 1935)

Wickwar, H. and M., *The Social Services* (London, 1949 revised edn)

Williams, Gertrude, *The State and the Standard of Living* (London, 1936)

Williams, K., *From Pauperism to Poverty* (London, 1981)

Wolfe, Willard, *From Radicalism to Socialism: Men and Ideas in the Formation of Fabian Socialist Doctrines, 1881-1889* (New Haven & London, 1975)

Wright, T.R., *The Religion of Humanity. The Impact of Comtean Positivism on Victorian Britain* (Cambridge, 1986)

Index of Names and Places

This index contains the names of individuals, institutions, places, societies and unions mentioned in the text and in substantive footnotes. London place-names are indexed under London. Titles of published works mentioned in the text are also included.

Index of Subjects

Please see Index of Names and Places for London place-names, persons, institutions and societies mentioned in the text.